Let Contention Cease

Let Contention Cease

The Dynamics of Dissent
in the
Reorganized Church of Jesus Christ
of Latter Day Saints

Edited by
Roger D. Launius
and
W.B. "Pat" Spillman

Graceland/Park Press
Independence, Missouri

Library of Congress Cataloging-in-Publication Data

Let Contention Cease: the Dynamics of Dissent in the Reorganized Church of Jesus Christ of Latter Day Saints / edited by Roger D. Launius and W.B. "Pat" Spillman.

    p.   cm.
  Includes bibliographical references.
  ISBN 0-8309-0592-8
  1. Reorganized Church of Jesus Christ of Latter Day Saints—Doctrines—History. 2. Dissenters, Religious—History. I. Launius. Roger D. II. Spillman, W. B.
  BX8675.L47   1991
  289.3'33—dc20   91-34038
                                         CIP

96 95 94 93   2 3 4 5

Table of Contents

Foreword

As the presidents of Graceland College and Park College, we are delighted to introduce this new publishing imprint as a joint venture: Graceland/Park Press.

Our hope is to encourage publication of scholarly and exploratory studies on religious topics, which relate directly or indirectly to the Reorganized Church of Jesus Christ of Latter Day Saints.

Faculty members at Park and Graceland are available for advice and consultation, if needed, depending on the disciplines involved in the work. Along with the editorial director of Herald Publishing House, we will continue to seek the work of reputable authors whose efforts exhibit the highest standards of academic integrity and honesty.

Barbara M. Higdon
Graceland College

Donald J. Breckon
Park College

Preface

For those who may wonder how books come about, this one is probably not atypical. The editors, Roger Launius and I, were sitting in my office in Temple School early in 1990 talking about some recent events in the history of the Reorganized Church of Jesus Christ of Latter Day Saints. The problem of dissent in the church was one of our significant concerns. As we discussed our observations, I mentioned that I was interested in writing an article about the subject. As usual, while encouraging me to do it, Roger said he was writing one, too. Roger is *always* writing something interesting. Before long we were considering the possibilities of other authors who might want to contribute to a collection of essays dealing with the problem of dissent. It did not take long to come up with a list of potential contributors. Most of those we approached took us up on the challenge. This book is the result of their efforts.

Our organizational scheme is partly chronological, partly topical. We consciously sought authors who would be in a position to contribute insights from their particular area of expertise. What we hoped to develop was a book that considered dissent from a variety of perspectives and opinions. We believe we have achieved that goal. Each author has presented his own ideas, ideas not necessarily representative of the opinions or positions of the editors, the other authors, the Reorganized Church, or either Park College or Graceland College. The differences in opinion and perspective presented in these pages represent the spectrum of thinking historically found in the church. The Reorganized Church of Jesus Christ of Latter Day Saints began as an organization of dissenters—those who disagreed with others who claimed to inherit the prophetic mantle after the assassination of Joseph Smith, Jr. Since its earliest days, members of the church have cherished their independence of thought and freedom of expression. To observers unacquainted with the church's history, many of its conferences may have seemed raucous and undisciplined as delegates shouted and contended with one another over minutia and significant issues alike. But readers must keep one thing in mind when reading these articles: For most of their history, Reorganized Latter Day Saints have continued to maintain loyalty to the church even when disagreeing among themselves and their leaders about directions and policies. Only rarely has dissent reached levels that large numbers of people found it necessary to effectively remove themselves from active participation in the church community. Regrettably, the late 1980s was one of those periods.

We hope readers will find this book thought provoking and edifying. The 1980s were a trying time for the church. The nature of religious dissent often leads to emotional response rather than rational thought. We trust the articles in this book will help reverse this process. We doubt that readers will agree with everything said within these pages. Frankly, we don't either. But each author has approached his thesis with scholarship and good intentions. We hope that as the church confronts its problems with objectivity and perspective, people on all sides of the various controversies will recognize the legitimate concerns and views of others with goodwill and charity. As they do, the church will continue to grow as a community of healthy diversity, in which people do not confuse means with ends, and in which the ultimate goal remains to bring the ministry of Jesus Christ to a world in great need.

W. B. "Pat" Spillman

Background on Contributors

Dr. Donald J. Breckon is president of Park College in Parkville, Missouri, one of the Reorganized Church's two institutions of higher learning. Breckon is the author of numerous articles and books on health education and related subjects, most significantly: *Matters of Life and Death* (Herald House, 1987); and with others, *Community Health Education: Settings, Roles, and Skills* (1989).

Larry W. Conrad is the pastor of Polk City, Iowa, United Methodist Church. A graduate of Candler School of Theology at Emory University in Atlanta, Conrad is a well-known analyst of contemporary Reorganization theology. His article, coauthored with Paul Shupe, "An RLDS Reformation: Construing the Task of RLDS Theology," *Dialogue: A Journal of Mormon Thought* 19 (Summer 1985): 92-103, was a pathbreaking work on the nature and direction of the church's theological task.

Dr. Maurice L. Draper is a former member of the Reorganized Church's First Presidency and Quorum of Twelve Apostles. He has written numerous important books and articles on the development of the church. Notable contributions published by Herald House include: *Marriage in the Restoration Movement* (1968), *Isles & Continents* (1982), *Credo, I Believe* (1983), and the forthcoming volume in the Administrative Biography Series, *The Founding Prophet: An Administrative Biography of Joseph Smith, Jr.* (December 1991).

Dr. Paul M. Edwards is Temple School Division director for the Reorganized Church and dean of the Park College Graduate School of Religion. He is the author of numerous works on history and philosophy. Among his more significant efforts are *Our Legacy of Faith: A Brief History of the Reorganized Church of Jesus Christ of Latter Day Saints* (Herald House, 1991), *The Chief: An Administrative Biography of Fred M. Smith* (Herald House, 1988), *Ethics: The Possibility of Moral Choice* (Herald House, 1987), and *Preface to Faith: A Philosophical Inquiry into RLDS Beliefs* (Signature Press, 1986). Edwards is a past president of the Mormon History Association and the John Whitmer Historical Association.

Dr. Roger D. Launius is chief historian for the National Aeronautics and Space Administration in Washington, D.C. Although a historian of science and technology, he investigates the history of Mormonism as an avocation and has published several articles and books relating to the subject. These include: *Joseph Smith III: Pragmatic Prophet* (University of Illinois Press, 1988), which received the Evans Biography Award and best-book award from the John Whitmer Historical Association; and *Father Figure: Joseph Smith III and the Creation of the Reorganized Church* (Herald House, 1990), which received the best-book award from the Mormon History Association. He is serving as president of the John Whitmer Historical Association during the 1990-1992 term.

Kenneth R. Mulliken recently completed his master's degree in American history at the University of Missouri at Columbia, and is currently studying environmental law at the University of Missouri at Kansas City. His previously published works include:

"A History of the Irrigation and Reclamation Projects in the State of Nevada," *The Nevada State Comprehensive Preservation Plan* (1989); and "Captain Harry's Battery D," in *A Centennial Tribute to Harry S. Truman* (1984).

William D. Russell is a faculty member of the Division of Social Sciences at Graceland College in Lamoni, Iowa. A past president of both the Mormon History Association and the John Whitmer Historical Association, he has published several articles about the development of Mormonism, notably, "History and the Mormon Scriptures," *Journal of Mormon History* 10 (1983): 53-63, his presidential address which caused considerable controversy in scholarly circles. He currently is working on a full-length history of the most recent fundamentalist dissent in the Reorganized Church.

Steven L. Shields is pastor of the Reorganized Church congregation at El Segundo, California. A writer of note in the history of Mormonism, Shields' most significant work is *Divergent Paths of the Restoration: A History of the Latter Day Saints* (Restoration Research, 1975; 4th ed., 1990). For many years he was the editor of *Restoration,* a journal committed to documenting the histories of the many dissident groups arising out of the Mormon experience. He currently is editor of the *Restoration Trail Forum.*

Dr. W. B. "Pat" Spillman is Real Estate Operations manager for the Reorganized Church. At the time this book was developed he was adult education director for the Temple School Division of the Reorganized Church. He is the author or editor of numerous books, articles, and curriculum materials, including the church's sesquicentennial reunion text, *A Great and Marvelous*

Work (Herald House, 1980), and the four-volume church-school survey history of the church, *Studies in Restoration History: The Hastening Time* (Herald House, 1987-1990).

Chapter 1

Guarding Prerogatives: Autonomy and Dissent in the Development of the Nineteenth-Century Reorganized Church*

by Roger D. Launius

Introduction

When Joseph Smith III lay on his deathbed during the last part of November and the first part of December 1914, he called his family and friends to him to offer whatever encouragement and guidance he might possess at that late stage of his life. On 29 November 1914 he invited his oldest son and designated successor to the presidential office, Frederick Madison Smith, into his chamber to offer him advice about church administration. Taking his son's hand, Joseph said:

*An earlier version appeared in *Journal of Mormon History* (1991) and is published here with permission. Some research was funded by a grant from the National Endowment for the Humanities.

Fred, a great opportunity lies before you. Better in some respects than lay before me, for, as I look back over history and the revelations that have been given to the church, and are on record since I have been presiding, they show me very clearly that a great many things which have been left open to misunderstanding have been cleared up in the revelations and in the letter of instruction.

The old prophet went on to urge his son to exercise patience in his relationship with church members. "Be steadfast and if the people are heady, if the church is heady, the eldership are heady and take the reins in their hands as they have done a little especially on the rules and regulations, rules of representation," he told Frederick, "don't worry, let it pass, let the church take the consequences and they will after a while grow out of it. ...It is better that way than to undertake to force them or coerce. That would be bad trouble."[1]

Dissent and Early Mormonism

Joseph Smith III recognized a fundamental principle of the Reorganized Church and sought to explain it to his son. The Reorganization, Joseph III understood, was made up of independent-minded people who could not be herded like mere sheep without questioning, could not be ordered like prison inmates, could not be controlled like automatons. The Reorganized Church was primarily an inheritor of a legacy of independent-mindedness that had been present as a minority movement within the early Mormon church. This legacy had manifested itself almost from the very beginnings of the church as a debate over the direction of church policy, organizational direction, and doctrinal conceptions. Joseph Smith, Jr., had sought to establish his control over each of these arenas of church life, and to a large extent he was successful in doing so.

Marvin S. Hill recently argued persuasively that these efforts should be viewed as an attempt to escape from American pluralism and secularism. According to Hill, the early Mormon attempt to develop a communal utopia under theocratic control during the 1830s and 1840s was partially a reaction against the increasing importance of democratic, competitive, secular tendencies and the overall decline of religion in American life. The Mormon church, therefore,

> sought to revitalize this magical world view [like had been present in medieval society], combine it with elements of more traditional Christianity, and establish a theocratic society where the unconverted, the poor, and the socially and religiously alienated could gather and find a refuge from the competing sects and the uncertainties they engendered. His efforts to do so would bring him into conflict with leaders and others of the established order who were otherwise-minded.[2]

The emerging emphasis on personal freedom, as expressed in Jacksonian democracy, then, was an unnerving ingredient in this, as was a general sense of alienation from other religious denominations, especially those that embraced the tendencies of larger society.[3]

The erection of a strong theocratic organization to counter these external pressures was imperative in this environment and social milieu. Consolidation of authority, therefore, became an early and persistent goal of the Mormon leadership. Perhaps the best examples of this were Smith's statements in the Doctrine and Covenants setting him up as the final authority on all matters in church government. For example, when

Hiram Page challenged, apparently with some success, Smith's right to receive revelations binding on the whole church in September 1830, the church founder dictated an emphatic revelation that ended Page's career as a prophet:

> But, behold, verily, verily I say unto thee, No one shall be appointed to receive commandments and revelations in this church excepting my servant Joseph Smith, Jr., for he receiveth them even as Moses; and thou shalt be obedient unto the things which I shall give unto him, even as Aaron, to declare faithfully the commandments and revelations, with power and authority unto the church.[4]

When a woman known only as Mrs. Hubble challenged Smith's authority to receive revelations a few months later he dictated an even stronger revelation. "But verily, verily I say unto you, that none else shall be appointed unto this gift [of revelation] except it be through him," the document stated, making it impossible for another person to assert authority as a prophet in the church.[5]

The differences over interpretation of church government and direction that Joseph Smith III recognized and appreciated in the Reorganized Church, as shown in his advice to his son, were part and parcel of the movement's history from its foundation in 1830. Some early Latter Day Saints less alienated from society emphasized the positive aspects of its pluralism and decried what they perceived as an omnipresent pressure to conform to unique characteristics. Over a period of years in the early Latter Day Saint movement, differences of opinion over the policies, doctrines, and direction of the church surfaced repeatedly. At times these differing elements contended one with another to the extent that a dissenting element was identifiable. Following the disastrous Zion's Camp expedition to Missouri in 1834, for example, several church officials in Kirtland, Ohio, challenged Smith's role in the church and brought charges against him.[6] They charged him with a variety of crimes ranging from important discrepancies in policy and doctrine to differences of opinion on insignificant issues. The dissent culminated in a serious rift in the ranks of the movement in 1837 and 1838. All three of the original witnesses to the divinity of the Book of Mormon—Oliver Cowdery, Martin Harris, and David Whitmer—withdrew from the church, as did more than half of the Quorum of Twelve Apostles and the ranking bishop, Edward Partridge. An unquantifiable number of members of lesser stature also withdrew or were excommunicated. The dissent was devastating to both the people affected and to the church they believed had the "fullness of the gospel."[7]

This question must be asked: "Why did the rift in the church take place?" The answers offered have ranged from a purely economic interpretation to explanations that create simple cause/effect dichotomies about the nature of apostasy and rebellion.[8] The issue, however, was much more complex than the specific complaints leveled. Marvin S. Hill has offered a compelling analysis of the dissent that was demonstrated in Kirtland. He found that the Saints' complaints about specific issues were only symptoms of a larger discontent over the fundamental nature of the church:

> In the upheaval at Kirtland, which carried over into Far West, Missouri, the degree of control to be possessed by the church and its leaders, the degree of consolidation in the kingdom was at stake. Dissenters like the Cowderys, the Whitmers, Burnet, McLellin and Brewster, wanted a more open society, closer to the values and

traditions of evangelical Protestantism, while those who supported Smith tolerated a more closed society based on higher law, where the Saints were of one mind an[d] one heart, ready to do battle against the ungodly.[9]

The Saints were concerned about the fundamental shape of the church in future years, and whether it would be a part of American religion or outside of it. The dissenting element of the church was an important part of the process of growth and direction and should be understood as an intrinsic part of the development of the early Latter Day Saint movement.

Many of these dissenters' comments were directed toward working out a position on the relationship of the church to society. Much of the concern revolved around the nature of church government, its role somewhere between authoritarianism and complete freedom for the members. Many dissenters expressed concern over what they thought was the development of a tyranny in the church and stood up to oppose it. Warren Cowdery, the brother of Oliver and editor of the *Messenger and Advocate*, warned against authoritarianism among the church leadership:

> If we gave all our privileges to one man, we virtually give him our money and our liberties, and make him our monarch, absolute and despotic, and ourselves abject slaves or fawning sycophants. If we grant privileges and monopolies to a few, they always continue to undermine the fundamental principles of freedom, and, sooner or later, convert the purest and most liberal form of Government into the rankest of aristocracy. ...Whenever a people have unlimited confidence in a civil or ecclesiastical ruler or rulers, who are but men like themselves, and begin to think they can do no wrong, they increase their tyranny and oppression and establish a principle that man, poor frail lump of mortality like themselves, is infallible.[10]

Benjamin Winchester said that Joseph Smith, Jr., while preaching in the Kirtland Temple, claimed that he "was authorized by God almighty to establish his kingdom — that he was God's prophet and God's agent and that he could do whatever he should choose to do, therefore the Church had NO RIGHT TO CALL INTO QUESTION anything he did, or to censure him for the reason that he was responsible to God Almighty only."[11] Winchester suggested that such an attitude demonstrated the fundamentally authoritarian direction toward which the church was moving. He could not accept it and withdrew from the movement.

These were fundamental questions that the Kirtland dissenters raised. They went far beyond the details of the events involved to consider the nature of church government and the direction of institutional development. The whole of the era added up to much more than simply the sum of the parts of individual dissent. Marvin Hill concluded, "Here were sown the seeds of ideological division which in time would lead to a split between the Reorganized branch of Mormonism, with its capitol at Independence amongst the gentile community, and the Utah branch of Mormonism, which became more isolated, self-contained and closed and somewhat more militant."[12] While there were a number of other events that had to take place and several additional factors that were involved in the creation of the Reorganized Church, Hill had found an important thread in the origins of the Reorganized Church. It is one that has been expressed in the Reorganization repeatedly, as episodes of dissent over the fundamental questions of authority, power, and control and its use or abuse cropped up between 1851 and the present.

The dissenting attitude in Kirtland continued in western Missouri during 1837 and 1838 as well and led to the development of such organizations as the Danites. This organization, led by an overzealous Sampson Avard, began with the intention of enforcing orthodoxy among the Mormon membership. It was, in essence, a regulator movement, with all the abuses that have attended those movements over the years. Most important, perhaps, its very appearance on the scene demonstrates that a significant minority of church members were unwilling to acquiesce in the direction the institutional church was heading.[13] Certainly the tradition of dissent was a persistent, if a minor, reality in the life of the church during that early period.

The undercurrent of concern over the direction of the movement was not washed away with a purging of dissenters from the church during the 1837-1838 time period. It arose again most forcefully in Nauvoo in the mid-1840s. Many influential Latter Day Saints, led by William Law, a counselor to Joseph Smith in the First Presidency for a time in the early 1840s, left the movement because they were convinced that the organization had departed from the true principles of the gospel. The dissenters also included Wilson Law, William's brother and a brigadier general in the Nauvoo Legion; Austin Cowles, a member of the Nauvoo Stake high council; and James Blakeslee, Robert D. Foster, Chauncey Higbee, and Charles Ivins, all prominent church members. This alternative position, therefore, was not led by rabble merely out to gain notoriety. Some of the most solid and dignified men in the community were involved. Perhaps, even, their secular stature contributed to their dissent; having a larger stake in mainstream American society than most of their Mormon brethren they may have been less willing to over-turn social, political, and economic institutions.[14]

These dissidents worked to expose what they considered the evils of the church in a newspaper called the *Nauvoo Expositor*. On 7 June 1844 they issued the paper's only number. This newspaper has been remembered largely for its affidavits about the practice of plural marriage by church officials and condemned as the catalyst for Smith's death. But digging below the surface of this controversial issue, the dissidents were protesting what they viewed as an erosion of the rights of the Saints to direct the church. The editors affirmed that they "know of a surety, that the religion of the Latter Day Saints as originally taught by Joseph Smith, which is contained in the Old and New Testament, Book of Covenants, and Book of Mormon, is true; and that the pure principles set forth in those books, are the immutable and eternal principles of Heaven, and speaks a language which, when spoken in truth and virtue, sinks deep into the heart of every honest man." Although accepting the purity of the movement at the beginning, these Saints asked Smith to function more democratically within the church. They claimed that he had become a tyrant who did as he pleased without the regard for others that a man of God must have. They added that he was mixing religion and politics, even to the extent of declaring himself a candidate for the presidency of the United States in the 1844 election. Furthermore, they complained that Smith had started teaching doctrines—plural marriage was only one of them—contrary to the gospel of God they had accepted in joining the church. Any who opposed Smith's actions, they suggested, were dealt with harshly by ecclesiastical authorities.[15]

The publication of the *Expositor* raised a furor in the community, and Smith, acting as mayor of Nauvoo, ordered that the press be silenced by city authorities. William Law immediately went to Carthage, the seat of Hancock County, to swear out a complaint against Smith for inciting a riot and unlawfully destroying property. State authorities arrested Smith on this charge, as well as some others drummed up later, and while incarcerated in the county jail a mob lynched him and his brother on 27 June 1844. In an irony of the foremost magnitude, whether one believes all the charges levied by William Law against Smith matters not, the prophet was vulnerable to the mob because he had been arrested for exercising injudiciously the very power Law accused him of exercising injudiciously.[16]

Those who represented the moderate elements of early Mormonism bequeathed a critical component to the Reorganized Church as it began to coalesce in the 1850s. They brought to the Reorganization a pluralism more in tune with the world around them and a commitment to more mainstream American religious ideals. Along with these attributes, developed largely to counter monolithic attitudes fostered in early Mormonism, Reorganized Church members possessed a fierce protectiveness of the individual rights of church members. To an extent that may be somewhat disturbing to modern Reorganized Latter Day Saints, the Reorganization was born out of the dissident elements of the early Latter Day Saint church. Its intellectual forebears—if not its actual ones, although sometimes they were actual—were the Oliver Cowderys and William Laws of the early church. Those people could not accept what they considered abuses of authority by the president, abuses that manifested themselves, they believed, in such arenas as church involvement in secular politics and economic activities and in the implementation of unusual religious practices and theological notions.[17]

The 1850s: The Golden Age of Reorganization Autonomy

The movement that coalesced around Jason W. Briggs and Zenos H. Gurley, Sr., in the 1850s was made up of cautious people who had embraced American pluralism and rejected the more extreme expressions of early Mormonism's religious commitment—specifically those theological ideals embraced and furthered by such factional leaders as Brigham Young. Reorganized Church members were repelled by the practice of temple rituals, plural marriage, and the emphasis on the political kingdom of God that they saw among the Utah Latter-day Saints. Early on they centered their beliefs on the lineal succession of one of the sons of the prophet—in the 1850s they were officially unwilling to limit the office to Joseph Smith III—on the right of the individual to make religious choices, and on the negatives of other Mormon groups.

The peculiarities of its historical development led the Reorganized Church to be much more democratically oriented than most of the other Latter Day Saint factions emerging after the death of Joseph Smith, Jr. There had always been a dynamic present within Mormonism creating an impetus toward a strong hierarchical structure versus the tradition of a strong congregational structure. The building of a formal priesthood hierarchy implied, of course, that authority tended to flow from the top to the bottom of the structure. Having a prophet who spoke for God at the top of the institutional pyramid only strengthened this predilection. At the same time, the church also possessed a tradition of congregationalism which suggested that the real authority of the movement rested with the individual members. The pushes and pulls of these two aspects of church government never were fully resolved during the lifetime of Joseph Smith, Jr., but a gradual centralizing of authority in the hands of the hierarchy did take place.[18]

This centralizing process, as pointed out concerning the dissent in the early church, did not take place without countering positions being advanced. There were three options in working through this question of who makes the decisions and directs the church. Thomas F. O'Dea, in a sociological study now more than thirty years old but still valuable, described the three approaches used:

> to apostatize (which was not infrequent), to persuade and limit authoritarian leadership by informal devices (which was done), or to claim that after some point in time Joseph (or Brigham) was a fallen prophet (which was also done). Informal devices to influence and limit the power of Joseph Smith, together with his own responsiveness to the expectations of his people and his lieutenants as he perceived these in the formal and informal contacts of daily life, were the really effective limitations on his power. The more these were successful, however, the more they strengthened the oligarchical structure of leadership and decision-making.[19]

In the end the early Saints worked out an arrangement in sharing authority that reconciled the democratic nature of the church membership with the authoritarian nature of the decision-making process. They called it "common consent," but in its practical application after the very earliest years of church development, it involved little more than the democratic ratification of decisions made elsewhere in the central hierarchy. As a result, for the early Mormons congregational authority became increasingly ceremonial as the years passed and real authority tended to flow to the hierarchy.[20]

Because of the uniqueness of its founding, the peculiarities of its early leadership, the fortunes of its environment, and the doctrinal biases of those making up the Reorganized Church as it emerged in the 1850s, the group embraced and gloried in a moderate expression of Mormonism in the American Midwest. Fundamental to its Weltanschauung was a commitment to greater membership involvement in the church's decision-making process.[21] For this branch of Mormonism, congregational authority was still considered an imperative and was never relegated to ceremonial roles. That was true for three basic reasons. Each of these were closely related and perhaps could be merged. However, I believe they were sufficiently distinct to warrant separate discussion.

First, after 1844 the stalemate between the two traditions—hierarchical versus congregational—quickly unraveled when strong individuals with definite ideals opposed the Mormon retreat from American pluralism. At least by 1846, when Brigham Young began the exodus to the Great Basin, according to Jan Shipps, "those whose understanding of the Mormon message as mainly metaphysical generally stayed behind."[22] The controversies over policy and doctrine, and the apparent high-handedness of the church leadership in dealing with those holding differing opinions, led to a schism that could never be bandaged. Brigham Young, probably taking a no-more-forceful action against dissenters than Joseph Smith, Jr., would have done had he still been alive, did not have the loyalty of the whole membership that the founder enjoyed and his actions were not so well tolerated. Because of what they perceived as abuses of authority by Brigham Young and others, individuals who eventually became members of the Reorganized Church were perhaps more jealous of their rights than they would have been otherwise. Burned by what they considered "would-be" prophets, the Reorganized Saints were notoriously cautious in turning authority for action over to leaders on a wholesale basis. For those Saints, therefore, the theory of "common consent" took on a much more important role than it had possessed either in the early Mormon church or in the faction that settled in the Great Basin. It approached the status of an inviolate right which was much more than majority rule, even with minority rights; it required a consensus arrived at by the whole body in free and equal debate.[23]

The experience of Jason W. Briggs provides an ideal case study of the makeup of those who would eventually enter the Reorganized Church.[24] Briggs had joined the Latter Day Saints on 6 June 1841 at Potosi, Wisconsin. Quickly ordained an elder, he became involved in the local congregation at Beloit, Wisconsin, and remained there until 1854. Although he visited Nauvoo in 1843, he never resided in the Mormon stronghold and was never a confidant of the prophet or privy to the inner workings of church government. He was, thus, a church member like most others of the period, having only intermittent contact with ranking officials and receiving most of his knowledge of the church's beliefs and practices from the written word, either in scripture or in periodical form, and from missionaries visiting the local area.

At the time of Joseph Smith, Jr.'s death, Briggs was faced with the difficult choice of following one of several claimants to the prophetic office. He used his best judgment, prayerfully rendered, and affiliated with a succession of individual factions until each espoused ideals of which he could not abide. One important ingredient of these various rejections was that the factional leaders each tried to force him to accept certain concepts or practices which he could not justify in his interpretation of scripture and practical experience. Only one of these was the doctrine of plural marriage, which most factional leaders at one time or another adopted. The crux of Briggs's inability to find a religious home in any of the Mormon factions revolved around who, how, and by what authority the doctrinal position was implemented. The issue of control and who had the lion's share of authority in decisions of importance to the movement was at center stage in Briggs's search for a successor to the early Latter Day Saint organization. Briggs, in addition, was a strong advocate of democratic tendencies and a proponent of American religious pluralism.

A second reason contributing to a strong sense of democracy in the Reorganized Church was the basically small and isolated nature of its congregations, sustained over a period of many years. The Reorganization, more than any other branch of Mormonism emerging from the 1844 divisions, was made up of members who were not gathered in central areas. Although no demographic studies exist over who united with the Reorganized Church in the 1850s—studies for which there is a pressing need—it seems that few members had been residents of Nauvoo or the communities immediately surrounding it. They were members of small, rural congregations scattered throughout the Midwest and held together by local priesthood. These congregational leaders may have affiliated with different factional leaders at various times, but by the early 1850s they and most of their members were fed up with the options open to them. Some of them renounced all allegiance beyond the local level and functioned as independent branches, sometimes for several years. The twin developments of frustration over what they saw happening to the Mormon movement as it fractured and the oftentimes lengthy period of independent branch action created a strong sense of democracy in the decision-making process. When the Reorganization began to coalesce in the early 1850s and members coming out of this experience affiliated with it, the result was an emphasis on individual and congregational rights and prerogatives, an emphasis that remained throughout the presidency of Joseph Smith III.[25]

The experience of one congregation that joined the Reorganized Church during this period is instructive. The Brush Creek branch of the church, located in the northwest corner of Wayne County, Illinois, about eighty miles east of St. Louis, had been founded in 1842. Jefferson Hunt, a missionary from Nauvoo, went throughout the area, baptized several members in Brush Creek township, and organized a congregation. Following the prophet's death in 1844, the Brush Creek congregation continued very much as it had before. Various members allied themselves with differing factional leaders periodically. For instance, one leading priesthood member, Nathan A. Morris, affiliated with Brigham Young's organization and with his family made the trek to Utah in 1864, only to become disgruntled. He and his family returned to Brush Creek three years later. Some members had relations with other factional movements, but most remained in the branch and operated as if no higher authority than that present in the congregation existed. Then, in June 1864 Reorganized Church missionaries William Anderson and Frank Reynolds visited Wayne County and discovered the Brush Creek branch by accident. They met with the Saints, told them about the claims of the Reorganization, and discussed at length the importance of Joseph Smith III's leadership to the church. More than sixty members of the Brush Creek Congregation as well as other early Saints scattered about the region immediately affiliated with the Reorganization on the strength of their original baptisms.[26] The experience of the Brush Creek Congregation was repeated many times in the early Reorganized Church by other independent branches.

This emphasis on congregational autonomy has been officially recognized as a prerogative within the Reorganization. In 1891 its leadership stated in a manual on church practice that local branches were "the primary and congregational organizations of the Church and may be formed wherever six or more members in good standing may be resident in any one neighborhood, one of whom must be an Elder, a Priest, a Teacher or a Deacon." It went on to define other organizational structures as "secondary and governmental organizations of the church."[27] As recently as 1972, the church's delegates in conference reaffirmed this position. On 13 April 1972 the body adopted a resolution which began: "The branch is the primary field organization of the church."[28] Such a tradition of local autonomy is not easily circumvented; Joseph Smith III recognized as much and sought gingerly to work with it.

Finally, the leadership of the early Reorganized Church must also be credited with the emphasis on democratic institutions in the movement. Unlike some egocentric and autocratic leaders of the other Mormon factions, those responsible for the coming together of the Reorganization had no personal ambitions and were cautious in their efforts. No evidence exists to suggest that either Jason W. Briggs or Zenos H. Gurley, Sr., the two individuals most responsible for the Reorganization beginning in 1851, ever sought status and power in the leadership of the church. They probably could have done so with some success, particularly by the late 1850s just before the accession of Joseph Smith III. These two men, and the others who were in the forefront of the reorganizing effort, were also seasoned by the same episodes and factors already mentioned and had no desire to create an institution that might not be responsive to the need of its membership.

William Marks, a former president of the Nauvoo Stake during the early 1840s who had united with the Reorganization in 1859, represented the mind-set of the entire Reorganization leadership when visiting Joseph Smith III on 20 March 1860. Smith had written to him and other church leaders about affiliating with their movement, and although they recognized him as the lineal successor of his father in the prophetic office, Marks matter-of-factly confronted him about his true intentions. "We have had enough of man-made prophets," he told Smith, "and don't want any more of that sort. If God has called you, we want to know it. If he has, the Church is ready to sustain you; if not we want nothing to do with you."[29] Smith, of course, convinced them of his commitment and calling and was ordained on 6 April 1860, but the caution, hesitancy, and concern for the church and its members' rights were of paramount importance in Marks's emphatic pronouncement.

Sociologists have suggested that organizations—any type, religious or otherwise—can exist only when leaders and members agree on how to distinguish themselves from the larger society and from other groups with similar ideas and goals. The general nature of the institution, its internal cohesion, and the relationship with its environment interplay with other issues of a less tangible nature to create and sustain the institution. The erection of boundaries between itself and its surroundings make possible the viability of organizations. Although these boundaries vary considerably from one organization to another, the firmness of them dictates the general strength of the organization. A strong organization, one that is firmly bounded, generally has rigorous entrance requirements, difficult standards for maintaining acceptability, and tolerates little dissent. A loosely bounded organization fosters simple entrance requirements, tolerates differing positions, and has fewer standards of conduct.[30]

Brigham Young and the Utah Mormons developed a firmly bounded organization with a high level of internal cohesion. Several elements—some of them imposed from outside, such as persecution—led to a high level of identity and singularity among the Mormons. These have been recognized both within and without that movement, and have led to a sense of separateness for the Latter-day Saints.[31] The event of the exodus from Nauvoo to the Great Basin, the requirement to work together to survive, and the strong sense of shared misery in it proved to be a *kairos* experience, an intense, compressed period of great and life-altering events, for those who participated. The Mormons began the intense process of becoming a unique people while leaving Nauvoo. In doing so they erected the greatest boundary to membership that could be fathomed: To be a member in good standing people had to forsake all that they held dear and journey for an unknown time, over an unknown distance, to an unknown land.[32]

The Reorganized Church, in part because of the circumstances discussed above, never developed strong boundaries between itself and the outside environment and religious experience. The Reorganized Church, instead, developed its personality out of the themes of dissent and American pluralism. The people of the Reorganized Church represented that strain of early Mormonism that was less extreme, more tolerant, and undeniably and incessantly democratic in its outlook. The early Reorganization embraced and celebrated those trends. A diversity of congregations, a diversity of personalities, a diversity of ideas all came together in only the loosest of organizations before the ordination of Joseph Smith III to the presidency. The Saints, proud of their diversity, jealous of their independence, and invocative of their prerogatives, created an organization that was not only loosely held together but even gloried in its internal divisions.[33]

The Reorganization manifested these pluralistic tendencies especially during its formative years in the manner in which it dealt (or did not deal) with issues. Until the entrance of Joseph Smith III into the movement there was really no body of accepted doctrine to which all agreed. A vague consensus existed for such general statements as a loose acceptance of the life and ministry of Joseph Smith, Jr.; the scriptures of the early church; the denunciation of all other Mormon factional leaders as apostates; the rejection of plural marriage; and the general, although by no means unanimous, belief that the successor of Joseph Smith, Jr., would be one of his descendants.[34] Virtually all other questions were wide open. Most important, church members explicitly and repeatedly asserted their individual rights to accept or reject all or part of any Reorganization conceptions, and in so doing they firmly ensconced the authority to make decisions in the hands of the rank-and-file membership.

A meeting—what Alma R. Blair has appropriately called the "founding conference of the Reorganization"—that took place in Zarahemla, Wisconsin, in April 1853 explicitly recognized the importance of control and who exercised it.[35] The actions emerging from it were all passed by a meeting of representatives, a democratic approach taken to ensure that nothing was done without the consent of those concerned, and they were always of a cautious nature so that vehement objections could be curtailed. Jason Briggs, named as the president pro tem of the movement, was especially cognizant that all things must be done cautiously and with the common consent of all. Virtually nothing took place in the Reorganization during the 1850s until it had first been sanctioned by conference action, and then the conferences were hesitant to act forcefully on any issue that might be potentially contentious among the membership.

In reality, the early Reorganized Church's commitment to absolute democracy and the pluralism that it embraced was something of an obstacle to accomplishing anything worthwhile. This was true for two essential reasons. First, Briggs and other Reorganization leaders looked for the day when the successor to the prophet would come to lead them and avoided making decisions that might run counter to the future prophet's wishes. In some respects this was an acceptable position because seeing the current administration as an interim government its leaders did not want to do anything that might injure the church and would have to be corrected by the successor, once he appeared.

There was a more important factor than the belief that the successor should be patiently awaited and he would put all in order, however. Inertia coming from fear of violating individual rights and prerogatives prohibited the Reorganized Church's leadership in the 1850s from accomplishing much of anything that might be considered worthwhile. Limited missionary outreach, virtually no publications program, and certainly no long-range planning for the organization took place during the decade. Briggs ran a caretaker government at best, one that kept the bills paid and the doors open, but without a plan for accomplishing and perhaps not even a vision of what the church was established to do.

The situation in the Reorganization in 1860 was very much like what the United States experienced during the confederation period before the implementation of the constitution in 1788. Under the Articles of Confederation, established during the revolutionary war, there had been only the smallest of federal establishments. What central government that existed was present in the Congress, which represented the people of the nation. But more of the authority for the direction of the nation resided at the state level, guarded jealously by governors and state assemblies. The lack of a central government strong enough to raise, equip, train, and employ military forces; forceful enough to make and enforce policy both at home and abroad; and stable enough to ensure that business ventures and economic activities could be protected forced the death of the confederation. As some historians have aptly phrased it, the government of the United States under the Articles of Confederation "died of an excess of democracy." With freedom and local autonomy came a certain amount of weakness, aimlessness, and inertia. The nation's Founding Fathers wrote the constitution as a means of correcting the weaknesses inherent in the Articles of Confederation, accepting a corresponding lessening of absolute democracy as a trade-off.[36]

Joseph Smith III and Reorganized Church Autonomy

Joseph Smith III, like Alexander Hamilton and other leading figures who wrote the U.S. Constitution, recognized that the administrative structure he presided over was weak and inefficient. He gradually, with a sense of honor and charity but also with a sense of purpose, worked during his early years as president to bring order to this church structure where little had existed before. Every time he issued a decision, every time he set a policy, every time he mediated a disagreement, virtually every time he took any action whatsoever Smith centralized in some way authority into his presidential office. And whenever Smith did that, whether by intent or without knowledge, he lessened the rights of individuals at local levels, in outside jurisdictions, or anywhere else in the church to choose for themselves. It was a decidedly evolutionary and subtle process but the accumulated efforts ensured that by the 1870s the membership was beginning to see that the wide-open democracy of the 1850s had become a thing of the past.[37] This was never an intention of Joseph Smith III; it was a by-product of his efforts to accomplish what he envisioned as the goals of the church. Perhaps he recognized, as most members of the Reorganization probably did not, that the opposite of dictatorship has never been democracy, but rather it is anarchy.[38] To accomplish the decidedly worthwhile goals of the movement meant that some of the local autonomy of church members had to be sacrificed for the greater good.

As one case study in this centralization effort, Joseph Smith III early recognized the necessity of placing the proper individuals in high church office, a measure that would ensure stable administration.[39] In October 1860, after six months as president of the Reorganization, Smith asked, in keeping with Reorganized Church practice, that the General Conference appoint a committee to nominate enough men to fill the Quorum of Twelve Apostles. Although this would have required the ordination of seven additional men, the committee called only three new members and later changed the meeting minutes so Smith's recommendation for ordination and the Conference's action coincided. Onto Smith's statement, "The Quorum of the Twelve should be filled," the 1861 Conference added, "as far as practicable."[40]

After several additional fits and starts, none of which were satisfactory to the prophet, Smith took forceful action in 1873 to secure appointments to the church's ruling quorums those people he believed God had called for service. Although he was concerned with the First Presidency and the Presiding Bishopric, the makeup and effectiveness of the Quorum of Twelve was probably the most pressing issue he wished to resolve. He prepared the way for this reorganization at the 1870

Conference by hinting that God would probably soon mandate changes in the quorums by revelation.[41] Smith followed through at the 1873 General Conference by delivering a revelation that completely revamped the church administrative officers. It filled the First Presidency by appointing two counselors, called seven men into the ranks of the Twelve, filled the Standing High Council, appointed numerous people to the Quorums of Seventy, and provided for the ordination of counselors in the Presiding Bishopric. Moreover, the document established the president as the supreme appointive power in the church and set the precedent for nearly all subsequent calls to the most important priesthood bodies in the church.[42] Since that time, all changes of personnel in the governing quorums have been made through the formal, written revelatory method adopted in 1873.

Investing the presidential office with the appointive and other powers ensured that Joseph Smith III over a period of years concentrated ever more authority in the church hierarchy and allowed Smith's handpicked associates to develop a more efficient ecclesiastical structure capable of carrying on ambitious programs and engaging in more forceful missionary endeavors. This action, and others centralizing authority in the hierarchy, contributed to a sense on the part of some members that the liberty of the 1850s to believe and conduct themselves as they saw fit was being eroded. Smith, as cautious and moderate as he really was, constantly had to be prepared to answer charges of tyranny, of trying to get his way without due consideration of the wishes of the general membership. Dealing with the persistent tradition of dissent was an ever-present part of his presidential administration.

The Briggs/Gurley Dissent from Institutional Hegemony

The church faced its most serious crisis during the latter 1870s and early 1880s when Jason W. Briggs and Zenos H. Gurley, Jr., two Reorganization apostles, challenged the hierarchy's rights to make fundamental decisions about policy and doctrine and aimed for a reformation that would redistribute ecclesiastical power among the membership. The crisis arose because Joseph Smith III had done such a fine job of building an administrative structure capable of carrying out church policy and enforcing orthodoxy. While it was a much more pluralistic administration than most other inheritors of the Mormon tradition, these Reorganization apostles and their followers were unwilling to accept even moderate circumscription of their rights.

The facts of the crisis known as the Briggs/Gurley affair in the Reorganization are well-known, having been discussed at length in several essays by recent chroniclers of the movement, and need not be completely recited here.[43] Instead, the following discussion will focus on the causes of the rebellion of two apostles and an untold number of other Reorganized Church members against the church hierarchy. The crisis originated directly as a result of supposed violations on the part of certain church leaders, especially by Joseph Smith III, of the cherished autonomy of the Saints. The commitment to individual autonomy and an acceptance of opposing positions that was so much a part of the Reorganization's heritage was being seriously and subversively challenged, Jason W. Briggs and Zenos H. Gurley, Jr., believed, by the overarching authority of the presidential office. Their reaction in this situation was predictable.

It was this centralization of leadership authority, Joseph Smith III's subtle and rational attempts to create an efficient organization, that Briggs and Gurley and their followers rebelled against during the 1870s and 1880s. Persistently and with a touch of remorse, Briggs and Gurley sounded the call against what they perceived as an erosion of tolerance for pluralism and democracy in the Reorganization and a centralization of authority in the prophetic office. Jason Briggs, the same man who had been so crucial to the formation of the Reorganized Church in the 1850s, upon occasion charged the presidency of the church with a latent Caesarism, condemning Joseph Smith III for pontificating about "my policy" and comments by Smith that the Saints "will not go far wrong if you will take brother *Joseph's Counsel.*"[44] He was suggesting by the 1870s that the Smith family was a detriment to the church—robbing the membership of autonomy—and Briggs called for an end to the "peculiar phaze [sic] of *Family Worship*" enjoyed by the Smiths in the Reorganization.[45]

At the center of Briggs' challenge to church government, doctrine, policy, and ideals was a fundamental commitment to think for himself and not to be, at least in his mind, dictated to by anyone else. Believing that personal reason and experience had to be the final arbiters of truth, Briggs found it increasingly easy to question the decisions of the Reorganization's leadership. He summed up his position in *The Messenger*, a Reorganized Church missionary periodical:

> Why do you make other men's dreams your law, but trust not your own? Prove all things, and whatever is

proved to be good, hold fast, and the rest...leave in the ante-room of inquiry, or let it slide....We often hear... "you must not trust your own judgment." But we ask whose then shall we trust?...If we are told to repudiate human judgment all together, we answer we have no other, and moreover that such is the platform of fools.[46]

It was a declaration of independence from the dictates of others for Briggs and for those of his ilk. In October 1876 Briggs wrote to William H. Kelley, president of the Quorum of Twelve, in an obvious state of disgust: "There is but little encouragement for an Elder who thinks as well as feels."[47]

Zenos Gurley's criticisms emanated from the same basic issue of authority in the church and to what extent its hierarchy was responsive to individuals. He believed Joseph Smith, Jr., had established a virtual dictatorship in the early Latter Day Saint movement, condemning this: "No servant of Christ should be a guide for you to follow, only as he follows Christ."[48] Unfortunately Joseph Smith's power in the early Restoration had been "omnipotent. It places him instead of God to us....If this be law,...then in that case our salvation depends upon belief in Joseph Smith."[49] The role of Joseph Smith III in exercising power was only moderately more restrained than had been his father's, Gurley charged, and the result, as Clare D. Vlahos wrote, was that "the real law of the church was not the designated Conference body but the prophet who could legislate with each revelation."[50] Joseph Smith III's ability to pronounce revelation, therefore, served as a catalyst for a whole range of lesser complaints about the church and its direction, policy, and doctrine.

Briggs and Gurley did not challenge directly Joseph Smith III's prophetic authority, the rights of the First

Presidency as a presiding unit, or the overall centralizing of functions that had once been in the hands of relatively autonomous local units if they were conducted at all, but the issues that they raised hit at the very heart of these conditions. They questioned the veracity of scripture and of various doctrines emerging from the Latter Day Saint experience, thereby casting doubt on the prophetic guidance of the church's leadership. They doubted some of the policies of the church, such as a commitment to the gathering, as a dubious and unwise position because of the opposition it invariably engendered from the external community. They thought and publicly stated that the church was building its reputation on faulty foundations by officially espousing that plural marriage had never been a part of early Mormonism. In each of these specific instances, as well as others not mentioned here, Briggs and Gurley believed Joseph Smith III had established the direction of the Reorganization by legal maneuver, cautious manipulation, or the force of his personality and prestige. In every case, additionally, he had taken from the church membership the right to make decisions that would fundamentally affect the movement. Although they did not explicitly state their criticisms in these terms, Briggs and Gurley recognized that the democracy present in the early Reorganized Church had been eroded. Members in the earlier period could hold a greater divergence of opinion and remain in good standing in the body, and decisions, if made at all, were made only in the conferences where all representatives had equal voice and vote.[51]

While Jason Briggs was a theoretician and rabble-rouser, Zenos Gurley was a tactician who devised an ingenious plan to curb the authority of Joseph Smith

III and the presidential office and at the same time make the General Conferences *the* policy-making body of the movement, as it had been in the 1850s. During the early 1880s he pushed for what amounted to an open season on all policies and doctrines of the church for one year. During that time everyone with anything to say on any issue would be allowed to do so using whatever avenue of expression they wished. Gurley, of course—and this was partly because Smith had already prohibited publication of some of his ideas in it—was committed to a completely free and open debate in the columns of the *Saints' Herald*. Gurley also demanded that, following this free discussion, the General Conference make definitive statements on all issues of importance to the Reorganization.[52]

This approach accomplished three crucial objectives from Gurley's perspective. First, he believed that with an open forum for the presentation of his criticisms and ideas for change he would be able to sway the church membership decisively toward the ideas he and Briggs shared for a better organization. Gurley genuinely believed his doctrinal conceptions were clearly superior to the myth and symbol that passed for Reorganized Church policy and doctrine at the time. But, equally important, he *knew* without any question that his rational presentation of the facts would convince the Saints of the virtue of his position. This was, perhaps, the ultimate evidence of Gurley's crucial dedication to a fearlessly democratic movement. Gurley had a basic trust in the people that if they were not manipulated in any way they would make right decisions. To paraphrase a common statement used in American politics, "Put the facts before the citizens and let the citizens decide, and they will not steer you wrong." Second, this approach reinstituted and solidified the critical role of the General Conference as the final authority for all that the Reorganization did, undertook, and stood for in the world. Finally, this strategy for reform had the especially attractive advantage for Gurley of lessening the hold of Smith on the direction of the church at the same time that the General Conferences asserted greater authority.

Joseph Smith III understood the challenge to the authority of the centralized presidency much more clearly than did most of the other people in the Reorganization at the time. Certainly, while he respected the viewpoints of Briggs and Gurley, he had no sympathy for the disharmony their criticisms engendered within the church and for the reform effort masterminded by Gurley. Smith's response recognized that if the Reorganized Church was to accomplish anything of worth it had to unify and focus its efforts along a concentrated path. To do so required enough centralized direction that the system functioned with a degree of efficiency. Tolerance and sympathy could be accepted, even demanded, but when it significantly impinged on the accomplishment of church objectives then it had to be curtailed.

Joseph Smith III expressed this basic belief about limited freedom in a letter to Briggs in 1877:

> I assume no right to dictate, but have supposed from the action of all the conferences since 1852, that if a matter was decided by the plain teaching of the books it was settled for all members of the Church. If this is not correct, nothing is gained by organization, for the word alone means nothing. However, I am a man for free speech and free inquiry, howbeit, he who mistakes *belief* for liberty will have a hard row to hoe.[53]

If this was not clear enough, Smith wrote near the same time to the president of Briggs's quorum about what was required of members. "I acknowledge the 'right of conscience' and I believe in its exercise," he commented, "but to allow that to dictate to, and dominate the rights of fellowship and ignore the bonds of Association, I cannot." Then he offered the clincher, which stated what he thought should happen to persistent malcontents: "If a man wants to retain and exercise *all* his individual rights, let him get by himself, where his elbows and knees will not hurt his neighbors."[54] Smith understood very well that the Saints had to give up some liberty for the sake of the movement's larger goals.

There is no doubt about Joseph Smith III's hostility to Briggs and Gurley's position; his ideas clearly opposed the two apostles, particularly when they voiced liberal theological positions.[55] He probably also had personality conflicts with the two men. These factors, coupled with his commitment to the maintenance of a reasonably well-centralized presidential office, forced Smith to develop and implement a strategy for defeat. He was tolerant for quite some time and tried to give the apostles the benefit of doubt in questionable instances, but he was dedicated from the outset to containing the reform effort.

Clare D. Vlahos has posited the creation of a protective envelope in which Smith placed the apostles, and he carefully guarded against their movement beyond it. He set up a situation in which the church would allow a certain level of tolerance. Vlahos argued:

> However, the protective barrier also extended in the other direction. Smith would allow deviations in thought but not where they might have too profound an influence. [W.W.] Blair rather than Briggs was called to

the position of counselor [in 1873] as a result. Some Gurley materials were allowed in the *Herald* but not those condemning Joseph Smith, Jr., for polygamy. Most importantly, President Smith acknowledged the potential impact of a Gurley-sponsored free debate in the *Herald*. He flatly refused to let it take place.[56]

Smith could not allow the Briggs/Gurley reform attempt to succeed, for it could only do so at the expense of his authority in the presidential office, something that could not happen, Smith believed, for the good of the church.

Joseph Smith III's handling of the Briggs/Gurley affair was masterful. He displayed a remarkable mastery of the nuances of the issues in contention. While decisive, Smith was also cautious in dealing with the malcontents to preserve as much internal harmony and order as possible. Eventually, only after years of controversy in which Smith worked behind the scenes to solidify his position and to erode that of Briggs and Gurley, the rebellion peaked at the April 1885 General Conference. As he wished, the meeting stripped Briggs and Gurley of their apostolic authority. The next year, these two malcontents—dissenters who had tried to redistribute political authority within the church in favor of the local members—and some of their adherents left the movement. Smith's victory was sure.

Smith believed his actions had ensured the stability of the church. He recounted in his memoirs a vision experienced before the April 1886 General Conference in which he and W.W. Blair were tending three charcoal pits. One pit began burning out of control and Smith and Briggs were forced to decide what to do, for the smoke and steam inside threatened to destroy the wood rather than char it. Smith decided to sacrifice some of the wood to correct the problem and save the rest. He hammered a large hole into the pit and allowed it to burn until under control. He wrote, "Thus the trouble threatened was avoided and the pit saved from destruction." Smith specifically equated the loss of Briggs and Gurley and their followers to the wood that was sacrificed so the remainder might achieve its intended purpose. The sum of the whole, and therefore the good of the whole, was greater than the sum or the wishes of any of its parts.[57]

Assessment

Did Smith's action end the dynamics of dissent and celebration of plurality in the Reorganization? Absolutely not! In spite of Briggs's and Gurley's withdrawals, the voices of freedom of thought and expression have remained an important part of the Reorganized Church down to the present.[58] When Joseph Smith III lay on his deathbed in 1914 and spoke to his son about the peculiarities of the Reorganization, he understood better than most that the church's membership was jealous of its autonomy. His cautions, therefore, were appropriate for his successor. Perhaps Frederick M. Smith, a man who possessed tendencies toward autocracy already, could learn from his father's experience.

Unfortunately, Reorganized Church presidents have been forced to relearn this lesson repeatedly in the twentieth century, and with every crisis the institution and membership has significantly suffered. These rebellions have always arisen when there is a perception that the church's leadership is moving in a direction or with a forcefulness that is unacceptable to many members. While the particulars of the controversies might change, always those who are discontented charge the church hierarchy with tyranny and rebel against a perceived violation of their rights to believe and act in a manner they consider in keeping with the Restoration movement. Most of the time the malcontents have been of minor importance and dismissed by the corporate church without serious consideration. Periodically, however, they become so loud and persistent and have such a large following that they cannot be ignored. The result has been a series of major crises in the church, all of which had the potential to rip it apart.[59]

During the last several years the Reorganized Church has been in the midst of yet another permutation of this tendency in the movement. Couched in terms of a rebellion against so-called ecumenical trends in the church, and fueled by the volatile issue of women's ordination, the fundamentalist controversy really rests on the issue over who controls events, the church hierarchy or the local membership. Several thousand Reorganized Church members have formed independent churches rather than submit to what they consider abuses of authority on the part of the institutional church.[60] In doing so they are exercising a cherished, long-standing tradition in the Reorganization. It was the tradition upon which the Reorganized Church was founded, and it was nourished in the leadership vacuum of the 1850s. Joseph Smith III recognized its central place in the movement and chose not to overturn it, although he certainly lessened its influence. At the same time, Smith understood how central the autonomy of individuals was and how it would always be a part of the movement, telling his son not to try "to force them or coerce. That would be bad trouble." He was right.

Notes

1. Joseph Smith III's Last Remarks to his Family (29 November 1914), Joseph Smith III Papers, Reorganized Church of Jesus Christ of Latter Day Saints Library-Archives, Independence, Missouri; "Statement of President Joseph Smith to his Son, Frederick M. Smith, Sunday, November 29, 1914," *Zion's Ensign* 26 (11 February 1914):1.

2. See the brilliant analysis of Marvin S. Hill, *Quest for Refuge: The Mormon Flight from American Pluralism* (Salt Lake City, Utah: Signature Books, 1989), quote from 17.

3. See the argument in Peter L. Berger, *The Sacred Canopy* (New York: Doubleday Anchor, 1969), 111-112.

4. Doctrine and Covenants 27:2a-b (Independence, Missouri: Herald Publishing House, 1970 ed.).

5. Ibid., 43:1b-2a.

6. For a fuller description of this event in Mormon history, see Roger D. Launius, *Zion's Camp: Expedition to Missouri, 1834* (Independence, Missouri: Herald Publishing House, 1984). The aftermath of the expedition is explained on 159-165.

7. The dissenting movement in Kirtland is admirably described in Milton V. Backman, *The Heaven's Resound: A History of the Latter-day Saints in Ohio, 1830-1838* (Salt Lake City, Utah: Deseret Book, 1983), 310-341.

8. The economic interpretation of Kirtland dissent is usually tied to the failure of the church-sponsored Kirtland Safety Society Anti-Banking Company. See Scott H. Partridge, "The Failure of the Kirtland Safety Society," *Brigham Young University Studies* 12 (Summer 1972): 437-454; Dean A Dudley, "Bank Born of Revelation: The Kirtland Safety Society Anti-Banking Company," *Journal of Economic History* 30 (December 1970): 848-853; Robert Kent Fielding, "The Mormon Economy in Kirtland, Ohio," *Utah Historical Quarterly* 27 (October 1959): 331-358; James B. Allen and Glen M. Leonard, *The Story of the Latter-day Saints* (Salt Lake City, Utah: Deseret Book, 1976), 113-114, for this view. The problem of apostasy is discussed in Leonard J. Arrington, "Centrifugal Tendencies in Mormon History," in Truman G. Madsen, ed., *To the Glory of God: Mormon Essays on Great Issues* (Salt Lake City, Utah: Deseret Book, 1972), 165-177.

9. Marvin S. Hill, "Cultural Crisis in the Mormon Kingdom: A Reconsideration of the Causes of Kirtland Dissent," *Church History* 49 (September 1980): 286-297, quote from 296.

10. *Latter Day Saint Messenger and Advocate* 3 (July 1837): 538.

11. Charles L. Woodward, "The First Half Century of Mormonism" (n.p.: New York Public Library), 195.

12. Hill, "Cultural Crisis in the Mormon Kingdom," 296.

13. Without going into a long recitation of this crisis in the church and the Danite operation in Missouri, I would commend Stephen C. LeSeuer's *The 1838 Mormon War of Missouri* (Columbia: University of Missouri Press, 1987). For a short general study of the crisis in Far West, see F. Mark McKiernan's dated essay, "Mormonism on the Defensive: Far West, 1838-1839" in F. Mark McKiernan, Alma R. Blair, and Paul M. Edwards, eds., *The Restoration Movement: Essays in Mormon History* (Lawrence, Kansas: Coronado Press, 1973), 121-140. A recent publication emphasizing his dissenting nature is Phillip R. Legg, *Oliver Cowdery: The Elusive Second Elder of the Restoration* (Independence, Missouri: Herald Publishing House, 1989).

14. On these men, see Lyndon W. Cook, "William Law, Nauvoo Dissenter," *Brigham Young University Studies* 22 (Winter 1982): 47-62; Robert Bruce Flanders, *Nauvoo: Kingdom on the Mississippi* (Urbana: University of Illinois Press, 1965), 305-310; John Fredrick Glaser, "The Disaffection of William Law," in Maurice L. Draper and Debra Combs, eds., *Restoration Studies III* (Independence, Missouri: Herald Publishing House, 1986), 163-175. Marvin Hill's *Quest for Refuge*, chapter 2, describes the early Saints as generally destitute and the social and economic policies of the church they embraced as radical, in part because there was little for the Saints to lose in a complete restructuring.

15. *Nauvoo Expositor* (7 June 1844).

16. Dallin H. Oaks, "The Suppression of the *Nauvoo Expositor*," *Utah Law Review* 9 (Winter 1966): 862-903; Dean C. Jessee, "Return to Carthage: Writing the History of Joseph Smith's Martyrdom," *Journal of Mormon History* 8 (1981): 3-21.

17. For an analysis of the Reorganization as a moderate movement, see Alma R. Blair, "Reorganized Church of Jesus Christ of Latter Day Saints: Moderate Mormons," in McKiernan, Blair, and Edwards, eds., *The Restoration Movement*, 207-230. Its dissenting nature has been discussed in Wayne Ham, "Let Contention Cease: An Overview of Past and Present Dissent Among the RLDS," unpublished address presented at the annual meeting of the Mormon History Association (5 May 1986), Salt Lake City, Utah, copy in possession of author.

18. Roger D. Launius, "Joseph Smith III and the Quest for a Centralized Organization, 1860-1873," in Maurice L. Draper and A. Bruce Lindgren, eds., *Restoration Studies II* (Independence, Missouri: Herald Publishing House, 1983), 104-120.

19. Thomas F. O'Dea, *The Mormons* (Chicago: University of Chicago Press, 1957), 160-165, quote from 164.

20. For a discussion of the flow of power to the ecclesia, see T. Edgar Lyon, "Nauvoo and the Council of the Twelve," in McKiernan, Blair, and Edwards, eds., *The Restoration Movement*, 167-205; D. Michael Quinn, "The Evolution of the Presiding of the LDS Church," *Journal of Mormon History* 1 (1974): 21-38; Ronald K. Esplin, "Joseph, Brigham, and the Twelve: A Succession of Continuity," *Brigham Young University Studies* 21 (Summer 1981): 301-341.

21. Maurice L. Draper, "Theocratic Democracy—Restoration Church Government," Part I *Saints' Herald* 115 (1 December 1968): 800-801, 814, 815; Part II, 115 (15 December 1968): 842-844.

22. Jan Shipps, *Mormonism: The Story of a New Religious Tradition* (Urbana: University of Illinois Press, 1985), 121.

23. "Common consent" was originally established in Doctrine and Covenants 25:1b. Something of its importance in the Reorganization can be gleaned from *Church Member's Manual* (Independence, Missouri: Herald Publishing House, 1957 ed.), 85-86. For an example of its excess see "Annual Conference," *The True Latter Day Saints' Herald* 9 (April 1866): 122.

24. The general outline of Briggs's life is taken from *The History of the Reorganized Church of Jesus Christ of Latter Day Saints* (Independence, Missouri: Herald Publishing House, 1967 ed.), 3:737-742; and Alma R. Blair, "The Tradition of Dissent—Jason W. Briggs," in Maurice L. Draper and Clare D. Vlahos, eds., *Restoration Studies I* (Independence, Missouri: Herald Publishing House, 1980), 146-161.

25. Douglas D. Alder and Paul M. Edwards, "Common Beginnings, Divergent Beliefs," *Dialogue: A Journal of Mormon Thought* 11 (Spring 1978): 18-28, especially 19.

26. Dale Warren, "1842 Branch Is Still Sharing 'The Good News'," *Restoration Trail Forum* 1 (August 1975): 3-4.

27. *A Manual of Practice and Rules of Order and Debate for Deliberative Assemblies of the Church of Jesus Christ of Latter Day Saints* (Lamoni, Iowa: Herald Publishing House, 1891), 9-10.

28. *Rules and Resolutions* (Independence, Missouri: Herald Publishing House, 1980 ed.,), GCR 1111, page 29.

29. *History of the Reorganized Church* 3:264-265; Joseph Smith III, "Autobiography of Joseph Smith," in Edward W. Tullidge, *The Life of Joseph the Prophet* (Plano, Illinois: Herald Publishing House, 1880), 774; *The True Latter Day Saints' Herald* 14 (1 October 1868): 105.

30. The importance of boundaries is shown in Max Weber, *The Theory of Social and Economic Organizations*, A. M. Henderson

and Talcott Parsons, trans. (New York: The Free Press, 1964), 139-143; Meyer N. Zeld and Roberta Ash, "Social Movement Organizations: Growth, Decay, and Change," *Social Forces* 44 (March 1966): 327-341; William R. Dill, "The Impact of Environment on Organizational Development," in Disney Mailik and Edward Van Ness, eds., *Concepts and Issues in Administrative Behavior* (Englewood Cliffs, New Jersey: Prentice-Hall, 1962), 94-109.

31. Robert R. King and Kay Atkinson King, "The Effect of Mormon Organizational Boundaries on Group Cohesion," *Dialogue: A Journal of Mormon Thought* 17 (Spring 1984): 61-75.

32. Elliot Aronson and Judson Mills, "The Effect of Severity of Initiation on Liking for a Group," *Journal of Abnormal and Social Psychology* 59 (September 1959): 177-181; Harold B. Gerard and Grover C. Mathewson, "The Effects of Severity of Initiation on Liking for a Group: A Replication," *Journal of Experimental Social Psychology* 2 (1966): 278-287; Jacob E. Hautaluoma and Helene Spungin, "Effects of Initiation Severity and Interest on Group Attitudes," *Journal of Social Psychology* 93 (1974): 245-259; Shipps, *Mormonism*, 121-123.

33. As only one example of this theme, see Norma Derry Hiles's tentative essay, "Lamoni: Crucible for Pluralism in the Reorganization Church," in Draper and Combs, eds., *Restoration Studies III*, 139-144. This argument can be extended for the whole of the Reorganized Church in the nineteenth century.

34. The differences within the Reorganization over matters of doctrine, policy, and organization during the 1850s have been discussed in Roger D. Launius, *Joseph Smith III: Pragmatic Prophet* (Urbana: Unviersity of Illinois Press, 1988).

35. Blair, "Reorganized Church of Jesus Christ of Latter Day Saints: Moderate Mormons," 216.

36. The most extensive analyses of the confederation period remain those by Merrill Jensen: *The Articles of Confederation: An Interpretation of the Social-Cultural History of the American Revolution, 1774-1781* (Madison: University of Wisconsin Press, 1940) and *The New Nation: A History of the United States During the Confederation, 1771-1779* (Madison: University of Wisconsin Press, 1950), which takes a decidedly pro-confederation position; and Gordon S. Wood, *The Creation of the American Republic, 1776-1787* (Chapel Hill: University of North Carolina Press, 1969), and Robert R. Palmer, *The Age of Democratic Revolution*, 2 vols. (Princeton, New Jersey: Princeton University Press, 1959-1964), which argue that the confederation was a less than fully effective governmental system.

37. Launius, "Joseph Smith III and the Quest for a Centralized Organization," 104-120. See also the critique of ecclesiastical structure in the Reorganized Church by William D. Russell, "The Latter Day Saint Priesthood: A Reflection of 'Catholic' Tendencies in Nineteenth Century American Religion," in Draper and Vlahos, eds., *Restoration Studies I*, 232-241.

38. Joseph Smith III was never subversive in this centralization process. He had a fundamental commitment to a basic democratic, pluralistic church government. In an 1899 editiorial in the *Saints' Herald*, Smith suggested the Saints should ensure that "Those who rule and those who administer must be held to a strict account of stewardship; no evasion of responsibility must be permitted, no misuse of power or position be tolerated." See Joseph Smith III, "Editorial," *Saints' Herald* 4 (October 1899), as quoted in *The History of the Reorganized Church of Jesus Christ of Latter Day Saints* 5:468-471.

    In 1905 Smith made an even stronger statement, and what made it an official pronouncement can be discovered from his signature, "Joseph Smith, President Reorganized Church." He wrote

    > In order that the people may be safe from the undue advantage of the position accorded to this leading quorum in case ambition seize them or any one of them to the overriding of the integrity of the others, two other quorums composed of larger numbers are provided, the members of which quorums hold the same priesthood as these presiding officers, each quorum being invested with equal authority in decision, so that if the three presidents should attempt to take from the people any, or all the liberties that membership in the church entitles them to, it is in the power of the Twelve and Seventy to check such ambition and secure the people from imposition.

    The checks and balances of the system, therefore, assured that democracy would be a real part of the institution. See Joseph Smith III, "Safeguards in Church Government: Are the People Safe?" *Saints' Herald* 52 (22 March 1905): 266-267.

39. Richard P. Howard, "Selection of Apostles 1835-1873: A Tradition Emerges," *Saints' Herald* 118 (April 1971): 48.

40. This has been changed in the handwritten "Early Reorganization Minutes," Book A (6 October 1860), Reorganized Church of Jesus Christ of Latter Day Saints Library-Archives, Independence, Missouri. The amendment is recorded in "Conference Minutes," *The True Latter Day Saints' Herald* 2 (May 1861): 67.

41. "Conference Minutes," *The True Latter Day Saints' Herald* 17 (15 April 1870): 243-244.

42. Doctrine and Covenants 117. On this benchmark revelation, see Richard P. Howard, "On the Background of Section 117," *Saints Herald* 124 (February 1977): 111.

43. I have no wish to duplicate—indeed, that is the best I could ever hope to do—such fine works as these which relate the details of the Briggs/Gurley affair: Blair, "Reorganized Church of Jesus Christ of Latter Day Saints: Moderate Mormons," in McKiernan, Blair, and Edwards, eds. *The Restoration Movement*, 207-230; Blair, "The Tradition of Dissent—Jason W. Briggs," in Draper and Vlahos,eds., *Restoration Studies I*, 146-161; and Clare D. Vlahos, "The Challenge to Centralized Power: Zenus H. Gurley, Jr., and the Prophet Office," *Courage: A Journal of History, Thought, and Action* 1 (March 1971): 141-158.

44. Jason W. Briggs to William H. Kelley (2 April 1877), William H. Kelley Papers, Reorganized Church of Jesus Christ of Latter Day Saints Library-Archives.

45. Ibid. (31 October 1875).

46. Jason W. Briggs, "Skepticism—Its Use," *The Messenger* 2 (Salt Lake City, Utah: 1876): 32.

47. Briggs to Kelley (15 October 1876).William H. Kelley Papers.

48. Zenos H. Gurley, Jr., to Fred Johnson (18 June 1886), Miscellaneous Letters and Papers, Reorganized Church Library-Archives.

49. Ibid.

50. Vlahos, "The Challenge to Centralized Power," 143.

51. Blair, "The Tradition of Dissent," *Restoration Studies I*, 146-161; Vlahos, "The Challenge to Centralized Power," 141-158.

52. Launius, *Joseph Smith III*, 283-285.

53. Joseph Smith III to Jason W. Briggs (22 January 1877), Joseph Smith III Letterbook #1, Reorganized Church Library-Archives.

54. Joseph Smith III to William H. Kelley (22 January 1880), William H. Kelley Papers.

55. Briggs and Gurley were quite progressive in their commitment to more advanced ways of looking at religious issues and in the use of the methodology of higher criticism then emerging. Smith did not understand and appreciate this approach. See William D. Russell, "The RLDS Church and Biblical Criticism: The Early Response," *The John Whitmer Historical Association Journal* 7 (1987): 62-68.

56. Vlahos, "The Challenge to Centralized Power," 149.

57. Joseph Smith III, "The Memoirs of President Joseph Smith (1832-1914)," *Saints' Herald* 83 (9 June 1936): 719-720.

58. Blair, "Reorganized Church of Jesus Christ of Latter Day Saints," 225.

59. For discussions of later episodes of dissent in the Reorganization, see Paul M. Edwards, "Theocratic-Democracy: Philosopher-King in the Reorganization," in McKiernan, Blair, and Edwards, eds. *The Restoration Movement*, 341-357; Larry E. Hunt, *F.M. Smith: Saint as Reformer*, 2 vols. (Independence, Missouri: Herald Publishing House, 1982); William J. Knapp, "Professionalizing Religious Education in the Church: The 'New Curriculum' Controversy," *The John Whitmer Historical Association Journal* 2 (1982): 47-59. In religious dissent generally, see Edwin Scott Gaustead, *Dissent in American Religion* (Chicago: University of Illinois Press, 1973).

60. William D. Russell is currently writing a history of the ongoing fundamentalist controversy in the Reorganized Church. This should be published in 1991. This rebellion was initiated by the perception that improper changes in policy and doctrine were being forced down the throats of the membership. On these changes, see Larry W. Conrad and Paul Shupe, "An RLDS Reformation: Construing the Task of RLDS Theology," *Dialogue: A Journal of Mormon Thought* 18 (Summer 1985): 92-103; and Howard J. Booth, "Recent Shifts in Restoration Thought," in *Restoration Studies I*, 162-175. For the fundamentalist response, see Richard Price, *Action Time* (Independence, Missouri: Price Publishing, 1985), and several periodicals: *Restoration Foundation Newsletter*, *The Herald Review*, *Restoration Voice*, and *Vision*, all published in Independence, Missouri.

Chapter 2

An Overview of Dissent in the Reorganization

by Steven L. Shields

Introduction

Given an understanding of the milieu of dissent in which Joseph Smith's religious ideas developed,[1] it is not surprising that the Latter Day Saint church is not one unified body but a movement comprised of many differing and sometimes competing organizations.[2] Joseph Smith, Jr., promoted a type of "priesthood of all believers" that was different from the mainline churches of his time; Smith taught that education was not necessarily related to divine sanction; that poor farmers and frontierspeople had as much claim on God as anyone else. Smith was not the only religious leader of his time promoting similar viewpoints, but the movement he founded is certainly one of the most enduring, if not the best known.[3]

During his fourteen-year administration of the church,[4] Joseph Smith's authority was challenged from within by at least ten identifiable movements that disassociated themselves from Smith's leadership and attempted to form independent churches. None of these movements survived Smith's death. At least four of these groups claimed independent revelation that appointed their leader as the prophet. Furthermore, two of the groups appear to have renounced all scripture except the Bible.[5]

Two of these uprisings were serious contenders for authority. The first was led by Warren Parrish in 1837[6] during a period of dissension within the church and economic crisis in the United States.[7] Parrish had been the cashier of the church's bank, the Kirtland Safety Society, and was accused by the church leadership of embezzlement. Within five years this movement had failed and Parrish was found preaching as a Baptist minister.[8]

The other dissident movement was established at Nauvoo, Illinois—then church headquarters—in 1844. William Law, a one-time counselor in the First Presidency of the church, along with several others, established an opposition church with Law as the new prophet. This group was behind the publication of the *Nauvoo Expositor*, an alternative newspaper that had as its purpose exposing alleged wrongdoings on the part of Joseph Smith, Jr., particularly the rumored practice of "spiritual wifery" which Law charged was being practiced by a small and select group of individuals within the ranks of the church leadership.[9]

Smith, as mayor of Nauvoo, persuaded the city council to declare the *Expositor* a public nuisance and ordered the printing press destroyed. Neighboring journalists were outraged and called citizens to arms. The incidents surrounding the destruction of the *Expositor* press contributed to strong public opinion against Joseph Smith, and a few short weeks later he was killed in Carthage, Illinois.[10]

The single most divisive issue the Latter Day Saint movement has ever dealt with was the untimely death of its founder. Had Smith lived out his years, the church probably would have continued under whatever direction Smith led it, with assorted and relatively small movements separating themselves from the mainstream from time to time as they had disagreement with policies, practices, or teachings. With Smith's death, however, the church had to deal with the matter of succession in its leadership. Smith did not leave explicit instructions, and with his demise what had once been more or less a unified church was to be reborn into a movement with various leaders claiming the prophetic "mantle."[11]

A Period of Fragmentation

This period of fragmentation in the church stretched essentially from the prophet's death in 1844 to about 1865 when the rival church organizations finally settled down to six main expressions of the original church. During the twenty-year period, at least twenty-five dissenting church organizations came directly out of the early Mormon movement. Each was led by an individual with his own claims as to why he should be the leader of the church. In almost every case these groups saw themselves as the only legitimate expression of the original church. Generally, each was loyal to its own understanding of Joseph Smith as a prophet and the work he had begun. Gradually, though, various smaller movements were caught up and absorbed into others—many into the Reorganized Church of Jesus Christ of Latter Day Saints, which began its emergence in 1850-1851 and became formally established when Joseph Smith III, son of the martyred prophet, became president in 1860.

The reasons for this fragmentation are varied and most can be traced directly to that milieu and its values from which the movement initially emerged. Humanity is inherently pluralistic. In the Latter Day Saint system it is theologically simple to conceptualize an alternative Christian vision. By the end of the fragmentation period there were six viable church organizations firmly established—each totally independent of the other; each launching a unique theological journey to the present day. And, in the same fashion that dissenters separated themselves from the original church, so also have dissenters continued to express their individuality by forming separate organizations off of these six organizations down to the present.

Dissident Movements in the Reorganized Church

As stated in other chapters, the Reorganized Church was born from the same dissenting tradition that is one of the hallmarks of the Latter Day Saint movement. Throughout its history, the Reorganized Church has struggled with issues of pluralism, attempting to provide the delicate balance of a middle ground. But, as history illustrates, this is a precariously difficult position to maintain. Some dissenters merely become disenchanted with the church and leave its fellowship only to disappear from all but the most personal of historical records; often other dissenters group others around them and form opposition movements.

Space does not permit even the most general of summaries of each and every dissenter who has gained the attention of the Reorganized Church. Succeeding chapters of this book will focus on specific eras of controversy. The balance of this chapter will provide a brief introduction to some of the main players in the schismatic history of the Reorganized Church.

Henry Harrison Deam

A prime illustration of the challenges of putting together the Reorganized Church from the collection of independent and autonomous congregations is the story of Henry H. Deam. Born in 1817, Deam joined the Mormon church about 1836 as a young man and was ordained an elder and served as a missionary. At Nauvoo Deam was ordained a high priest. After Joseph Smith's death Deam became one of those seeking what they considered to be the legitimate successor to the original church. Unable to follow Brigham Young for what he perceived as doctrinal innovations, Deam spent some time investigating the church organization under the leadership of James J. Strang but ascertained that it too was not the "true" church.[12]

Deam enthusiastically embraced the basic principles of the reorganizers in the early 1850s, and on 8 April 1853 was ordained an apostle in the "New Organization" of the church. In fact, the "New Organization" began its formal organizational procedures based on a revelation Deam had presented to a church conference in 1852. This inspiration was received in answer to the deep-felt question of the reorganizers on how they should go about establishing an institution:

Verily, thus saith the Lord, as I have said unto my servant Moses, "See thou do all things according to the pattern, given to you." Behold the pattern is before you. It is my will that you respect authority in my church, therefore let the greatest among you preside at your Conference. Let three men be appointed by the Conference to select seven men from among you, who shall compose a majority of the Twelve, for it is my will that quorum should not be filled up at present. Let the President of the Conference, assisted by ten others, ordain them. The senior of them shall stand as the representative. Let them select twelve men from among you, and ordain them to compose my High Council. Behold ye understand the order of the Bishopric, the Seventies, the Elders, the Priests, Teachers and Deacons. Therefore, organize according to the pattern, behold I will be with you unto the end, even so. Amen.[13]

Seven were chosen and ordained as apostles during the April 1853 Conference. The presidency of the quorum was offered, in succession, to the oldest member of the group: Zenos Gurley, Sr., who declined; then H. H. Deam, who also declined; and finally Jason W. Briggs, who accepted the presidency of the apostolic quorum as well as the presidency pro tem of the church. Briggs led the church in this capacity for the next seven years.[14]

When Joseph Smith III proved to be reluctant in accepting the presidency of this newly forming church, Deam became increasingly impatient. Believing that the Latter Day Saint structure required a First Presidency as the leading body of the church, Deam proposed that Briggs be sustained as president of the church. He also promoted the doctrine of rebaptism, which was not then accepted by the Reorganizers and never would be.[15]

Rebuffed in his attempt to see the church more fully organized, Deam and several others formed the first organized schism in the Reorganization. Emerging over several months, the effort culminated on 6 October 1854 when Deam and his followers held a separate conference. H. H. Deam was ordained president of the church, with Aaron Smith the first of his two counselors. The Reorganization met in its conference a few months later and had the dismal task of expelling Deam and John Cunningham from their positions as apostles as well as from their membership in the church, the first such action in Reorganized Church history. The charge was "apostasy and an assumption of authority."[16] Deam died in May 1860, just one month after Joseph Smith III accepted the presidency of the Reorganization. His church does not seem to have survived his demise.

Jason W. Briggs and Zenos H. Gurley, Jr.

Jason W. Briggs was one of the main promoters of the Reorganization. It was Briggs who received a revelation in November 1851 that provided impetus for the first tentative reorganizing efforts. Briggs served as president pro tem of the church from 1853 to 1860. Gurley was the son of Zenos H. Gurley, Sr., who was a close associate of Briggs. Both were members of the Reorganization's Quorum of Twelve Apostles, Briggs serving as quorum president from 1853 to 1886 when both withdrew from the church. He and Gurley, the son of his former associate, both became increasingly concerned about policy interpretations in the church in the 1870s and 1880s.[17] It eventually led to their dissent and withdrawal from the Reorganized Church, but neither sought to establish his own religious organizations.

The Priesthood Company

A minor local rift in the church occurred in French Polynesia in 1907. French Polynesia has been one of the most successful missionary fields for the Reorganized Church. It is certainly one of the largest areas of membership in the church today outside of the United States and Canada.[18]

About 1905 several church members in French Polynesia began an involvement with spiritualism. They organized themselves as the "Priesthood Company" and began holding meetings separate from the Reorganized Church. In 1907 the church took formal action against fifty-two church members who were actively involved in this new movement. Many of these appealed to church officials in the United States, stating they wished to remain as members of the church but wanted the freedom to worship as they pleased.

The elders involved with this movement issued revelations and held a powerful influence over their people. Unlike true spiritualists, though, this movement was founded in the scriptures. In 1912 Reorganization Apostle Gomer T. Griffiths was sent to the islands with instructions to deal with the dissenters. Griffiths was successful in bringing all the members of the Priesthood Company back into full fellowship in the church, whereupon the movement ceased to exist.[19]

Richard C. Evans

R. C. Evans was born in 1861 in Canada and became a member of the Reorganized Church in November 1876 when he and his mother were baptized. Over the next forty years, Evans rose through the ranks of the church's leadership, gaining fame as a preacher of great eloquence. His personal success fed a strong ego. Some of his actions created a rift within the institutional hierarchy that could not be healed. In 1919 Evans renounced the church, rejected all of its distinctive tenets, and organized his own church, the Church of the Christian Brotherhood, in Toronto, Ontario.[20]

Evans served with distinction in various priesthood offices, culminating in his selection and ordination as a counselor to Joseph Smith III in the First Presidency. According to Roger D. Launius, Evans eventually believed himself in such a position of leadership that he might be chosen by Smith to be the next prophet of the Reorganized Church.[21] When Smith's son was appointed in 1906, Evans was disappointed and considered resigning from the First Presidency in 1907. He was eventually released in 1909 and at that time became bishop of Canada.

Although Evans was actively involved in church work in Canada, reports began reaching headquarters that caused concern. Allegations of financial mismanagement and other inappropriate activities were leveled against Evans. These and other problems caused the leadership of the church to review Evans' ministry and membership, and in March 1919 Evans was disfellowshiped by the church. Several Reorganized Church members followed the charismatic Evans in forming a new religious institution.[22]

Perhaps the most important of Evans' published works is his *Forty Years in the Mormon Church: Why I Left It*, published in 1920, the year after he was removed from church membership. The title of the book is interesting because Reorganized Church members have not commonly referred to themselves as "Mormon" or to the Reorganization as the "Mormon Church." From his introduction, however, it is clear that Evans no longer saw any difference between the two and was writing his book to appeal to a broader audience.[23] This book was an essentially dishonest defense of his actions in separating from the Reorganization. He wrote:

> I have endeavored to give the true history of Mormonism, quoting very largely from their own works, and bringing into prominence the teaching of the Prophets, Seers and Revelators and other leading ministers ... having been ordained to seven different offices in the Mormon Priesthood, from Priest to Presidency of the church, standing next to Joseph Smith himself in the Highest Council of the church, the world is wise to read the facts from one who has escaped from the Mormon thraldom. ... I have tried to keep my heart from bitterness, but have, in this little volume, endeavored to show that Mormonism is the lying wonder of the Latter Days, with the hope that the honest in heart, now under the yoke of bondage will, like tens of thousands before them, make their escape and find peace and joy in the gospel of Christ as revealed in the Bible.[24]

Throughout the book Evans harped on the well-known inconsistencies and exotic doctrines adopted by some Mormon organizations but failed to explain in any true sense his own dissent, although it could have been defended on its own merits.

T. W. Williams, an apostle, took charge of the Reorganization's rebuilding process in Toronto after Evans left. He launched a vigorous preaching and pamphleteering campaign against Evans which only served to worsen the situation caused by Evans' dissent.[25] Ironically, Williams would leave the Reorganized Church only five years later and establish his own opposition movement. Evans died unexpectedly of pneumonia on 18 January 1921. His church also died shortly afterward.[26]

John Zahnd

Although apparently unrelated to the Evans case, John Zahnd separated himself from the Reorganized Church at about the same time and formed his own church, "The Church of Christ, The Order of Zion." Zahnd believed the Reorganized Church was not practicing what it was preaching concerning the building of Zion. He believed the church should be living the United Order, interpreted as having all things in common. He also rejected the office of high priest and the Quorum of the First Presidency, believing instead that the church should be led by a Quorum of Twelve Apostles.

Zahnd's new church had its first meeting at Kansas City, Missouri, in September 1918. Zahnd claimed revelation and presented documents to his church as scripture. Unfortunately, there are no records indicating how long Zahnd's organization survived and to what degree it gained followers. It would seem to have received but little attention by the Reorganization at large. By November 1928 Zahnd appears as an author in the periodical of T. W. Williams' Church of Jesus Christ.[27]

Thomas W. Williams

Thomas W. Williams was born in Utah in 1866 and baptized into the Reorganization in 1875.[28] His family were already members of the Reorganized Church before his birth. He began his church service when he was ordained a priest in 1887 and in 1889 received his first missionary assignment. He served the church in various positions throughout the United States. Between 1910 and 1916 Williams made his home in California where he became involved in politics and worked as the secretary of the California State Socialist Party. When the difficulties with R. C. Evans occurred in Toronto, it was Williams who was sent in by the church to take charge of its programs there.

Williams became an apostle in 1920 and spent almost two years in Europe with President Frederick M. Smith who was then on an extended tour. In 1924 a new management policy was adopted by the church leadership and Williams publicly opposed it. He traveled throughout the United States and Canada attempting to gain support for his position. When the church met in conference in 1925, the policy was adopted by the church, whereupon Williams was not sustained as a member of the Quorum of Twelve Apostles. Williams quickly gathered his supporters into a protest movement.[29]

Although this controversy will be discussed in a later chapter, a brief summary of Supreme Directional Control and the history surrounding the events that took place prior to and following the 1925 General Conference will be helpful. These events not only affected Williams, his religious group, and the Reorganization, but also the Church of Christ (Temple Lot), a small organization that had established itself under the leadership of Granville Hedrick in Independence, Missouri, by 1867.[30] Until the Supreme Directional Control controversy erupted in 1925, the Church of Christ had been a small family church with barely a hundred members.

This small organization had a theology and organizational structure that was not incompatible with the Reorganization, and many people believed that in time the followers of Granville Hedrick could be incorporated into the Reorganized Church. In 1918 agreements were reached between the Reorganized Church and the Temple Lot group that permitted transfers of membership from the church without affecting an individual's membership in the Reorganization.[31] After the 1925 Conference, however, hundreds of Reorganization leaders and members transferred their membership to the Temple Lot church, including some prominent appointee ministers. Church of Christ (Temple Lot) membership swelled to more than 3,000 by 1928. Experiencing its first real numerical growth, the Church of Christ chose seven apostles at its conference in April 1926. Two years later, the church reported that the quorum was complete, with a total of twelve members. It was in this group that the church vested all its leadership authority.[32]

With the relations between the Reorganization and Temple Lot groups thus changed, the leaders of the Reorganized Church acted to rescind the 1918 agreement. With its formalizing of its own leadership, the Church of Christ (Temple Lot) no longer appeared fruitful for unification with the Reorganized Church.[33]

It was into this arena that Williams stepped with his strong pronouncements against the new management policies of the Reorganized Church. Williams and his followers realized that reconciliation with the Reorganized Church was impossible and they organized the Church of Jesus Christ. Hundreds of Reorganization members put their signatures to Williams' "Protest Document," which denounced the leadership practices of Frederick M. Smith and other key church officials.[34] Many members were active in both Williams' movement as well as in the Temple Lot church; joint meetings were often held. The structure of Williams' movement was quite informal; he did not consider himself a prophet. Leadership was vested in an executive committee and regular conferences were held in April and October. After a few years, though, conferences began to be called only in the event of a special need. Williams returned to his home in Los Angeles, California, where he served on the city council. He died in Los Angeles on 11 April 1931. His followers disbanded, many uniting with the Temple Lot church.[35]

The Fallout from Increasing Liberalism

For some reason—probably the deliberately moderate policies of the church hierarchy designed to forestall dissent—separatist movements seem to have been rather quiet for almost forty years. Minor incidents of a local nature may have occurred, but very little attention seems to have been paid by the overall church. The Reorganized Church began a move toward increasing liberalism in the 1950s, however, having confronted for the first time the needs of persons outside the Christian world. Many in leadership positions believed it was time for a theological reassessment, and over a period of several years in the mid-1960s, new statements were drawn up for consideration by church leadership. Ultimately these statements gave direction to the church's curriculum and program development, which caused concern for some in the church who felt that the "old Jerusalem gospel" was being abandoned.[36] This fallout process continued from 1969 through the controversy surrounding Wallace B. Smith's revelation of 1984, which provided for the ordination of women to the church's priesthood. Many who were uncomfortable with the "new curriculum" found this event to be the "last straw," and a burgeoning of separatist movements followed. Some who had separated previous to 1984 found a new rallying cause, and the second greatest threat to the stability of the Reorganized Church was launched, the first being the Supreme Directional Control controversy of the 1920s.

Barney Fuller

Barney Fuller and others organized a group called World Redemption in Glendale, California, in 1969. This organization was not a church but was formed to present to the church membership what Fuller and his associates believed were important issues regarding what was seen as a dangerously fast-growing liberalism within the Reorganized Church. One aim of the group was to bring church members into line with the scriptures, at least as Fuller and his associates interpreted them, so they might once again enjoy the "workings of the Holy Spirit and come to know Christ as the Savior." Although Fuller had been "silenced" by the Reorganized Church (officially unable to exercise priesthood authority), he and his associates reached church members through a periodical called *Zion's Warning*, which was published from 1970 until mid-1976.

World Redemption came to an end when Fuller and others organized the New Jerusalem Church of Jesus Christ on April 18, 1975. In 1976 Fuller dropped all the Latter Day Saint scriptures, causing most of his members to leave. By 1977 only a small group remained. They disbanded shortly afterward.[37]

Stanley M. King

Another reaction to these developments in the direction of the Reorganized Church's mission was the organization of the Church of Jesus Christ Restored, under the leadership of Stanley M. King. On 26 April 1970, a group of members of the Reorganized Church in Owen Sound, Ontario, Canada, began holding meetings separate from the church. Six weeks later, on 6 June 1970, Stanley M. King was called by this group to preside over the newly organized church and took steps to complete its organization and missionary efforts. King claimed direct revelation that God had rejected the Reorganized Church and was creating a third chosen organization (the original church having been the first).[38]

A brief recitation of the group's history provides some insight into their motivation and rationale for organizing a new church. One observer said that at Owen Sound, Ontario, in January 1967

> outstanding spiritual leadership in the local branch [was] being thwarted by tradition-bound, carnal-minded men who years ago had received the Melchisedec priesthood, but who had forgotten (maybe never realized) the intent of their calling nor the intent of the Gospel of Christ. These were not all local men but individuals whose "interference" from the district and WORLD church was called "ministry."
>
> In the midst of this opposition, one man stood up in the congregation and diligently administered the law. His name? Elder Stan King. The fruits of the Holy Spirit attended his Godly counsel. His ministry consisted of encouragement, comfort, and chastisement; and for the latter he paid dearly.

According to King and his followers there was a "tremendous gulf between the glorious Church of Christ, with its blessings all so *full* and free and the administration and theology of the RLDS church. We could see, even then, the liberal, social gospel of man taking over the church we believe(d) was Christ's." Although King and his followers remained active in the Reorganization for the next two years, they were told to "work within the framework of the church, until I shall call you out from under her." It was an uneasy relationship, but King's associates remained a part of the Reorganized branch in the area, all the time the two views of where the church should be heading was debated within.[39]

During this period King developed a highly organized movement, albeit one that was small in numbers. He claimed, however, to have thousands of followers in India. Two issues that distinguished King's movement from the mainstream Reorganization was his announcement that Joseph Smith, Jr., had no successor, and that the church must build temples.[40] On this latter issue King wrote in a letter to the author dated 25 March 1975:

> The fullness of the gospel cannot be achieved without temples. They are the only Houses of worship which were employed in the first church. They did not build churches after the fashion of the world...The Temple had many functions which are not well understood by the people of the restoration, and those people who do believe in them, and those who do build them do not build them like the ones built in the old days. Neither are they used for entirely the same purpose or for the same reasons....
>
> Temples are Holy Houses. ...These are the only places which God can come to, and reveal his presence. Temples are the only places where the high ordinances can be performed...such as, the anointings, washings, receiving of the endowment [not the same as taught by the Utah church],baptism for the dead, and the receiving of the Holy Spirit of Promise, which in effect, is the Sealing Ordinance performed by the Patriarch, which is the sealing up unto eternal life, which is being saved, or as the scriptures more often call it, being sanctified.

King died on 5 October 1986 and was succeeded in the leadership of this church by his son. It still claims a small following.[41]

Paul Fishel

Late in 1976 the Reorganized Church silenced Paul E. Fishel of Vancouver, Washington. Fishel had been a member of the church since his youth, and was a patriarch at the time of his silence. In a statement issued to Fishel at that time, local Reorganized Church leaders declared that Fishel "lean[ed] toward the puritanistic stand, frequently applying labels of 'liberals' to those with whom you disagree and your ministry has assumed a 'meddlesome' conscience." The statement continued: "You have taken it upon yourself to make unauthorized visits in church member homes for the purpose of exposing supposed apostasy taking place among church leadership."[42]

The resulting furor in the Vancouver Reorganized Church led to the disorganizing of the branch. The split created a division, with many following Fishel's leadership. Initially the new group attempted to carry on with the Reorganization's name, but legal requirements forced it to incorporate under the name, "Church of Christ Restored." The new group attracted many other independent separatist branches who have gathered under its banner.

Fishel wrote, "The division resulted from the introduction of new doctrinal teaching which are contrary to those taught by the church as reorganized. They were first introduced in the 'Position Papers' in 1969."[43] Since that time Fishel's group has been meeting but has not grown much beyond its initial membership.

Women's Ordination Fallout

After the 1984 revelation mandating the ordination of women in the Reorganized Church, a sizable number of members could not square the action with their traditional interpretations of scripture, church history, and Christian doctrine. For too many it was the "last straw" in a long series of actions on the part of the church hierarchy aimed at rejecting the "truths" of the Restoration. The result has been a larger number of dissenting movements, some claiming outright rejection of the Reorganization, others seeking to remain a part of the organization and attempting to change it from within. A later chapter will explore this recent movement in detail, but the following discussion provides an overview.

Restoration Branches Movement

With the 1984 revelation by Wallace B. Smith allowing women to hold the priesthood, many in the church began to look elsewhere for religious expression. Believing that the Reorganized Church is the One True Church, many of these dissatisfied people have organized branches outside, at the same time claiming to be the true church. These separatist movements are led mainly by men who have been removed from priesthood ministry by the hierarchy—the legality of those actions being denied by the promoters of fundamentalism. Richard Price, a long-time advocate of the "independent" branch movement, has written of this activity:

> During the past quarter of a century, the highest officials of the Reorganized Church of Jesus Christ of Latter Day Saints have introduced liberalism, humanism, and ecumenism into the Church. They have also conspired to gradually remove all traces of the Restoration Movement of 1830 from the Church's beliefs. After women's ordination was officially adopted by the World Conference of 1984, it became apparent that the Liberal

Faction had permanently departed from the Faith and entered into complete apostasy. It also became apparent that the Church (the saints as a body) is now divided, and that the only part of it that shall survive this apostasy is that part which shall reject the liberal officials and their paid appointees, and shall cling to the original beliefs of the Church as they are found in the Three Standard Books of Scripture. The division in the Church has now reached permanent proportions.

To add to this confusion and sorrow which the Liberal Faction has caused, over a dozen fundamental men have arisen, each claiming to be the new God-given leader. Each claimed to be the "One Mighty and Strong," or the prophet, a mighty bishop, messenger, or restorer. Because these leaders have pulled the saints in different directions, and also because they and/or others have introduced strange doctrines, the RLDS fundamentalists are now divided into a number of separate camps. ...

Almost simultaneously the Lord has inspired groups of saints in a number of places to begin holding their own services, in which they are worshiping according to the original beliefs and practices of the only True Church—the true RLDS Church. These faithful souls, though plagued with disdain from the Liberalists and the Pro-liberalist "fence sitters" alike, have found a new freedom and a greater degree of the Holy Spirit in their midst.

Thus, a new movement is being born in the Church—silently and inconspicuously. It is the independent Restoration Branches Movement.[44]

Price has explicitly modeled his call for church reform after the efforts of the early Reorganized Church.

At the 1986 World Conference of the Reorganized Church, various groups attempted to rescind the actions of the 1984 Conference by placing in legislation several proposed resolutions. Each of these was declared out of order by the chair. When the chair's ruling was challenged, the vote overwhelmingly upheld the decision of the chair, and, thus, the actions taken in 1984 were revalidated.[45] Insufficient time has passed to determine what course ultimately will be taken by those associated with the Restoration branches movement in the Reorganization.

A. Lee Abramson

Formerly a seventy in the Reorganization, A. Lee Abramson is a key leader in the "Church of Jesus Christ, the Lamb of God." Abramson, although affirming direction by the Holy Spirit, has not claimed to be a prophet or otherwise specially appointed leader. Based first in Maine and now in Oak Grove, Missouri, this church claims several branches across the United States. Originally the group felt it should remain faithful to the Reorganized Church, but recently its members have come to believe that by maintaining membership but not activity in the organization they are supporting it. Although explorations for uniting with the Church of Christ, Restored in Vancouver, Washington, have been conducted, this church seems to be continuing as an independent organization.[46]

John M. Cato

Organized shortly after the breakup of the International Elder's Conference—a movement advocating a position similar to that of the "Restoration Branches Movement"—in April 1986, John M. Cato emerged as the prophet of a new church, the Church of Jesus Christ, Zion's Branch, headquartered in Independence, Missouri. Several revelations were issued by Cato in 1986 and 1987. However, sometime before 1988 Cato and his entire family left the church and joined the

Mormon church. In spring 1989 the church issued a statement that it no longer believes in the office of president or high priest, which, in essence, aligns them with the Church of Christ (Temple Lot) position on the matter. A doctrinal statement, published in 1988, stated:

> We of Zion's Branch have existed in a state of waiting...hoping to see an indication of repentance on the part of the leadership and membership of the RLDS organization and a commitment to once again represent Jesus Christ and the fullness of truth before the world. We have reached an understanding that the RLDS organization has not, nor appears ever will, return to the Holy task for which it was established, for their pollution of the Holy Priesthood was culminated as of April, 1984.[47]

Robert E. Baker

Robert E. Baker, a former Reorganization seventy, and others organized "The Church of Christ—His Zion's Remnant" on 15 October 1989. Baker claimed two visitations from Jesus Christ which authorized him in these actions. The position of this young organization has been:

> By His own patterns, God has allowed His Prophets to continue in leadership of the church until death. The only exception to this is if the Prophet is in transgression. ... On March 29, 1976, W. Wallace Smith, President of the Church, stated that he was naming his successor in accordance with Section 43:2a. This was a public admission of transgression and that the gift had been "taken from him." According to the law, the only thing he could have done was to name his successor. However, he then proceeded to give what he called a revelation to the church—a gift he no longer had. In that document he assigned Wallace B. Smith to a priesthood

office that did not exist: "prophet and president designate." Many other things were presented and several changes called for in the quorums. (See Section 152.) The conference approved of these unlawful actions and seemed very joyous in doing so.

Two years later, after his unlawful "ordination" as President of the Church, Wallace B. Smith immediately presented a document to be accepted as revelation which named his father, W. Wallace to another new office of the priesthood: "President Emeritus." So, the RLDS had two presidents. One was in transgression and had no authority except to name his successor, and the other, a president in name only, with no authority at all.

...W. Wallace was the only President of the Church. And only he could have saved the RLDS as being the true church. However, on August 4, 1989, W. Wallace Smith died, and the true RLDS Church died with him. This, similar to the days after the death of Joseph left the church without a Prophet and President, but more important, left the people without a church. ... But, God immediately did what He has always done. He revealed His will be begun again, a Second Time. He has established His Church once more in the same manner.[48]

The church also made some pointed remarks to those who adhere to the "Restoration Branches Movement" idea of organizing independent branches outside of the Reorganized Church, while yet claiming to be the "true" church:

Many "restorationists" are still confused, however. They have been led to believe that the RLDS church is still the Lord's church, even though it has completely strayed from the Gospel of Jesus Christ. They use the term "independent" branch. By law, there is no such thing as an "independent" branch of the church. Either there is a branch or there is not. And a branch cannot stand alone. It must be a branch of something. Study all of God's Word and you will find that this is so. If a judge or lawyer were to ask you if you consider yourself

81

to be a member of the RLDS Church and one of its branches, and you answered in the affirmative, then you would be bound by the current laws and directives of that church.[49]

Clearly there is dissension among the ranks of the dissenters, and much remains to happen before any real strength to the movement can be developed.

Other Separatist Movements

There have been others who, for various reasons, have established movements separate from the Reorganized Church but based generally on Latter Day Saint principles. The following two examples appear to have had reasons entirely different from the recent controversies, although these factors may have entered into the equation.

David B. Clark

The organization founded by Clark is not actually classed in the same group with other separatists who disagree with the issue of women's ordination. However, this church did emerge during the time period of the controversy and is included here chronologically. David B. Clark and his wife founded the Church of Christ at Oak Grove, Missouri, in November 1985. In essence, the church has attempted to establish itself along the same lines as the primitive Mormon church in 1830. David Whitmer advocated a similar organization. In a letter to the author, Clark stated his position:

> This Church of Christ has much in common with the Church of Christ that was founded by Alma I. As a result of intensive study of so-called "restoration" church history, and earnest study of the scriptures, it became

apparent to David Clark that the Latter Day Saint churches were very dissimilar to the Church of Christ that was established in 1829, and had all evolved from it over the years, adding spurious offices, doctrines, and ritual ordinances. He discovered that Latter Day Saint doctrines are rooted in the teachings of Joseph Smith and his various successors, and have very little in common with the doctrine of Jesus Christ as proclaimed in the Book of Mormon and the Bible. In a sense, the Bible, Book of Mormon, and David Whitmer's Address were to David Clark as Abinadi was to Alma. As the result of much study, fasting and prayer, the Lord drew him and his wife, Gwyn, out of the RLDS Church. In November, 1985, organized Sunday morning scripture studies began to be held regularly. The Lord eventually led David to build up a Church of Christ, in a manner similar to Alma I.

The Church of Christ is not an "off-shoot" of any of the "Latter Day Saint" churches; it is not a "dissident protest group"; in other words, it is not a "modification" or a "reorganization" of any of those existing church organizations. ... [50]

Just what it might become remains to be seen.

Christopher C. Warren

Christopher C. Warren established the Independent Church of Jesus Christ of Latter Day Saints in November 1986 at Oxford, England. As with the organization established by David C. Clark, mentioned previously, notes on this movement are included chronologically and do not necessarily indicate that Warren is a protesting group because of the ordination of women in the Reorganized Church.

Warren was a member of the Mormon church who later joined the Reorganized Church before establishing his own organization. In 1988 Warren moved his church headquarters to Oslo, Norway, where the church has had some success in attracting members. Warren claims to receive revelation. He argues, like Stanley M. King and others, that two latter-day apostasies were foretold. With the death of Joseph Smith, the original church was rejected and Brigham Young introduced heresies into the church. The Reorganized Church, then, originally taught the truth, but it, too, since 1958, has shifted into apostasy.[51]

Conclusion

As the 1980s came to a close, the world saw a resurgence of the human quest for dignity and freedom of choice, especially in Eastern Europe. The concept is not really new. From the beginning, humanity was given the inherent right to choose its own destiny. The United States was founded on the principles of self-determination, which were enshrined in the two great documents of freedom: the Declaration of Independence and the U. S. Constitution, accompanied by the Bill of Rights. On this foundation the Latter Day Saint movement was founded; its adherents still proudly proclaim the divinely granted right of "free agency"—the ability to choose for oneself the direction of one's life and ambitions. Ultimately it is upon this principle that dissent in the Reorganization is based. In its efforts to maintain a pluralistic theology, the Reorganization as an institution has fostered separatist movements.

Although throughout the history of the church there have been and undoubtedly will continue to be those who disagree, there have been two major arenas of dissent—both of which have taken place in the twentieth century, barely fifty years apart from each other. The first was the 1925 controversy concerning the principles of church administration, commonly called Supreme Directional Control. The choice of words used by the church leadership in describing the new policy was unfortunate. Other descriptions might have been less explosive. The dissent that erupted as a result of the new policy, however, was the single-most divisive issue in the history of the Reorganization to that point. The protest that followed was fairly well organized and reasonably unified. Many high-ranking church officials found themselves aligned with the protest. It also illustrated the limits of the pluralistic stance of the institution. The protestors clearly disagreed with the leadership of the church, specifically its president.

The next divisive controversy has been the ordination of women, which was prefaced by a drawn-out opposition to the increasing liberalization that developed after the church reassessed its theological position in the late 1960s. However, the major difference between this latest controversy and Supreme Directional Control is that the dissent is not unified, and there appears to be little hope for the dissenters at gaining unity. In addition, none of the high-ranking leaders of the church are on the "outside" in this disagreement.

The Latter Day Saint mind-set seems irrevocably centered on the leadership of a prophet-president. Without this individual leader upon which all the current dissenters can focus, their efforts will continue to be fragmented and contentious one with another. However, should the majority of dissenters find one person in whom they could all have faith as the prophet, such as the Reorganized Church found in the person of Joseph Smith III, this latest controversy has the potential of being extremely damaging to the Reorganized Church in the long term. While the 1925 dissent was over policy, the 1980s disagreement revolves around theology and the fundamental direction of the church.

For most Latter Day Saints, it seems, theology is paramount. By and large the current dissenters still cling tenaciously to the theology of the Reorganized Church as it was expressed in the 1950s. They reject out of hand the entire prophetic administrations of W. Wallace Smith (who served from 1958 to 1978) and Wallace B. Smith (who has been president since 1978); they still believe there is only one "true" church (meaning denomination) and that all other Christian organizations are "false"; they refuse to acknowledge historical facts concerning details of the church during the Nauvoo era (1839-1846) and Joseph Smith's involvement in various theological explorations; they are generally scriptural literalists but are not always unified on interpretation.

In almost every instance, from the examples shown in this chapter, certain individuals or groups of individuals have found themselves to be in disagreement with the leadership of the church. Regardless of how democratic church procedures may be, there are some differences between the way the church is governed and how the United States and other democratic republics are governed. And this may be part of the reason for dissenters finding it necessary to separate themselves from the institution and establish alternative organizations. Although delegates to the Reorganization's biennial World Conferences have opportunity to sustain or reject the general officers of the church, they do not have alternate choices as usually occurs in a general political election. A key difference, of course, is the Latter Day Saint principle of revelation and the belief that the general officers are, in fact, called by God, rather than merely selected from among the body of the church by the members themselves. In some respects, this tenet of faith runs counter to the principles of self-determination and free choice; it makes it easy for dissenters to act on their own "authority from God" to establish an opposition movement whose policies are more in line with the thinking of those involved.

Notes

1. See Dan Vogel, *Religious Seekers and the Advent of Mormonism* (Salt Lake City, Utah: Signature Books, 1988) for an excellent treatise of some of the attitudes surrounding the Smith family and their social circumstances.

2. See Steven L. Shields, *Divergent Paths of the Restoration* (Los Angeles, California: Restoration Research, 1990 ed.) for a catolog of most of the Latter Day Saint churches and related organizations. See also Steven L. Shields, *The Latter Day Saint Churches: An Annotated Bibliography* (New York: Garland, 1987).

3. Joseph Smith expressed his story of the coming forth of the church in several different versions. The most commonly known story was first published in 1842. See *Times and Seasons* 3 (1 March 1842): 706-710, and 3 (1 April 1842): 748. Succeeding issues of this periodical contained installments of Joseph Smith's history and the history of the church. This record has formed the basis for much of the official history of the Latter Day Saint church from its inception up to Smith's death in 1844. In Smith's interpretation and practice of priesthood, any male member of the church who was deemed worthy could be ordained as a minister without requirements of a seminary degree or other formal education. Certain priesthood were designated to officiate in sacramental roles, reserved only to those so appointed. However, the responsibility of all church members, by virtue of their baptism, to provide ministry to other persons has been an important concept in the church since its earliest days.

4. The fourteen years is marked from the legal organization of the church as of 6 April 1830. Contemporary records of persons associated with the church at the time contend that the church existed before that date by at least a year or possibly more and that the action of 6 April 1830 was taken to satisfy the requirements of the law. See David Whitmer, *An Address to All Believers in Christ* (Richmond, Missouri: n.p., 1887), 32-33.

5. See Shields, *Divergent Paths of the Restoration*, 21-29 for further details.

6. Ibid., 22.

7. This period was a time of great crisis in the church. All of the three witnesses to the Book of Mormon, four apostles, several presidents of Seventy, and one member of the First Presidency left the church. See Milton V. Backman, Jr., *The Heavens Resound: A History of the Latter-day Saints in Ohio* (Salt Lake City, Utah: Deseret Book, 1983), 327-329.

8. Shields, *Divergent Paths*, 23. See also *Latter Day Saints Elders' Journal* 1 (August 1838): 55-60 for a contemporary narrative regarding Parrish's separatist movement.

9. For an interesting and scholarly analysis of this topic see Richard P. Howard, "The Changing RLDS Response to Mormon Polygamy: A Preliminary Analysis," *The John Whitmer Historical Association Journal* 3 (1983): 14-29.

10. Details of Smith's death are readily available in numerous resources which deal with Latter Day Saint history. Shields, *Divergent Paths of the Restoration*, 29-30, quotes Thomas C. Sharp's stinging renunciation of Smith's actions and a call to arms.

11. For details on the succession crisis, see D. Michael Quinn, "Joseph Smith III's [1844] Blessing and the Mormons of Utah," *The John Whitmer Historical Association Journal* 1 (1981): 12-27.

12. *The History of the Reorganized Church of Jesus Christ of Latter Day Saints* (Independence, Missouri: Herald Publishing House, 1967 ed.) 3: 732-737.

13. Zenos H. Gurley, Sr., "History of the New Organization of the Church," *The True Latter Day Saints' Herald* 1 (March 1860): 55.

14. W. B. "Pat" Spillman, *Studies in Restoration History: The Hastening Time, Volume 3* (Independence, Missouri: Herald Publishing House, 1988), 13.

15. Persons who had been baptized in the original church could, upon request, be granted full membership in the Reorganized Church. Other claimants to succession required that all be rebaptized to reaffirm their commitments.

16. *History of the Reorganized Church* 3: 226-231.

17. Ibid., 3: 737-742.

18. World Conference Reports (March 1990), 109-126.

19. F. Edward Butterworth, *Roots of the Reorganization: French Polynesia* (Independence, Missouri: Herald Publishing House, 1977), 197-217.

20. For a treatise of Evans's life and ministry, see Roger D. Launius, "R. C. Evans: Boy Orator of the Reorganization," *The John Whitmer Historical Association Journal* 3 (1983): 40-50.

21. Ibid., 43.

22. Ibid.; *History of the Reorganized Church* 7:297-99.

23. R. C. Evans, *Forty Years in the Mormon Church: Why I Left It* (Shreveport, Louisiana: Lambert Book, 1976 ed.), 3.

24. Ibid.

25. Several undated tracts were published by the Reorganized Church in Canada, all authored by Williams. See a partial listing in Shields, *The Latter Day Saint Churches: An Annotated Bibliography*, 220-221.

26. *History of the Reorganized Church* 7: 460-461.

27. Shields, *Divergent Paths of the Restoration*, 118-119.

28. *History of the Reorganized Church* 7:705.

29. Ibid., 7: 659, 706-707.

30. B. C. Flint, *An Outline History of the Church of Christ (Temple Lot)* (Independence, Missouri: Church of Christ, 1953), 102, 106-111.

31. *History of the Reorganized Church* 7: 667.

32. Flint, *Outline History*, 140-141.

33. *History of the Reorganized Church* 8: 66-69, 77.

34. This "Protest Document" was published in Independence, Missouri, in *The Messenger* 1 (October 1925): 1, 5.

35. Shields, *Divergent Paths of the Restoration*, 120-123.

36. Copies of the 1969 "Position Papers" found their way outside the offices of the church leadership and were published clandestinely.

37. Shields, *Divergent Paths of the Restoration*, 182-183, 202.

38. Ibid., 183.

39. Bruce Swackhammer, "History," *The New Times and Seasons* 1 (January 1974): 7-8. Published at Owen Sound, Ontario, by the Church of Jesus Christ Restored.

40. Ibid., 10-12.

41. Shields, *Divergent Paths of the Restoration*, 284.

42. On this issue, see Russ Fishel, *The Vancouver Story* (Vancouver, Washington: n.p., 1978).

43. *Restoration* 4 (July 1985): 7.

44. Richard Price and Larry Harlacher, *Restoration Branches Movement: Pamphlet #1—Forming of Restoration Branches* (Independence, Missouri: Price Publishing, 1986), 1-3.

45. World Conference *Bulletin* (1986): 288-289.

46. *Restoration Foundation Newsletter* (Independence, Missouri: August 1985); *Restoration* 4 (October 1985): 5, 7, (January 1988): 18.

47. Quoted in *Restoration* 7 (October 1988): 27, 28.

48. "An Open Letter to All Restorationists," *The Examiner* (Independence, Missouri: 11 November 1989).

49. Ibid.

50. See *Restoration* 5 (October 1986): 4, 17; 6 (April 1987): 8; 7 (January 1988): 18; 7 (October 1988): 2.
51. Ibid., 5 (October 1986): 22, 28; 6 (April 1987):12, 13; 6 (July 1987): 2, 5; 7 (July 1988): 11.

Chapter 3

The Supreme Directional Control Controversy: Theocracy Versus Democracy in the Reorganized Church, 1915-1925

by Kenneth R. Mulliken

Introduction

The Reorganized Church of Jesus Christ of Latter Day Saints inherited from the original church the paradoxical doctrine of theocratic-democracy. This policy formed the basis for a series of rivalries from 1915 to 1925 between the First Presidency, specifically Frederick Madison Smith, and leading members of the other two branches of the Joint Council: the Quorum of Twelve Apostles and the Presiding Bishopric. These conflicts were fueled primarily by Frederick Smith's rigid and authoritarian view of church hierarchy and his use of power, which became known among the membership as "Supreme Directional Control."[1]

To fully understand the problematic contentions of Supreme Directional Control, one must examine the various undercurrents that caused the friction. These included the nature of theo-democratic religion and the vague and somewhat ambiguous definition of presidential responsibility within the Reorganized Church in 1915, the details of the six controversies of the larger Supreme Directional Control controversy in which Smith acted as aggressor in all but one case, and the various reasons President Frederick M. Smith claimed divine authority and chose to express it through this particular use of power. Among these reasons are Smith's view of Zion, his use of reform (progressive) methods reflecting external social trends to meet his utopian goals, his view of financial stewardship, and Smith's childhood and education. Finally, one must briefly probe the personalities opposing Smith, specifically Apostles T. W. Williams and John Rushton and Presiding Bishop Benjamin R. McGuire. This essay examines these topics and delineates some of the issues and concerns of leadership dynamics within the Reorganized Church structure.[2]

Inherent Conflicts of the Presidential Function

From its legal inception on 6 April 1830, the Restoration movement accepted as law the unique doctrine of theocratic-democracy. This practice was based on the church's interpretation of Christ's teachings as recorded in the New Testament and the Book of Mormon. Following both the death of Joseph Smith, Jr., in 1844 and the reorganization of the church under the leadership of his son Joseph Smith III in 1860, the theo-democratic aspect of the religion was maintained.

Theocratic-democracy represented the early Restorationists' attempt to realize authoritative governance for the church, combining the rule of God (theocracy) with the ratifying power of the people (democracy). Members of the church could express their common consent to, or dissent from, theocratic rule in conference sessions. At these sessions members voted to sustain the general authorities of the church, made legislative proposals, passed on priesthood calls, and accepted revelations of God's will presented to the church by the prophet.[3]

In a theocratic-democracy, divine authority reached downward from God through priesthood or prophetic utterance, while democratic voice reached upward from the membership in their collective approval or disapproval.[4] This right of the people to express their democratic ideas as to what should transpire within the structure of the church, coupled with a lack of specific laws governing the president's power and the force of his own personality, created great potential for conflict. The question was this: With whom did the final authority rest—the president and prophet or the people? The tension in this situation has been dealt with according to the various attitudes of differing presidents and their constituencies.[5]

I will focus here primarily on the three leading quorums of the Reorganized Church during Frederick M. Smith's rule. The relationships of the First Presidency, the Presiding Bishopric, and the Quorum of Twelve Apostles have always been critical to understanding the governance of the church, for these three quorums form the administrative Joint Council from which much authority emanates.[6] The Twelve, charged with conducting all missionary endeavors as "traveling councilors" and special witnesses of Christ throughout the world, approached issues of government from a perspective oriented toward missionary outreach. The Presiding Bishopric, composed of a presiding bishop and his two counselors, was responsible for the economic affairs of the church, and emphasized those more practical concerns in many of their dealings.[7] The First Presidency of three men held responsibility for the overall direction of the church. The president, in this case Frederick M. Smith, presided over the high priests specifically and also over the entire general church. His two counselors were to help him with decisions as he needed them. His only restrictions were stated in church scripture:

> And inasmuch as a president of the high priesthood shall transgress, he shall be had in remembrance before the common council of the church, who shall be assisted by twelve councilors of the high priesthood; and their decision upon his head shall be an end of controversy concerning him.[8]

The three main quorums of the church were full-time officers and had no outside employment, whereas most other priesthood members were lay priesthood earning their livelihoods outside the church but ministering as time and energy permitted.

The principal First Presidency members involved in this controversy were Frederick M. Smith, who served between 1915 and 1946, and Elbert A. Smith (1915-1938). They were essentially united in position throughout the debate. In addition, from the Quorum of Twelve Apostles John Rushton (1902-1947), Thomas W. Williams (1920-1925), and F. Henry Edwards (1922-1938) were intimately involved in the Supreme Directional Control controversy. Not always did they speak with one voice even among themselves, and certainly there was less than complete consensus among the entire Twelve. The Presiding Bishopric, on the other hand, was generally united in opposition to the Presidency's supposition that it possessed the authority necessary to chart the total direction of the church. Presiding Bishop Benjamin R. McGuire (1916-1925) and his associates, Israel A. Smith (1920-1925) and James Keir (1916-1925), presented a united front opposing the Supreme Directional Control concept.

During the presidencies of Joseph Smith, Jr. (1830-1844) and Joseph Smith III (1860-1914), there had been some difficulties in balancing theocracy and democracy in equal proportions, especially during the years 1876-1902. The gentle pragmatism of Joseph III, however, mitigated much of the controversy that might have surfaced under more authoritarian leadership. With the accession of Frederick Madison Smith to the presidency in 1915, however, controversy quickly arose largely because there was less desire on both sides to find compromises to differences. This set the stage for six friction-filled events that would plague the church for the next ten years: (1) administrative centralization of power under the president, 1917-1919; (2) General Conference actions, 1922; (3) the question of common consent and nomination, 1923; (4) the *Herald* controversy, 1924; (5) Joint Council debates, 1924; and (6) General Conference actions, 1925.

The Supreme Directional Control Rivalries (1915-1925)

A closer focus on the specific events of the Supreme Directional Control rivalries reveals the nature of dissent within the Reorganized Church from 1915 to its peak in 1925. In 1915 the Reorganized Church numbered slightly more than 70,000 members. President Frederick M. Smith envisioned the relatively modest resources of this group better and more efficiently used by consolidating services and centralizing energy. The roots of Smith's first effort to centralize the power of the church under the Presidency can be traced to 1902 when Smith was a counselor to his father, Joseph Smith III. At this time he instituted a monthly and quarterly reporting system for all church appointees (full-time church ministers) and for the officers of stakes, districts, and congregations. Church work often faltered, he assumed, due to "a lack of proper coordination" of the priesthood on all levels. The new system, he hoped, would help ensure new cooperation through the central authority of the institution.[9] Smith desired organization and order, and with it would come, he believed, efficiency and accomplishment.

Although compliance was uniform, many men working for the church took notice of the approach and questioned the method. In part, this approach was unpopular because change was being imposed from the top downward. Previously no one monitored their work directly, and some officers felt it somewhat insulting that the "young man" in the First Presidency suddenly required such reports.

A genuine clash of power did not occur until 1917, however. By this time Smith had finished his doctoral dissertation in social psychology at Clark University titled, "The Higher Powers of Man," and had turned his attention to the task of leading the church. His choice of theme for his dissertation and his choice of social psychology for his doctorate point to Smith's thinking, which he carried into his church work.

In March 1917 Smith sent a letter to the Quorum of Twelve which was assembled in pre-Conference meetings. In this letter he asked that all information regarding administrative or personnel changes be cleared through his office before action.[10] This had not been the usual procedure, and the Twelve objected to the change in their traditional responsibilities as missionary and administrative officers. Smith also ruled that the Twelve were being withdrawn from their traditional role of supervising geographic fields and missionary areas, instead taking their assignments directly from the First Presidency. They grudgingly yielded to Smith's direction. At best they considered this an "experiment." Two years passed before the next General Conference, during which time the Twelve saw Smith change missionary boundaries, extend the demarcation between local administration and missionary work, and reduce the number of stipendiaries.[11]

In February 1919 the Twelve again met in pre-Conference meetings with the expressed intention of discussing the "experiment" being forced on them, noting that it was not a result of revelation and therefore debatable. Among themselves the apostles agreed that some innovations were needed in the working system of the church but disapproved of Smith's approach of executive fiat. Rather, they would have preferred these innovations to arise through joint democratic discussions between themselves and the Presidency as had been the case under Frederick's father.[12]

The passive approach the Twelve had employed in relation to the changes that Smith had instituted suddenly vanished on 11 February 1917. On that date the

97

Quorum of Twelve issued a brief openly protesting centralization and the method that it had been introduced. It stated in part:

> It is the opinion of this Quorum that the entire field of ministerial labor should be placed directly under the supervision...of the Twelve, and so discharge the obligation imposed upon them...by the First Presidency.... Further, the appointment of the missionary corps and the direct supervision and active oversight of these men in their fields of labor be undertaken by the Quorum of Twelve as provided for in the law.[13]

They buttressed their case by citing scriptural references, specifically from the Doctrine and Covenants. The Twelve suggested that the church was built on democracy and common consent and that recent actions by the president had violated some of these cherished principles.

More important, toward the end of this document the Twelve inserted an additional concern. Each of the eighteen church officials comprising the Joint Council received an allowance for expenses. This allowance had no maximum limits. However, officials were expected to act responsibly and keep an itemized account of expenses. Using church treasury records, the Twelve now attempted to put the president on the defensive concerning his finances, contending that he was using too much money personally. "Inasmuch as there is increased dissatisfaction more or less widespread because of your annual expenses," they wrote, "we request that you submit to the Quorum an itemized account of your expenses for 1918, including family and personal."[14] Implicitly, they were suggesting that if the Twelve were to be accountable to President Smith, whose expenditures far exceeded other appointees, he should be equally accountable to them.

Table 1

Expense Allowances for
Leading Reorganization Officials, 1916-1918[15]

Year	F. M. Smith Finances	Amount Exceeding Average Church Official Finances
1916	$3,978.07	$3,014.07
1917	5,652.19	4,063.27
1918	5,995.84	3,809.95

Whether this disagreement stemmed from economic or more personal reasons, the emergence of financial statistics not only widened the rift between the president and Twelve, it also suggested two distinct attitudes toward the path the church should take: Smith's bold, experimental approach versus the Twelve's traditional, conservative approach. The cleavage was to intensify in later conflicts of Supreme Directional Control into a clear split among members of the Joint Council and the General Church membership. Meantime, Smith's curt response to such questioning two weeks later stated: "The conclusions reached in that document are due to ... losing sight of the proper perspective of the provisions of the law which place upon the Presidency the responsibility of supervision of the work of the church in all the world."[15]

The Twelve continued their discussions. Privately some spoke out against the usurpation of power by the Smith regime, which they viewed as unsatisfactory. Apostle Paul M. Hanson gave a speech during the General Conference that was typical of these interpretations. He said:

Under the present system matters of importance are allowed to drag on from year to year to the danger of the

church. Experience seems to show that the President
has too big a job on his hands. Everything goes to the
Presidency and nothing to the Twelve and under the
present system we cannot plan our work.

The disposition of the President to approve of all
recommendations for ordination seems to be an inva-
sion of our previous custom ... and the present system is
causing discouragement among influential men of the
church.[16]

Hanson concluded that Smith's conduct was dictatorial
and attempted to thwart the power and responsibility
of the apostolic calling. He spoke for the quorum when
he refused to surrender its individuality, thus reducing
influence from the First Presidency.[17]

For his part Frederick M. Smith was deeply frustrated
by what he viewed as stubbornness, old-fashionedness,
and even betrayal of loyalty from the Twelve, as is
evident from his writings of the time. In the church's
missionary magazine, *Zion's Ensign* (8 May 1919), he
recorded a vision of immense growth for the church if
only, he believed, the other members of the Joint Council would cooperate to increase efficiency under one
solid manager. He envisaged tremendous church expansion through a new generation of missionaries who
were to be fluent in foreign languages, church doctrine,
history, and the sociopolitical views of the people to
whom they would be sent.[18] Naturally they would utilize
facilities at the church-owned Graceland College in
Lamoni, Iowa, for study and preparation. He had great
plans for the church. Clearly Smith saw himself as the
captain and the church as the ship that he steered.

The 1919 General Conference, held in Lamoni,
brought further frustrations to Smith. In a brilliant
maneuver to gain the allegiance of the general membership, however, Smith gained the upper hand. He asked,

"Is your leader ... to be a real executive or a mere receiver of reports?" He went on to portray himself as a loyal and dedicated servant of Christ (an assertion with which few would have argued even if they disagreed with his methods) who had to deal not only with the criticism from outside the church but within the church as well. Smith stated, "In the executive or administrative line the Twelve are in all respects subordinate to, and under the direction of the Presidency, and this includes missionary as well as local work."[19] He concluded that compromise was impossible and that "The work of the church is such that confidence in your officers is demanded. And of no officer is that more true of than your chief executive ... and to make it easy for you to select some other in whom you can place this confidence if you have not in the present incumbent, I have presented my resignation."[20] Never before had such a situation occurred in the fifty-nine years since the Reorganization.

The Reorganized Church was very young, and no precedent had been established for presidential resignation. Smith, as everyone in the General Conference knew, succeeded his father. The Conference, which legally possessed the power to designate a new leader, embraced a tradition of church leadership being passed from father to son so strongly as to accept it as bordering on law. In addition, there was no one else to be president except one of Fred's younger brothers, none of whom were considered by the Conference to be legitimate candidates while Fred was still living.

Comparatively, interference in the missionary administration was of far lesser significance to the Twelve than the potential chaos of a leaderless institution. Two important events at the Conference immediately followed. The first was the unanimous ratification of an agreement which stated "The work of the Twelve is under the direction of the Presidency in the administrative or executive work of the church both in missionary and local lines."[21] In his book, *F. M. Smith: Saint as Reformer*, Larry E. Hunt characterized this agreement by saying, "No longer were they [the Twelve] to be appointed to specific fields as individuals; the Presidency decided where and to whom they were sent, for what purposes, and the length of appointment. Once local organization was effected by the missionary corps of the church," Hunt emphasized, "local leaders, not missionaries or the Twelve, were in charge of their operations."[22] Herein lay the seed for later controversy.

The other major event of the Conference, and of more immediate importance, was the rejection of Smith's resignation and a resolution declaring, "By this vote we express our confidence in him as a prophet, seer, and revelator to the church and as the President thereof."[23] Because of Smith's skillful manipulation, the doctrine of inherent succession, and the delegates' trust in Smith's divine authority, he triumphed in this first major battle.

The next three years were fairly uneventful. However, an undercurrent of tension manifested itself on 2 October 1922 when President Smith presented a revelation to the General Conference. This document released four men from their responsibilities as apostles. During 1921 one had died and another had resigned, leaving a vacancy of six in the quorum. The four men released, by the acceptance of the document of revelation, were the leading protestors to Smith's increasing administrative control. In accordance with usual procedure, the document had been referred to the various quorums for perusal and recommendations to the General Conference delegates concerning its validity. The Quorum of Twelve, the Quorums of Seventy, and the Presiding Bishopric joined in recommending that any action on it be deferred pending settlement of important matters before the Joint Council. Debate of this substantial matter had broadened into a review of the entire administration of the First Presidency and the divinity of the revelation. The document, however, was approved on 12 October by a vote of 656 to 452.[24] Smith won but at the same time lost ground in comparison to the 1919 General Conference since his actions were challenged by a strong minority of the delegates (more than 40 percent). Other indicators of the underlying dissatisfaction were substantial loss in revenues received through tithing and a drop in the number of baptisms registered in the net gain of members.

Table 2[25] Net Gain of Members 1918-1922	Table 3[26] Income Through Tithing 1920-1923
1918 - 4,565	1920 - $493,325.84
1919 - 1,921	1921 - 417,049.99
1920 - 1,120	1922 - 309,085.44
1921 - 1,630	1923 - 291,539.42
1922 - (131)	

The "Net Gain of Members" table reflects baptisms (anyone baptized into the church) less deaths and withdrawals. It is quite possible that discontent with church policies was a factor in the inconsistency of missionary effectiveness in conversions. This is especially true as one compares the net gain of 4,565 members in 1918 with the net loss of 131 members in 1922. The tithing income table more directly demonstrates the discontent among the membership with the direction taken by church officials. While tithing (one-tenth of financial income remaining after meeting basic needs) was expected from each member, it was not mandatory. No punishment resulted from ignoring one's stewardship/tithing responsibility. Thus it was the easiest form of protest within the institution. It should be noted, however, that this was a time of serious financial crises in the United States economy. While the 1920s are generally viewed by economic historians as a prosperous decade for most Americans, it certainly was not for many outside urban centers, and the economy was a bit sluggish in converting from wartime to peacetime. Ironically, as revenues dwindled, Smith reached for increased power.

The third major confrontation of the Supreme Directional Control controversy arose in 1923 over the issue of common consent. Leading up to the 1923 Conference, Smith had organized a committee which directly oversaw the six critical church departments in Independence, Missouri: Sunday school, Religio (study and activity for youth), women's auxiliary, education, publication, and remedial and corrective agencies. Smith nominated the executive officers for the approval of the General Conference, and all subordinate officers were chosen by Smith's handpicked committee (which included his wife). The next target he set his sights on was the ecclesiastical structure of congregations, stakes, and districts. This was known as the controversy of "common consent."

The question this issue raised: Should the administration nominate local officers—to place the best

trained and educated men in positions of authority—
then turn to.the membership only for approval, or did
the people have the right to both nominate and approve
their leaders on a local level? At this point a real tug of
war emerged between those supporting Smith and
those supporting the membership. This was the major
test that ultimately would determine how theocratic-democracy would be defined by the church.

In the 25 April 1923 *Saints' Herald,* Smith called for
"a more definite coordination of the departments in Zion
and a more uniform method of procedure in selecting
officers."[27] Subsequently, a proposed policy was given
to the local Independence conference by Apostle Daniel
T. Williams which included the following:

> 1. The heads of the general departments of the
> church and the pastor in Zion (Independence Stake) in
> consultation with the First Presidency shall nominate
> the heads of departments in Zion, subject to ratification
> by the Conference in Zion.
> 2. The four department heads in Zion shall then in
> consultation with the pastor in Zion select the heads of
> departments in the various congregations, the pastor in
> each congregation to be duly consulted. These selec-
> tions shall be presented to the Conference for approval.
> 3. In each local congregation the four local heads of
> departments together with the pastor shall appoint all
> subordinate officers and teachers.[28]

However, a substitute refined this proposal and won
support. This substitute asserted that nomination by
the membership took precedence over virtue of office,
but this was only for local congregations; the substitute
granted the president the right to nominate officers to
stake positions. The compromise only heightened the
debate for the 1923 General Conference and prompted
organized opposition to Smith led by some of the apos-

tles. A resolution by members of the Twelve blasted the proposal of administerial nomination. They pointed to the recognized practice and custom of nomination through membership and expressed "disapproval of any centralization of power in the hands of any administrative officer, or officers, whereby the expression of free choice and the deliberate will of the body may be invaded or abridged."[29] They cited various scriptures and precedents, most of which affirmed the voice of the people.[30] Yet, this was part of the problem. Scripture could be interpreted to support either side of the common consent issue.

This issue captured the full attention of the Reorganization's membership in the series of Supreme Directional Control rivalries. Two indicators of widespread interest were evidenced in the extensive debate on the subject on the Conference floor of the Stone Church in Independence between numerous delegates and the rejection of a Conference proposal to print only a few of the speeches of the twenty-two major church officials who addressed the issue. Although Smith wanted none of the discussions published, he eventually agreed to a compromise to print the twenty-two essays in the *Saints' Herald* during the following year. There is no doubt the rift grew as an increasing number of the membership became familiar with the division and funneled their opinions into the debates. In its extremes, one side saw the issue as democracy versus a tyrannical leader; the other saw it as efficiently establishing the kingdom of Zion versus chaos and hindrance of God's will.

Throughout the 1923 General Conference disagreements over this issue continued to rage on the Conference floor. Before the stated resolution could be accepted or rejected, however, two other members of the Twelve introduced a substitute. This, too, held up the idea of common consent but endorsed the will of God as "executed by divinely appointed ministers with the consent of the people."[31] In this approach the church members need not worry with the responsibility of active engagement in church activities, but they did hold the final authority because they reserved the right to say no. Finally an end to the debate was reached. Apostle F. Henry Edwards, Smith's son-in-law, offered an amendment to the substitute motion which in essence allowed both presiding officers and local membership to nominate with the people's voice as the final authority. Although this amendment passed, actually little changed in the practice of nominating local officers and all that was accomplished was an increase in bitterness and an uneasy truce.

The next major controversy focused on the Herald Publishing House—the publishing division of the church. A five-member board had been designated by the 1923 Conference to establish and execute managerial and editorial policies. Despite Resolution 361, passed by the 1891 Conference, clearly stating that the "editorship of the *Herald* was not inherent in the powers of any office," the reality was that the First Presidency (under both Joseph Smith III and Frederick) participated actively in editorial direction of the *Saints' Herald*.[32] On the surface this 1924 *Herald* struggle involved editorial rights of the board versus those of President Smith. At a broader, more fundamental level it involved one leader's attempt to control expression within the Reorganized Church.

In response to ten years of declining *Saints' Herald* sales and subscriptions, the Board of Publication determined (through neutral questionnaires to all church appointees and local, self-sustaining officers) that the content of the magazine was too one-sided, favoring views of the First Presidency without giving equal voice to contrary opinions. It was also worded in a lofty, eloquent manner that was difficult for the ordinary person to understand and appreciate. By combining the *Saints' Herald* (a family publication geared toward adults), *Zion's Ensign* (a childrens' magazine), and *Autumn Leaves* (a young adult publication) under one managing editor, the board hoped to appeal to a wider range of membership and to increase sales. Smith claimed the board's actions assumed "unwarranted powers" and changed the character of the *Herald* so radically that its editorial columns no longer represented the First Presidency.[33] In fact, the power of editorial management had always rested in the Board of Publication but, in practice, the president had played an explicit role in approving content.[34] The board felt that a change from the status quo was now needed, and it was not afraid to stand up to opposition from the First Presidency to make what it reasoned were worthwhile changes. In the end the *Herald* controversy left Smith's previous editorial power in the hands of the Board of Publication. It was the only aggressive victory for the democratic forces in the Supreme Directional Control controversies.

But this wrestling of authority from the First Presidency created ill will and controversy throughout the church. For instance, numerous tracts and pamphlets appeared, focusing on the various interpretations of the changes that many felt had penetrated the church since 1915. "Centralization," "theocracy," "authority," and "tradition" were terms common to these pamphlets, and the theme of Smith's perceived abuse of power was found in all of them. Interestingly, many of these political tracts were written by "ranking" priesthood members. Some tracts were direct and centered on beliefs or facts; but others, soliciting specific support for an issue, were weak and lacking substance. These later pamphlets usually attacked some personal aspect of President Smith, such as his extensive traveling or his involvement in the Masonic Order as High Potentate of the Kansas City area. This latter charge was especially troubling to some Saints because they believed that Masonic involvement had added to corruption in Nauvoo, Illinois, in Joseph Smith, Jr.'s era. This had been interpreted by some as a stigma or as "evil." One noteworthy pamphlet was titled *Let the Facts Be Known*, by Fred M.'s brother, Israel A. Smith, then a member of the Presiding Bishopric. It was indicative of the fact that Supreme Directional Control split families as well as friends and members in their viewpoints. The two brothers were in clearly divided camps within the Reorganization hierarchy—one supported the traditional method of operation while the other advocated a move toward sweeping reforms and presumed higher purpose.[35]

The previous month, April 1924, Frederick M. Smith had presented for consideration a "Document on Church Government." It was from this that the term "Supreme Directional Control" emerged. Basically this document restated the ideas Smith had been promoting for the past seven years. However, he inserted an important addition. He asserted that the president could carry out policies determined by prophetic insight and legislative enactment as he deemed appropriate during the period between General Conferences.[36] Implicitly he referred to the economic problems the church faced, which he believed necessitated control of monies by the First Presidency. In doing so, Smith, in many Saints' minds, reached for power which was not inherent to his office. The presiding bishop, for example, opposed this pronouncement by insisting that the Presiding Bishopric was solely responsible for the financial affairs of the church. The 1872 "Articles of Incorporation," the 1878 "Basis of Agreement," an 1881 General Conference resolution, and various other church documents all supported the Bishopric's stance.[37] While opposition to the document was strong and broad, Smith's determination, personal persuasion, revered station in the church, and pedigree served him well. With neither legal right nor traditional precedent Smith gained a narrow acceptance of the "Document on Church Government" at the 1924 General Conference. As a result, a stalemate arose between Smith and Presiding Bishop Benjamin R. McGuire that was not resolved until the 1925 General Conference when McGuire was forced by Smith to resign his position.

The sixth and final battle in the conflict over the Supreme Directional Control issue occurred at the 1925 General Conference. The narrow passage of Smith's "Document on Church Government" the previous year made it the first major issue on the docket. Despite widespread debate, on reconsideration it passed in the Twelve and in the high priests' and elders' quorums by wide margins. Thus, it passed its second crucial test and lay at the hands of the delegates, but before it could pass this third and final test, two apostles offered a substitute. This emphasized the Saints' ultimate authority over the church's executive structure, while downplaying obedience of priesthood. After days of discussion, the Conference carried the document by a vote of 919 to 405, while rejecting the substitute 942 to 394.[38] Almost without mention while this debate took place, Smith gained passage of a structural change to the Board of Publication that changed the composition of the board to include one member of each of the quorums in the Joint Council and two members elected by the Conference. More importantly, it officially recognized the First Presidency as the editors-in-chief of all church publications, reversing the open press policy of the democratic forces, and returned the power of the written word in the Reorganization to the hands of Frederick M. Smith.[39]

Forces opposing Smith mounted a final united effort against the theocratic emphasis of "Supreme Directional Control." In a series of meetings this group of about 300 signed a formal protest drafted by Apostle Thomas W. Williams and twenty-four supporters charging the Smith "regime" with a host of authoritarian crimes: ruthlessly eliminating opposition, illegally selecting delegates to the Conference, limiting the legislative function of the Conference to mere assent of executive fiat, and centralizing power in the hands of one man.[40] The group managed to read the protest on the Conference floor and have it entered into the official minutes. Smith's supporters at the Conference far overpowered them, however. Recognizing Smith's triumph, the entire Presiding Bishopric submitted its resignation to the General Conference which, in turn, referred the matter to the prophet to seek counsel and inspiration from the Lord. The revelation Smith offered in response, on 18 April stated:

> It is wisdom that the brethren of the present Presiding Bishopric be released from further responsibility in that

office, and that Albert Carmichael be ordained to act in
the office of Presiding Bishop for a time, he to choose
from among the bishops two to act as counselors. It is
well that the documents from the joint council of April,
1924, have been approved; and the church is admonished once again that the great task laid upon it cannot
be accomplished if contention continues.[41]

The delegates embraced the new document by a vote of
351 to 97.

One more hurdle lay ahead for Smith before a total
victory for his policy of greater presidential control was
realized. While many called for peace and reconciliation, as the revelation had asked, some were still disgruntled, even hostile. This group called for sustaining
all general officers on an individual basis. One aspect
of the democratic side of theocratic-democracy as practiced by the Reorganized Church, which even Smith
endorsed, was the sustaining of officers. However, the
traditional practice focused on the Joint Council as a
whole, and never before had such a vote centered on
individuals. Although unprecedented in Conference
history, the proposal was accepted. In the closing session of the General Conference a radical speech was
directed at Smith by James E. Yates, an appointee
minister. He said, "I vote against sustaining the President, and will wholly disavow and repudiate his monar-
chial claims to supremacy of control of the Church of
Jesus Christ even though the audacious claim be supported by this illegally constituted ... Conference."[42] The
President was upheld by the vote, but those within the
Joint Council who opposed him did not fare as well. As
reported in the 22 April edition of the *Independence
Examiner*, Apostle John Rushton "ended his speech by
telling of an interview in the office of the Presidency ... in
which after a discussion of his present attitude toward

certain questions in the church...was told that it was not satisfactory. His resignation was asked for and immediately given."[43] Another apostle, T. W. Williams, shared a similar experience but he responded differently. "I did not give it to the President," said Williams, "because I owe my position as an apostle to the General Conference and not to the President. I leave myself in the hands of the General Conference to do as it sees best."[44] He failed to be sustained by a vote of 173 to 114.

With these actions the triumph of Supreme Directional Control was complete. From this point forward Smith enjoyed almost unchallenged power within the church. Administratively he controlled all quorums, councils, and territories; he appointed missionaries, department heads, stake and district presidents, and pastors in the Independence Stake. He could allocate or withhold finances during the inter-Conference period, and he was the editor-in-chief of all church publications. He exercised profound legislative strength by initiating legislation through his dominance of the Joint Council, presenting revelations in which the prophetic voice was accepted or rejected by a majority, and chairing Conference meetings in which he controlled the debate as parliamentarian. Finally, in a judicial respect, Smith presided over the Standing High Council, the court of high appeal in the church.[45]

It would seem that the people had spoken their will; but the 1925 General Conference had not accurately reflected the extent of the discontent among the church membership. During that Conference nearly 60 percent of the voting delegates represented delegations outside the Independence/Kansas City, Missouri, and Lamoni, Iowa, areas.[46] This was not proportional to the population of members and differed from previous Conference representations. From 1915 to 1925 delegates were chosen on a local level by vote from members in the areas to be represented—the administration had nothing to do with who was elected. The number of seats allotted to each delegation, however, was based on recommendations of a credentials committee. No mention is made in church history of a significant change in members immediately before the 1925 Conference, which would suggest a direct link between Smith and the "rigging" of the Conference. Garland E. Tickemyer, assistant to Smith during the 1930s and 1940s, claimed: "President Smith was not responsible for the 1925 Conference delegates nor the Credentials Committee."[47] Allegations to the contrary cannot be proven with any degree of certainty, but the effect leads one to conclude that Smith took every opportunity to ensure that delegates to Conference were sympathetic to his position.

For two years following the 1925 Conference, T. W. Williams and others organized a protest movement. This numbered about 600 persons and opposed "innovations creeping into the church in the past ten years, and the principle of centralized government being so definitely established in the action of the 1925 General Conference."[48] Still, they had no desire to splinter from the main body of the church and petitioned to stay within the Reorganization, conducting services in a separate building under officers of their own choosing.[49] Smith paid little attention to this group of malcontents and let them carry on as they wished. Gradually the group dissipated.[50]

Frederick M. Smith's Authoritarian Views

Having described the basic facts of the Supreme Directional Control controversy, it is now important to turn our attention to why Frederick M. Smith took the approach of greater centralization and authority in the presidential office. "Zion" was the subject of many of Smith's sermons, lectures, and writings. Inez Smith Davis described his character and background in these terms:

> Frederick M. Smith came to the leadership of the church, the inheritor of a dream unfulfilled, and to no one have the spires of Zion-to-be gleamed in the distance with more glory than they have to him; not with the call to dream on, but with the challenge to make his dreams real. ...At the very heart of President F. M. Smith's hopes for the church was the passionate longing for Zion [the spiritual and economic brotherhood], which moved his forebears.[51]

Indeed, Smith was by no means a dreamer content with the status quo. He fervently wanted to build God's perfect intended social order in Independence.

The Writings of President Frederick M. Smith: The Zionic Enterprise is a collection of his works dealing exclusively with the topic of Zion. It convinces the reader that Smith deeply dedicated himself to establishing the heavenly kingdom of God on earth. Not unlike the vision that some Jewish leaders (such as Chaim Weizmann and Henrietta Szold) of that time had for Israel, Smith's goal was to build an ideal Latter Day Saint community in Independence, Missouri. He knew this would require great economic and social change, but he believed it was possible to realize if the Saints dedicated themselves fully to the cause. Smith's writings reflect his opinion that it was his responsibility to instruct the membership and to give them hope and a sense of purpose. He sought to utilize the church's manpower and financial resources to their maximum potential in relation to his dream of Zion.[52]

External social trends, no doubt, had some influence on Smith's view of and desire for Zion. As outlined in historian Robert H. Wiebe's *The Search for Order, 1877-1920*, the first two decades following the turn of the century faced great social change. The rise of big business, temperance/women's movements, science, pluralism, isolation, and decreasing morality were all trends feeding the broader theme or transition of America's middle class.[53] Wiebe used the ideas of sociologist Max Weber to show how modern institutions were created and periodically recreated to bring discipline and meaning to the social order.

Smith's *Saints' Herald* writings, such as "Care of the Poor" (August 1925), "Loss of Time in Labor Disputes" (July 1928), and "Christianity and Present Day Problems" (September 1926), all addressed in some way or another the "Zionic answers" to current social concerns, at least as he viewed them. Smith searched for positive service to address evident social problems. He saw the church as the tool by which the evils plaguing the world could be resolved, but he failed to see that it was not his personal tool for the reformation process.

Smith's upbringing undoubtedly played a great role in molding and shaping the president's perspective and views in later life. Before a General Conference he stated: "I have been cognizant of the responsibility that I have taken upon me. ...I have given up...ambition in making something for myself like most young men do; but I gladly do it for the sake of the work, and trust that what little I shall be able to do will be for the good of the cause."[54] Frederick was his father's heir apparent, and out of this he grew to accept not only responsibility but authority. He was inexorably locked into a commitment and a structure that determined the course of his life. His career was institutionally predetermined.

Recently Wallace B. Smith, current president of the Reorganized Church, explained how Frederick's inheritance affected his own attitudes.

> My experience in becoming president was very different from that of Fred M. I established a successful medical practice and had no intention of succeeding my father. My parents encouraged my development of skills in my interests, which were not church-related. I never aspired to the Presidency—I wasn't groomed for it. However, since childhood Fred believed he would be the next president, and trained himself for that position. Then, toward the end of Joseph III's administration (as his health failed) Fred viewed the church from within as counselor to his father. There is no doubt that Fred felt frustrated as he saw things needing to be done but feeling the lack of authority to do them. Perhaps this is why he surged ahead so vehemently once taking office in 1915. ...In Fred's formative years the rule of primogeniture was still in effect and this must have had an influence on his perspective.[55]

A vital part of his upbringing, Fred's education was pertinent to the attitude he held concerning his authority and superiority. In 1894-1895 Smith attended Iowa City Academy, the State University of Iowa, where he was elected class president and gave a graduation day speech.[56] The following year he transferred to the newly opened church-owned Graceland College. There he was an honor student. In 1898 he graduated with a bachelor of science degree and remained the following year to teach mathematics. In 1911 Smith received his master of arts degree from the University of Kansas, after taking research courses with Frank Blackmar in sociology with an emphasis on cooperative movements in doctrines of socialism.[57] These studies laid the foundation from which Smith would write his doctoral dissertation at Clark University. His mentor there was psychologist G. Stanley Hall, the president of Clark University, who established the first research laboratory for psychology at Johns Hopkins University and founded the *American Journal of Psychology.*

In his dissertation, "The Higher Powers of Man," Smith held that the innate potential of the human being enabled him to surpass his habitual mediocre plateaus once it was tapped, resulting in higher energization of consciousness and ever more transcendent levels of achievement.[58] Smith accepted the ideas of Sigmund Freud, who had lectured at Clark in 1909 and who asserted that persons, once recognizing their impulses and drives for what they were, could control them for personal development and social good. This theme was echoed time and again in his writings—urging Saints to educate themselves, to overcome their faults for the social good—for Zion! Zion seemed even more a possibility once Smith finished his education and accepted the role of acting president.

Three aspects combined to motivate him. The first was the pressure he felt to follow his father. He was chosen by birth to lead the church and had, he believed, exclusive authority to direct the business and planning of the institution for the welfare of all. The second aspect was the development of his keen mind. By the time he received his doctorate, Smith was probably the best educated and well-read member of the church. Thus superior, formal education enhanced and buttressed his attitude that he alone was qualified to guide the church. Third, Smith's research work under G. Stanley Hall provided him with conviction that Zion was possible, based on psychological and sociological theories. He believed his own personal religious ideas had basis in scientific principles. Perhaps this prompted Smith to act in such aggressive and manipulative ways. He felt he was legitimately justified in taking whatever action was needed to achieve his plan for Zion. Smith's mistakes were believing that his way was the only way and attempting to order people's actions rather than guide them.

Sporting the alert, sharp mind of a man sixty years his junior, ninety-year-old F. Henry Edwards (member of the Quorum of Twelve from 1922-1938; member of the First Presidency from 1946-1966) affirmed this view of Smith in a personal interview. He said:

> Fred M. never wanted the tension that arose in the church during those years...at that time there was a strong feeling of fundamentalism in the church—a feeling that the scriptures held more importance than "the knowledge of man." Rushton, Gillen, and myself all had higher education...soon, there developed resentment among those in the church who felt they were not being used because, they believed, appointment was tied into the amount of schooling one had. ...Fred felt deeply we should have the best. Bishop McGuire felt Fred was spending too much. On a personal level there was no real animosity, but on a professional level McGuire felt Fred was acting irresponsibly."[59]

This insight shows cause for the Joint Council debate controversy of April 1924 and may indicate why the "Brief Submitted by the Quorum of Twelve" in 1919 called for an itemized account of Smith's personal expenditures. At any rate, financial differences separated the president from the Presiding Bishopric (McGuire, Israel Smith, and Keir) and were largely responsible for the noncooperation of the two groups, especially during 1924 and 1925.

Finally, a brief look at Smith's most ardent opponent, T. W. Williams, should be undertaken. Williams worked in a coal mine in Iowa from 1883-1889 when he accepted church appointment. From 1889 to 1920 (when he became a member of the Twelve) he had responsibilities in the United States and Canada. It is not clear why he vocalized his disdain for the Smith policies at every opportunity. One clue researchers have concerning why Williams came to epitomize the resistance to Smith's authority is that he was deeply interested in labor organization, and from 1910 to 1916 he served as secretary for the California State Socialist Party. It is possible that through his involvement with the socialist movement Williams gained a different interpretation of what Zion should be and what it would require than what was taught by Smith.[60]

Conclusion

This paper suggests that the conflicting doctrine of theocratic-democracy and the vaguely defined function of the Reorganized Church presidential office lay as seedbeds ripe for conflict during the second and third decades of this century within the Reorganization. The six major controversies of Supreme Directional Control emerged as such a conflict that ravaged the institution for ten years, at its worst toward the end. These rivalries stemmed from Smith's deep desire for building the economic and social brotherhood of Zion, which he would plan and direct, a belief that Zion was possible—an exemplary, utopian kingdom of God based on his educational research.

Whether one views him as a visionary leader ahead of his time or as a power-seeking theocratic tyrant, President Frederick M. Smith led the Reorganized

Church of Jesus Christ of Latter Day Saints through the nineteenth to twentieth-century transition with direction and purpose. He was not unlike social reformers such as Jane Addams or managerial reformers such as Gifford Pinchot in his desire to create a new institution based on the existing chaos or inefficiency of the past. His legacy of education, expansion, and moral perfection continue to live in the minds of the current generation who have studied his leadership. His approach toward issues solidified the authority to act within the Reorganized Church more firmly within the First Presidency. After the Supreme Directional Control controversy, a greater control was present at the top of the institution than at any period from its coalescing in the 1850s. The gentle, pragmatic democracy of Joseph Smith III was replaced by a more modern form of authority that recognized explicitly the right of the First Presidency to direct church affairs.

Notes

1. Frederick M. Smith, "Document on Church Government" (April 1924), Reorganized Church of Jesus Christ of Latter Day Saints Library-Archives, the Auditorium, Independence, Missouri.
2. For other discussions of this issue, see Paul M. Edwards, "Theocratic-Democracy: Philosopher-King in the Reorganization," in F. Mark McKiernan, Alma R. Blair, and Paul M. Edwards, eds. *The Restoration Movement: Essays in Mormon History* (Lawrence, Kansas: Coronado Press, 1973), 341-357; Larry E. Hunt, *F. M. Smith: Saint as Reformer*, 2 vols. (Independence, Missouri: Herald Publishing House, 1982). On religious dissent generally, see Edwin Scott Gaustead, *Dissent in American Religion* (Chicago: University of Illinois Press, 1973).
3. Edward A. Warner, "Mormon Theodemocracy: Theocratic and Democratic Elements in Early Latter-Day Saint Ideology, 1827-1846," (Ph.D. Dissertation, University of Iowa, 1973), 36, 42-43.
4. Ibid., 43; Maurice L. Draper, "Theocratic Democracy—Restoration Church Government," Part I, *Saints Herald* 115 (1 December 1968): 800-801; Part II, 115 (15 December 1968): 842-844.

5. Thomas F. O'Dea, "Sources of Strain in Mormonism Reconsidered," in Marvin S. Hill and James B. Allen, eds., *Mormonism and American Culture* (New York: Harper & Row, 1972), 149-155; Mark P. Leone, *Roots of Modern Mormonism* (Cambridge, Massachusetts: Harvard University Press, 1979), 148-166.

6. On the formation of this structure, see D. Michael Quinn, "The Evolution of Presiding Quorums of the LDS Church," *Journal of Mormon History* 1 (1974): 21-38. On the Reorganization's development of these, see Roger D. Launius, *Faither Figure: Joseph Smith III and the Creation of the Reorganized Church* (Independence, Missouri: Herald Publishing House, 1990), especially chapter 4; William D. Russell, "The Latter Day Saint Priesthood: A Reflection of 'Catholic' Tendencies in Nineteenth Century American Religion," in Maurice L. Draper and Clare D. Vlahos, eds., *Restoration Studies I* (Independence, Missouri: Herald Publishing House, 1980), 232-241.

7. Doctrine and Covenants 104:32c, 129:7c (Independence, Missouri: Herald Publishing House, 1970 ed.).

8. Doctrine and Covenants 104:37a.

9. Frederick M. Smith, "Reports," General Conference Minutes (6 April 1914), 1801, Reorganized Church Library-Archives.

10. Quorum of Twelve Minutes (April 1917), Reorganized Church Library-Archives.

11. "President's Address to the Conference," *Saints' Herald* 64 (11 April 1917): 341.

12. Quorum of Twelve Minutes (April 1917), Reorganized Church Library-Archives.

13. Brief submitted by the Quorum of Twelve Apostles (11 February 1919), 1-2, Reorganized Church Library-Archives.

14. Ibid., 4.

15. Frederick M. Smith, "Response to the Quorum of Twelve" (24 February 1919), 8, Reorganized Church Library-Archives.

16. Quorum of Twelve Minutes (12 February 1919), 8.

17. Ibid., 8.

18. Frederick M. Smith, "The President's Call," *Zion's Ensign* 30 (8 May 1919): 289.

19. General Conference Minutes (April 1919), 2696-2698, Reorganized Church Library-Archives.

20. Frederick M. Smith, "The President's Message to Conference" (April 1919), 6, Reorganized Church Library-Archives.

21. Elbert A. Smith and John Rushton, "Ministerial Policy," General Conference Minutes (15 April 1919), 2295-2296, Reorganized Church Library-Archives.

22. Larry E. Hunt, *F. M. Smith: Saint as Reformer* (Independence, Missouri: Herald Publishing House, 1982), 273.

23. General Conference Minutes (17 April 1919), 2800-2801.

24. General Conference Minutes (15 October 1922), 3279-3280.

25. Archive File, n.d., Membership Records Office, the Auditorium, Independence, Missouri.

26. *The History of the Reorganized Church of Jesus Christ of Latter Day Saints* (Independence, Missouri: Herald Publishing House, 1968) 7: passim.

27. Frederick M. Smith, "Independence," *Saints' Herald* 70 (25 April 1923): 405.

28. Daniel T. Williams, General Conference Minutes (6 October 1923), 3546.

29. J. F. Curtis and T. W. Williams, General Conference Minutes (4 October 1923), 3450.

30. *Saints' Herald* 39 (16 July 1892): 454-455, cited in speeches by Curtis and Williams.

31. General Conference Minutes (6 October 1923), 3457.

32. "Report of the Board of Publication," 3709, Reorganized Church Library-Archives.

33. Frederick M. Smith, "Official," *Saints' Herald* 71 (18 June 1924): 578-579.

34. Benjamin R. McGuire and A. E. McKim, "The Facts of the Case" (Tract—Publisher Unknown), recorded in *Saints' Herald* 71 (25 June 1924): 604-605.

35. Most of these pamphlets are available in the Library-Archives of the Reorganized Church in Independence, Missouri.

36. Smith, "Document on Church Government," 3803-3804.

37. Hunt, *F. M. Smith*, 303.

38. General Conference Minutes (11 April 1925), 1.

39. *Independence Examiner* (8 April 1925): 1.

40. Hunt, *F. M. Smith*, 315.

41. Doctrine and Covenants 135:1-2a.

42. James E. Yates, *Refusal to Sustain Doctrine of Supremacy of Church President* (Independence, Missouri: n.p., 1925), 1-3.

43. "Storming to the Last," *Independence Examiner* (22 April 1925): 1-3.

44. Ibid.

45. Paul M. Hanson, "Statement, Protest, and Notification," *Messenger* 1 (October 1926): 1; T. W. Williams, E. D. Moore, and Vida E. Smith, "Under Supreme Directional Control," *Messenger* 1 (April 1926): 83; Edwards, "Philosopher King," 355-356; Daniel T. Williams, "Oral History Memoir," 39-41, 62-63, Reorganized Church Library-Archives.

46. *History of the Reorganized Church* 7: 623-624.

47. Interview with Garland E. Tickemyer (10 November 1988), Independence, Missouri.

48. E. D. Moore, "Detailed Record of Protesting Group of Latter Day Saints in Independence" (29 June 1925), 1, Reorganized Church Library-Archives.

49. Ibid., 4.

50. Steven L. Shields, *Divergent Paths of the Restoration: A History of the Latter Day Saint Movement* 3rd ed. (Bountiful, Utah: Restoration Research, 1982), 116-123.

51. Inez Smith Davis, *The Story of the Church* (Independence, Missouri: Herald Publishing House, 1976 ed.), 517.

52. Norman D. Ruoff, comp., *The Writings of President Frederick M. Smith: The Zionic Enterprise*, Volume 3 (Independence, Missouri: Herald Publishing House, 1981).

53. Robert H. Wiebe, *The Search for Order, 1877-1920* (New York: Hill and Wang, 1967), 1-10.

54. "General Conference," *Saints' Herald* 50 (15 April 1903): 331.

55. Interview with Wallace B. Smith (9 November 1988), Independence, Missouri.

56. Ruth Lyman Smith, *Concerning the Prophet: Fredrick [sic] Madison Smith* (Kansas City, Missouri: Burton Publishing, 1924), 27-28.

57. Hunt, *F. M. Smith*, 67.

58. Ibid., 72; Frederick M. Smith, *The Higher Powers of Man* (Independence, Missouri: Herald Publishing House, 1968 ed.).

59. Interview with F. Henry Edwards (10 November 1988), Independence, Missouri.

60. *History of the Reorganized Church* 7: 705-706.

Chapter 4

The Fundamentalist Schism, 1958-Present[1]

by William D. Russell

Over the past thirty years or so there has been a deepening theological division within the ranks of the Reorganized Church of Jesus Christ of Latter Day Saints. A growing professionalism in the top leadership of the church has led to a more liberal or ecumenical approach to theological issues. This has meant that those aspects of Reorganization belief held in common with other Christians have been given comparatively more emphasis and those aspects of church thought which are unique have been given less emphasis.[2] An example of this would be the idea of the restoration of a primitive Christian Church that had fallen into apostasy and was later restored. When the Saints draw on ideas from other denominations, they use what could be called an ecumenical approach. By way of contrast, the fundamentalists believe the Reorganized Church should draw only on its own tradition.

This deemphasis on certain Restoration fundamentals has quite naturally been resisted by people who are sometimes called conservatives or traditionalists.[3] Most often they are called fundamentalists, because they want to hold fast to certain fundamental doctrines and practices that they feel are absolutely essential for the faithful to retain. I prefer to use the term fundamentalist for this school of thought, a label the fundamentalists themselves seem to accept. I also prefer the term "ecumenist" rather than liberal for the other point of view. Some ecumenical thinking is not necessarily liberal, although liberal is the more commonly used term for the left wing of the church.

The fundamentalists believe the leaders of the Reorganized Church have been moving away from many unique or distinctive features of Reorganized thought and, in the process, becoming more like mainstream Protestantism. The fundamentalists assume the three standard books of the Reorganized Church (that is, the canon of scripture) are writings that are fully accurate, reliable guides for our individual and corporate lives. They read the scriptures in a strict, literal fashion, with some exceptions such as those canonical writings that were clearly intended by the author in another sense.[4]

The Reorganization fundamentalists regard ecumenism as apostasy, because for them ecumenism represents a moving away from the unique Latter Day Saint distinctives that have traditionally been at the heart of Restoration thought. Thus, many fundamentalists hold that church leaders with liberal, ecumenical views are in apostasy.

The issues for the Reorganization, therefore, are fairly similar to those that divide fundamentalist and liberal Protestants. The central issue in both the Protestant and Reorganization cases is the authority of scripture, with fundamentalists explicitly or implicitly adopting some form of the idea of biblical inerrancy or infallibility, while the liberals regard scripture as conditioned by human fallibility and historical circumstances.[5] To borrow terminology from constitutional history and law, the fundamentalists are "strict constructionists" of the scriptures, like the Jeffersonians were on constitutional interpretation, while the ecumenists tend to be "loose constructionists" of the scriptures, much like the Hamiltonians were in constitutional interpretation.

In Latter Day Saintism the fundamental/liberal division has an additional dimension: Biblical inerrancy is expanded to include the Book of Mormon and the revelations to the latter-day prophets. The fundamentalists take these additional scriptures as fully trustworthy while the liberals contend that they are also conditioned by history and human fallibility.

Latter Day Saint ecumenists have an additional problem: The unique Latter Day Saint scriptures support the fundamentalist interpretation of the Bible. For example, scriptures produced by Joseph Smith, Jr., assume that Moses wrote the Pentateuch[6] and that the Book of Isaiah had a single author.[7] These assumptions are contrary to the majority consensus of biblical scholars on these issues.

In the mainline Protestant denominations the fundamental/liberal controversy was fought in the early decades of the twentieth century, with the liberals prevailing in most cases by the end of the 1920s.[8] But unlike those churches, an appropriate date to begin an overview of the developing controversy in the Reorganized Church is 1958. A considerable number of Saints on both sides of this issue see the beginning of the presidency of W. Wallace Smith as the point when these issues began to emerge in a serious way.

At the October 1958 General Conference when W. Wallace Smith was ordained prophet, he retained F. Henry Edwards as a first counselor and named Apostle Maurice L. Draper as his second counselor. At the same time, Smith called Clifford A. Cole and Charles D. Neff to the Quorum of Twelve Apostles.[9] He also broke lineage in the office of presiding patriarch by calling Roy A. Cheville to that office, passing over Lynn Smith—son of the outgoing patriarch, Elbert A. Smith, grandson of David H. Smith, and great-grandson of Joseph the Martyr. Thus, in 1958 Lynn Smith was the heir apparent to the office of presiding patriarch. While the Reorganization presiding patriarch does not have much power, the appointment of Cheville was a break with a significant tradition. It was a symbol of change.[10] In fact, some fundamentalists have suggested that passing over Lynn Smith for presiding patriarch was the first sign that President W. Wallace Smith was in apostasy. Each of these gentlemen called to high office by W. Wallace Smith played significant roles in the movement of the Reorganized Church toward a more ecumenical understanding of the nature of the gospel and of the church.

In the early years of W. Wallace's presidency, staff members at some of the offices at World Headquarters in Independence began to take graduate courses at Saint Paul School of Theology, a Methodist seminary in Kansas City, which opened its doors in 1959. A few members of the Department of Religious Education began taking courses the first year it was in operation, and several staff members graduated with the master of divinity degree from Saint Paul.[11]

Formal theological training of church staff members had a liberalizing effect on the materials published for church school use and on the materials published in the *Saints' Herald* and other church publications.[12] These trends were apparent at least as early as fall 1960 when the Department of Religious Education published a yearlong series of quarterlies on the Old Testament for senior high students. These quarterlies adopted an essentially evolutionary view of the Old Testament. Written by Garland E. Tickemyer, then the president of the Quorum of High Priests, these quarterlies created controversy in the church. Some congregations refused to use them. Some members of the Quorums of Seventy were quite vocal in their opposition to the interpretation of the Bible set forth by Tickemyer.[13]

In summer 1960 Chris B. Hartshorn retired as editor of the *Saints' Herald*, the official publication of the church. A seventy-two-year-old conservative, Hartshorn was replaced by twenty-nine-year-old Roger Yarrington, a professional journalist with a moderately liberal theology.[14] Previously the editors had scrutinized articles submitted for possible publication to see if there were statements that were "not in harmony" with traditional Reorganization teachings. Unlike Hartshorn, Yarrington did not see his editorial role as that of a protector of the traditional faith.

Largely because of Yarrington's approach to editorial tasks, as well as that of his successor, Paul Wellington, there were a number of liberal articles in the *Saints' Herald* in the early 1960s. Probably the two most controversial were by James E. Lancaster and Lloyd R.

Young. Lancaster, in "By the Gift and Power of God," concluded that the Book of Mormon was translated with Joseph Smith sitting with his face buried in a hat, dictating to his scribe, with the plates under cover on a nearby table.[15] This was a shock to many Latter Day Saints schooled in the traditional story where Joseph viewed the golden plates through a spectaclelike Urim and Thummim, translating the reformed Egyptian characters into English.[16] Lloyd R. Young's article, "Concerning the Virgin Birth," cautiously suggested that the historical evidence for Mary's virginity at the time of Jesus' birth was not strong.[17] Letters of protest poured into Herald House when these two articles were published.

Finally, in the period 1958-1960, Graceland College hired four new faculty members to teach religion and philosophy: Lloyd R. Young, Paul M. Edwards, Robert Speaks, and Leland Negaard. These men were regarded as liberal in their beliefs, and it showed through in their teaching. Speaks and Negaard had graduate degrees from two of the leading Protestant theological seminaries in the country: the University of Chicago and Union Theological Seminary in New York respectively. And a few years before their arrival, two historians, Robert Bruce Flanders and Alma R. Blair, began to examine Latter Day Saint history critically with the tools of their discipline.[18] Criticism of these faculty for undermining the faith of students was often heard in the early 1960s.

I have focused this discussion of liberalizing tendencies in the Reorganized Church on the Department of Religious Education and Herald House in Independence and the faculty in religious studies at Graceland College because one could generalize by saying that in the 1960s the fundamentalists were primarily concerned about the liberal theology coming out in the church school curriculum materials, the *Saints' Herald*, and in religiously oriented courses at Graceland College. In other words, the threat to orthodoxy was coming from the well-educated staffs of church departments and institutions but not from the top leaders themselves. At that point the fundamentalists seemed to see it as their mission to inform the leaders as to the dangerous things that their underlings seemed to be teaching.

In the next decade, the 1970s, the fundamentalists became increasingly concerned that possibly the liberal theology that certain staff members had articulated in the 1960s was now being accepted by the top leadership—the First Presidency and the Quorum of Twelve Apostles particularly. This concern was triggered by the discovery about 1969 by the fundamentalists of certain facts relating to a new curriculum that the Department of Religious Education was developing. Certain theological papers—"Position Papers"—had been authored by members of a curriculum committee, which contained some members of the First Presidency and the Quorum of Twelve. When these papers were leaked to the church public, fundamentalist Saints were shocked at their extremely liberal contents. One example will illustrate the point quite well. In the paper on the Book of Mormon, for instance, the author viewed the book as fiction and Joseph Smith as the author.[19]

Most of these papers were written by Department of Religious Education staff members Donald D. Landon, Geoffrey F. Spencer, Wayne A. Ham, and Vernone Sparkes. Sparkes was a graduate of Union Theological Seminary in New York; Spencer and Ham were graduates of Saint Paul School of Theology in Kansas City.[20]

Meanwhile, in the late 1960s, another significant development was quietly occurring. Before his departure from the Department of Religious Education in 1966, Richard B. Lancaster had begun discussions with faculty and administrators at Saint Paul School of Theology about having some private seminars with the eighteen members of the church's Joint Council of the First Presidency, Quorum of Twelve Apostles, and Presiding Bishopric.[21] Before leaving church appointment in 1966 Lancaster had been the director of the Department of Religious Education and had completed a master of divinity degree from Saint Paul, graduating first in the class of 1965. As a result, beginning in 1967 a series of seminars was held in which faculty members at Saint Paul School of Theology, such as theologian Paul Jones and religious historian Carl Bangs, tutored the church's top leaders on issues in theology and history.[22] The seminars focused on the concept of incarnation, stressing that the church is "true" only to the extent that it reflects the spirit and personality of Jesus Christ.[23] When fundamentalists later heard about these seminars, they were appalled. As one delegate told the 1970 World Conference: "These other schools have nothing to teach us," referring to Protestant seminaries like Saint Paul.[24] They were afraid that the church would abandon its Restoration distinctives in favor of ecumenical Protestantism.

In 1978 W. Wallace Smith's son, Wallace B. Smith, was ordained president, and it was becoming clear that the top leadership was espousing the ecumenical approach. The fears of Reorganized Church fundamentalists seemed to be coming true. Whereas the "Position Papers" of the late 1960s could be dismissed as the work of staff members, in 1979 the First Presidency had delivered a series of lectures that espoused similar ecumenical or liberal views. The "Presidential Papers," as they were called, brought the fundamentalists' search for heresy right to the door of the prophet and his counselors.[25]

The early 1970s also saw the first significant separatist or schismatic movements resulting from the theological shift. In 1970 Barney Fuller began publishing *Zion's Warning* as a fundamentalist newspaper challenging the liberal direction the church leadership was taking. Before long he had organized a congregation of fundamentalists in Independence, Missouri, who rented a building for Sunday morning worship services. Fuller himself eventually rejected Joseph Smith and the Restoration faith entirely, becoming an evangelical Protestant preacher.[26] But his associate, Eugene Walton, eventually proclaimed himself a prophet and now heads a very small Reorganization splinter group. Walton has produced several revelations and continues to led a small group of believers.[27]

At this point most fundamentalists had little desire to separate from the church. They continued to have hope for the institutional church. But they longed to hear the "old Jerusalem gospel" preached. So in September 1978, a Restoration Festival was held, which consisted of a weekend of preaching, praying, and testifying in the church's old tradition. Led by Greg Donovan of Detroit, this independent group of fundamentalists rented facilities at Graceland College for the event. It attracted about 2,000 worshipers.[28]

The first Restoration Festival was a huge success, and its organizers repeated it several times thereafter. The Restoration Festival became a nonprofit organization with a board of directors, holding similar weekend retreats about twice a year. Some of its supporters began publishing a monthly magazine, the *Restoration Voice*, which included a lot of articles reprinted from the *Saints' Herald* of the 1940s and 1950s, just before W. Wallace Smith's presidency.[29]

There were only a few small fundamentalist groups meeting outside the authority of the institutional church when Wallace B. Smith announced his revelation permitting the ordination of women in 1984. For many fundamentalists, this was the last straw. To their way of thinking the gospel is unchangeable. They argued that no women had been called before, and therefore it was obvious that God did not want them in the priesthood.[30]

In the years since the women's ordination revelation was announced, many separatist branches and congregations have been organized. At the present time I have identified more than 200 independent local groups in thirty-two states, Canada, and Australia. Fifty-five of these groups are in Missouri, many in the Independence area. Other states with large numbers of such groups are Michigan, Oklahoma, and Texas.

The word "branch" is used to designate a group of people who organize themselves in a fashion comparable to a regular congregation; they have elected officers and regular worship and study meetings. Many of these branches administer Communion, baptisms, ordinations, and weddings, even though they are not recognized by the Reorganized Church and even though many of the priesthood administering these ordinances have been silenced by the institutional church, that is, they have had their priesthood authority removed.[31]

There are also several hundred groups of Reorganized Church members meeting informally. A "group" is simply a collection of people who meet for study or worship, but have not as yet organized in the form of a congregation with elected offices. Frequently they are a small group who meet in homes for scripture study or prayer. In some cases they simply have no priesthood leaders. In Salinas, California, for example, there were about twelve fundamentalist schismatics as of March 1990. A "schismatic" person is willing to break with the church—some fundamentalists still attend the regular Reorganization congregations and thus are not schismatic. The Salinas group has only one priesthood member, a teenage deacon, so it cannot have regular congregational worship activities. It cannot perform any sacraments or ordinances. But the members meet regularly for scripture study and travel to other branches to participate in the Sacrament of the Lord's Supper. These branches and groups are independent of the institutional church and normally hold their classes and worship services at the same time as the institutional church (church school and preaching on Sunday morning and prayer-and-testimony meetings on Wednesday night).

Reorganized Church Apostle William T. Higdon has suggested that the fundamentalist reaction to the ordination of women has come in three waves, responding to the biennial World Conferences of the church held in 1984, 1986, and 1988.[32] In the first wave, immediately after the revelation approved at the 1984 Conference, there were not a lot of people yet ready to leave the church or organize separate branches. Higdon estimated there were only about a hundred formal withdrawals from the church caused directly by Section 156 permitting women's ordination. While formal withdrawals are only the tip of the iceberg, the important point is that there were few local schismatic groups formed in those early months. There were many meetings of concerned fundamentalists, such as a series of International Elders Conferences held in Independence, but little formal schism. Many fundamentalists still thought Wallace B. Smith was a prophet; he had just made a mistake and it would be corrected, probably at the 1986 World Conference. They came ready to attempt to get the Conference to formally rescind Section 156. But President Smith ruled that a motion from a stake to rescind a revelation in the Doctrine and Covenants was out of order. Because only the prophet can propose a revelation, only a prophet can initiate a move to rescind a revelation, Smith reasoned. About 90 percent of the Conference delegates supported his ruling, creating a precedent that increased the power of the prophet. As so often happens to organizations in a crisis, the power of the leader is strengthened as a result of actions taken to deal with the crisis.[33]

This action meant that the fundamentalists could not look to the World Conference to remedy the situation, since opposing parties could not initiate a rescission of a revelation, and even if they did, they would not have the votes needed to succeed. In the wake of this action, the fundamentalists developed a strategy of preserving beachheads or enclaves in the church where "true Saints"—fundamentalists—could maintain local congregations or stakes that would resist liberalism and resist ordaining women or using women in priestly capacities. In a stake, for example, they might all gravitate to the congregation that was the most fundamental. That congregation could decline to call any women to the priesthood, and when priesthood women moved into the congregation they would not be asked to preach, serve the sacraments, or be allowed to participate in any priesthood capacity. In such situations liberals in the congregation would tend to transfer to other congregations that were not so fundamental.[34]

These beachheads or enclaves would allow both fundamentalists and liberals to remain within the church. Indeed, it appeared to be a reasonable compromise to a delicate situation. Furthermore, fundamentalists observed that several jurisdictions in the church had allowed such enclaves for persons whose views were more liberal than the institution's mainstream to exist for years without interference.[35]

There were a lot of issues involved in the fundamental/liberal struggle of the 1980s, but the ordination of women became a convenient symbol. If a congregation had not ordained any women and was not using women in priesthood capacities, it was regarded as fundamental, while those ordaining women were regarded as liberal. But in the latter camp there were people who were not truly ecumenical; they were simply loyal to the institution.

Many fundamentalists saw Blue Valley and Central Missouri stakes as such beachheads. The delegations from these two western Missouri stakes had been strongly fundamentalist at the 1986 World Conference. At stake conferences they were able to vote down all priesthood calls for women that were presented for vote. Both stakes are also close to Independence. Members from outside the Center Place (Independence), therefore, could "gather to Zion" by moving to the Independence area, and then attend congregations in one of these two stakes.[36] And fundamentalist members already living in nearby stakes could transfer their membership to congregations in the Blue Valley or Central

Missouri stakes and not have to drive far to their new congregation. As a measure of this approach, in a three-month period after the 1986 World Conference, about 600 persons transferred their memberships into Blue Valley Stake.[37]

But the church leadership decided not to allow fundamentalist enclaves or beachheads to exist. Some congregations controlled by fundamentalists were dissolved or reduced to mission status, or the leadership replaced fundamentalist pastors with pastors who were either liberal or at least supported the World Church leadership, especially on the use of women in priesthood capacities. In addition to the use of ordained women, other tests of loyalty to the World Church have been whether congregations use the 1981 hymnal (*Hymns of the Saints*) and the church's curriculum materials (the "Living Faith Series"), and whether they follow the priesthood guidelines established since 1984. When a "loyal" pastor was installed, in many cases the fundamentalists walked out and formed their own separate branch.[38]

The 1988 World Conference upheld the actions of church leaders that had denied the right to maintain enclaves of fundamentalists who did not support the World Church.[39] And as a result, a third wave of schism has occurred. Many fundamentalists who previously had held out hope, after 1988 now saw no reason to stay in the church if fundamentalist beachheads were not to be allowed. They saw little option but to leave the church altogether or worship in separate congregations unauthorized by the Reorganized Church but faithful to a fundamentalist Reorganization interpretation of the gospel.

The 1990 World Conference did not produce a fourth wave of fundamentalist defection. The fundamentalists were hardly noticed, if they had a presence at all. But certainly the defection has not run its course yet. There are still fundamentalists who have not yet made a final decision as to which way they will go. It is a difficult break to make because the Reorganized Church is an organization that places a high premium on the authority of the institutional church and the need for loyalty to it. Their dilemma is this: The more firmly a person believes the traditional message of the church the more likely they are disturbed by the direction the church has headed, but the more firmly they believe the traditional message of the church the more difficult it is for them to break with the authority of the church because they take that authority so seriously.

Possibly most of the defection that will occur has taken place by now. The question is whether the fundamentalists will become stable and cooperate with one another. So far they seem to be achieving that objective, although certainly there are rifts within the fundamentalist community. Another question is whether by missionary efforts they can grow in the future.

Three types of schism have developed regarding the fundamentalist controversy in the Reorganized Church. By far the largest group is what I call the "nonseparatists." The leading spokesman for this type is Richard Price. The second type is called "separatists" and finally, the "self-proclaimed prophets."

As indicated earlier, at the present time I have identified more than 200 local independent branches or groups. Many of these local groups of fundamentalists seem to be aligned in a loose way with the Association of Independent Groups and Branches, called the "Association." The Association takes what I call the "nonseparatist strategy." The founder of the Association, Terry Emerick, and its leading strategist and spokesman, Richard Price, are both from Independence, Missouri. It publishes a newsletter, the *Restoration Messenger*, and seeks to maintain a communications network among the fundamentalist community.[40] Its strategy has always been to consider its members fully a part of the Reorganization. They are the true Reorganized Church because they hold to the true Reorganization gospel. The Reorganized Church's hierarchy is considered the "liberal faction" of the church and is held to be in apostasy. Therefore, these nonseparatist fundamentalists do not attend regular Reorganization congregations because they see them as being controlled by an apostate hierarchy. Neither do they pay tithing or give other financial support to the institutional church. They do, however, retain their Reorganization membership and priesthood.[41] It is true that in many cases the regular church leaders have silenced fundamentalist priesthood. And in a few cases they have expelled them from church membership.[42] But the fundamentalists simply don't recognize these silencings or expulsions as valid, because they were performed by church leaders who have gone into apostasy and therefore lost their authority. Indeed, it has become for some a badge of honor to have been silenced.[43]

The Association of Independent Groups and Branches is somewhat like the Southern Baptist Convention—a loose association of local congregations, each of which retains its local autonomy. But Latter Day Saints believe in having a prophet and apostles and bishops. So the Reorganization fundamentalists do not expect to remain in independent Restoration branches forever. They believe God will someday move to purify the Reorganized Church, either by removing Wallace B. Smith and his liberal associates, by causing Wallace to repent and return to the true gospel, or by raising up a new prophet. If someone arises proclaiming himself or someone else to be the true prophet, the Association would take no position on the question as to the validity of such a claim. If everyone in the Association accepted the claims of that prophet, however, then the Association would cease to serve a function and dissolve.[44]

If the time comes that all members of the Association accept one or more persons' claims to be the prophet, the Association will no longer need to exist, as its purpose is only to serve in the interim while the most prudent thing to do is to organize independent Restoration branches because of the lack of World Church leadership with proper authority.

The vast majority of fundamentalist schismatics are taking this nonseparatist strategy. But a second and different approach—which I call the separatist approach—is taken by some fundamentalists. They are considerably less numerous than the nonseparatists. The separatists consider the Reorganized Church hopeless. They believe God has given up on the Reorganization and that true Saints should leave the Reorganized Church and look for God to call a new prophet, apostles, and the other officers of the General Church. A major difference between the separatists and the nonseparatists is that the nonseparatists do not do anything more than that which a local branch can do by itself. They will ordain up to the office of elder but will not ordain to any of the high priestly offices, or to the office of seventy. They will not create any organization higher than the local branch. They have local automomy, similar to the Baptists and other denominations with congregational church government.

But the separatists are organizing beyond the local level. The best example so far is the Church of Christ, Restored, with its base in Michigan. Their leader is Leroy "Bud" Ormsbee from Cheboygan in northern Michigan. They have more than a dozen congregations and have ordained eight apostles, one of whom is now deceased. All persons must formally withdraw from the Reorganized Church before they can vote in their meetings. Although they have a separate church organization, they have no prophet. When they feel that God has designated his choice for prophet, they will proceed to recognize him.

A similar group is the Church of Jesus Christ, the Lamb of God, which originated in Maine, and has a stronghold in the state of Washington. They urge their people to withdraw from the Reorganized Church, which they feel is dead. They have ordained new seventies. Many believe they will formally organize as a new church before long. It is expected that their Quorum of Seventy will call a General Assembly to set the church in order, and the General Assembly will vote to proceed with the process of fully reorganizing the church.[45]

There is a third approach to schism: schismatic movements led by a self-proclaimed prophet. The Church of Christ, Restored, in Michigan and the Church of Jesus Christ, the Lamb of God, do not yet have a prophet. They are building a church first and anticipate that a prophet will arise. But some men have stepped forward and proclaimed themselves prophets. For them, building an organization comes later, if at all.

Eugene Walton, a former Reorganization seventy, is a self-proclaimed prophet who has produced revelations. His following is tiny, however—only about six members. His ability to get out and win yet more converts was hampered by six months served in jail for refusing to pay alimony to his ex-wife. He refused on the grounds that God had instructed him to spend full-time preaching, and therefore he could not earn the money necessary to meet the alimony obligation.[46]

Another reasonably well-known would-be prophet was John Cato, who in 1986 proclaimed himself prophet and also produced revelations. His group, the Church of Christ, Zion's Branch, published a newsletter that has included John's revelations.[47] His term as prophet was short-lived, however, as less than a year after his calling he left Zion's Branch and joined the Mormon Church. Zion's Branch survives, but without a prophet to lead it. Another well-known prophet is Bob Baker. He had a considerable following, but his support has dwindled and is now very small since he announced that he has been called to be the prophet.

Several lesser-known figures have asserted their prophetic claims. A couple of them have died before getting much earthly recognition of their calling. But certainly the best-known is Jeffery Lundgren, who with twelve of his followers was indicted for the April 1989 murder of a family of five in Kirtland, Ohio. Lundgren was dissatisfied with the direction the church was headed and felt himself called to Kirtland because he believed that would be the location of Christ's return to earth. He gathered a following in Kirtland, mainly among persons similarly dissatisfied. He had a revelation which asserted that ten people needed to die to purify his community. Once that purification took place, they would receive the sword of Laban in the Book of Mormon and the lost plates containing hitherto unknown holy scriptures. He read something in the scriptures that made him conclude that the number to be killed could be cut in half, so the five members of the family of Dennis and Cheryl Avery were murdered. His group split up a few weeks before the bodies were found and murder indictments were issued in January 1990. It remains to be seen whether any of his followers will remain loyal to a prophet/seer who will almost certainly languish in prison until his death.[48]

Ron Livingston has a group of followers living on 240 acres of land east of Lamoni, Iowa. Livingston and his people apparently have no quarrel with ordaining women. But their group does seem to fit within the confines of this study, which is about the fundamentalist reaction to the growing liberalism or ecumenism in the church. Part of the fundamentalist critique is the apparent deemphasis on the Book of Mormon in the Reorganized Church, and Livingston—who has rejected his name and all secular recognition and has signed his name as "the Brother of Clark"—is above all a Book of Mormon zealot. And many of the people he has attracted are fundamental and strong Book of Mormon advocates. In spring 1990 Livingston produced a prophecy suggesting that the Russians were going to wipe out many people in the Midwest during April. Many thought it was expected to occur during the Reorganized Church's World Conference, and most probably on April 6, the birthday of the church and the day of the groundbreaking for the new Independence Temple. Some of Livingston's disciples urged their parents to come out to "the land" for safety during the month. But the day, week, and month passed with no apparent devious actions by the Soviet Union, whose leaders were plenty busy dealing with a crumbling empire.[49]

Looking now at the whole movement, I cannot at this point see any strong leader emerging to unite the Reorganization fundamentalists. The largest single figure in the movement is Richard Price. He has earned his prominence from his three books and many other writings, including quite a few full-page *Independence Examiner* advertisements, long articles criticizing Reorganized Church actions. But Price is a quiet, little man. Most observers do not think he has the charisma necessary to be a prophet himself. And Price himself looks for a descendant of Joseph the Martyr, one named Smith, to be the next true prophet. Where he will find him is difficult to imagine. But Price's strategy of retaining the true faith in independent local Restoration branches is a satisfactory strategy for those who are comfortable having the church exist on the local level only. They are comfortable with the American tradition of congregationalism—of local control. While the Reorganization scriptures call for central authority in various General Church offices and officers, perhaps many of these people are really Southern Baptists with two extra books of scripture to interpret strictly. And because they have had a problem with General Church officers thwarting their efforts to preserve the gospel as they know it in their local congregations, they have no wish to be in a hurry to create a new central bureaucracy that might frustrate them all over again. Far wiser to take time and be sure before accepting anyone's claim to be prophet. Better beware of those who attempt to create a central organization, collecting tithing and the like, before God has clearly signaled the time has come for such actions. Meanwhile, local leaders can retain control of their own groups and preach the true gospel as they see it.

A nonseparatist strategy can enable the Reorganization fundamentalists to survive for a reasonable period, although their numbers may not grow large. Those who claim to be prophets so far have achieved little success. Nonseparatists, of course, are always capable of becoming separatists any time a prophet arises in whom they can place their trust. If a charismatic leader does not arise as prophet, drawing many of the separatists and nonseparatists to his side, the Reorganization fundamentalists will continue to be split in many directions. Eventually even the more prudent faction informally led by Richard Price might dwindle as they wait for a prophet. I assume they cannot wait forever. But it is true that even today James J. Strang's followers still await the calling of another prophet to succeed Strang, and Strang died in 1856. That really takes patience. But there are about 300 people patient enough to continue the vigil, 134 years after Strang's death.[50]

Notes

1. An earlier version of this paper appeared in *Sunstone* vol. 14, no. 3 (June 1990): 14-19.

2. Some of these trends are traced in Howard J. Booth, "Shifts in Restoration Thought," *Dialogue: A Journal of Mormon Thought* 13 (Fall 1980): 79-92.

3. One of the chief protagonists from a fundamentalist perspective has been Richard Price, a retired Bendix employee who has written several books and articles noting the "errors" of the church's directions. See Richard Price, *Decision Time* (Independence, Missouri: Cumorah Books, 1975); Richard Price, *The Saints at the Crossroads* (Independence, Missouri: Cumorah Books, 1974); Richard Price, *Action Time* (Independence, Missouri: Price Publishing, 1985).

4. On the issue of scriptural literalism/interpretation, see William D. Russell, "Beyond Literalism," *Dialogue: A Journal of Mormon Thought* 19 (Spring 1986); 57-68; Larry W. Conrad and Paul Shupe, "An RLDS Reformation? Construing the Task of RLDS Theology," *Dialogue: A Journal of Mormon Thought* 18 (Summer 1985): 92-103.

5. On this issue in the larger Christian community, see John MacQuarrie, *Twentieth Century Religious Thought* (New York: Harper & Row, 1963); James Barr, *The Scope and Authority of the Bible* (Philadelphia: Westminster Press, 1980); Paul Tillich, *Biblical Religion and the Search for Ultimate Reality* (Chicago: University of Chicago Press, 1955).

6. See, for example, Book of Mormon (Independence, Missouri: Herald Publishing House, 1966), I Nephi 1:159: "He beheld that they contained the five books of Moses, which gave an account of the creation of the world." See also I Nephi 6:3, 7:43; Alma 16:191; Helaman 3:46-49; II Nephi 7:9.

7. The Book of Mormon assumes that the last half of Isaiah could not have been written around 540 B.C., as scholars assume, because in the Book of Mormon Lehi and family left Israel about 600 B.C. for their journey to the New World. They brought with them the Isaiah prophecies, including many from the last half of Isaiah. For discussions of these issues, see William D. Russell, "History and the Mormon Scriptures," *Journal of Mormon History* 10 (1983): 53-63; William D. Russell, "A Further Inquiry into the Historicity of the Book of Mormon," *Sunstone* 7 (September-October 1982): 20-27; Wayne Ham, "Problems in Interpreting the Book of Mormon as History," *Courage: A Journal of History, Thought and Action* 1 (September 1970): 15-22.

8. On this issue, see Norman F. Furniss, *The Fundamentalist Controversy, 1918-1931* (New Haven, Connecticut: Yale University Press, 1954); Ernest R. Sandeen, *The Roots of Fundamentalism: British and American Millenarianism, 1800-1930* (Chicago: University of Chicago Press, 1970); Willard J. Gatewood, Jr., ed., *Controversy in the Twenties: Fundamentalism, Modernism, and Evolution* (Nashville, Tennessee: Abingdon, 1969); Martin E. Marty, *Modern American Religion, Volume 1: The Irony of It All, 1893-1919* (Chicago: University of Chicago Press, 1986); George R. Marsden, *Fundamentalism and American Culture: The Shaping of Twentieth-Century Evangelicalism* (New York: Oxford University Press, 1980).

9. Doctrine and Covenants 145. This revelation was given in October 1958.

147

10. On the historical development and responsibilities of the presiding patriarch, see Reed M. Holmes, ed., *The Patriarch* (Independence, Missouri: Herald Publishing House, 1978).

11. Richard B. Lancaster and Clifford Buck graduated from Saint Paul School of Theology, Kansas City, Missouri, in 1965, the first Reorganization graduates of the Methodist-sponsored seminary. Both men were church appointees assigned to the Department of Religious Education at the Auditorium, Independence, Missouri.

12. This issue, and the fundamentalist backlash from it, is explored in an outstanding article: William J. Knapp, "Professionalizing Religious Education in the Church: The 'New Curriculum' Controversy," *The John Whitmer Historical Association Journal* 2 (1982): 47-59.

13. Garland E. Tickemyer, *The Old Testament Speaks to Our Day* (Independence, Missouri: Herald Publishing House, 1960-1961), four quarterlies for senior high students.

14. Indicative of Yarrington's standards were his observations on ethics. See Roger Yarrington, *Restoration Ethics Today* (Independence, Missouri: Herald Publishing House, 1963).

15. James E. Lancaster, "By the Gift and Power of God," *Saints' Herald* 109 (15 November 1962): 798-802, 806, 817; reprinted with minor revisions as "The Method of Translation of the Book of Mormon" in *The John Whitmer Historical Association Journal* 3 (1983): 51-61.

16. An example of the traditional Reorganization understanding is that of Clair E. Weldon, "Two Transparent Stones: The Story of the Urim and Thummim," *Saints' Herald* 109 (1 September 1962): 616-620, 623.

17. Lloyd R. Young, "Concerning the Virgin Birth: Comments on the Doctrine," *Saints' Herald* 111 (1 February 1964): 77-78, 94.

18. Robert Bruce Flanders, especially, excited the ire of the more traditional Saints by suggesting that, among other less-attractive features of his persona, Joseph Smith, Jr., had instituted the Mormon practice of polygamy. See Robert Bruce Flanders, *Nauvoo: Kingdom on the Mississippi* (Urbana: University of Illinois Press, 1965).

19. Price Publishing Company in Independence, Missouri, published *The Position Papers*, which can be purchased through the Restoration Bookstore. The paper on the Book of Mormon was also published. See Wayne Ham, "Problems in Interpreting the Book of Mormon as History."

20. Vernone M. Sparkes raised his own controversy when he wrote a moderately liberal book, *The Theological Enterprise* (Independence, Missouri: Herald Publishing House, 1969). Wayne Ham

did much the same by taking seriously the claims of other religions in *Man's Living Religions* (Independence, Missouri: Herald Publishing House, 1966).

21. Donald D. Landon, *A History of Donald D. Landon While Under General Conference Appointment, 1951-1970: An Oral History Memoir* (Independence, Missouri: Department of History, Reorganized Church of Jesus Christ of Latter Day Saints, 1970), 94.

22. Knapp, "Professionalizing Religious Education," 49.

23. Ibid., 49; Donald D. Landon to William D. Russell (28 January 1987).

24. William D. Russell, "Reorganized Mormons Beset by Controversy," *Christian Century* (17 June 1970): 770.

25. Price Publishing Company has also published the "Presidential Papers," which can be purchased through the Restoration Bookstore.

26. Barney Fuller and Glen Stout were the first editors of *Zion's Warning*, whose first issue appeared in February 1970. Fuller's career is reviewed in Steven L. Shields' article in this volume.

27. On his early career, see Eugene Oliver Walton, *God Is Alive* (Independence, Missouri: Vantage Press, 1970).

28. This group published the proceedings of the meeting. See *The Restoration Festival* (Independence, Missouri: Restoration Festival, 1978).

29. *Restoration Voice* continues to be the flagship for communicating the message of the fundamentalist dissent in the Reorganized Church. It is a slick paper, four-color, thirty-two-page magazine. It has always been supported by donations and is mailed free of charge to anyone who wants to receive it. A recent publication, also by the same people, is *Vision*, oriented more directly toward the news of independent branches.

30. See Merva Bird, *Women's Ordination—NO!* (Independence, Missouri: School of the Saints, 1980), which sets out the problems as the fundamentalists viewed them. See also Richard Price, *Action Time.*

31. Certificates for blessing, baptism, ordination, and marriages performed in independent Restoration branches can be purchased through the Restoration Bookstore in Independence.

32. Interview with William T. Higdon (17 August 1989), Independence, Missouri.

33. 1986 World Conference *Bulletin* (Independence, Missouri: Reorganized Church of Jesus Christ of Latter Day Saints, 1986): 288-289.

34. Richard Price developed a set of independent branches packages containing information for fundamentalists to aid them in devel-

oping and maintaining their independent groups. These have been available through the Restoration Bookstore in Independence since the mid-1980s.

35. Examples include the Oland Mission in Lamoni Stake and the Santa Fe Stake Mission. While they are hard to categorize on a right-to-left continuum, the Contemporary Christian Centers are another example of how the institutional church had catered to small groups with unique viewpoints.

36. Unlike the Utah-based Latter-day Saint church, the Reorganized Church does not insist that a member attend the congregation (ward) closest to his or her home.

37. Interview with William T. Higdon.

38. The most widely known example was the ouster of four fundamentalist presiding elders in Blue Valley Stake in January 1987.

39. 1988 World Conference *Bulletin* (Independence, Missouri: Reorganized Church of Jesus Christ of Latter Day Saints, 1988): 325.

40. *The Restoration Messenger* began publishing as a quarterly newsletter in January 1987.

41. Richard Price and Larry Harlacher, *Restoration Branches Movement* (Independence, Missouri: Price Publishing, 1986); *Join None of Them* (Independence, Missouri: Cumorah Books, n.d.).

42. I am aware of only eight expulsions resulting from the fundamentalist controversy.

43. One prominent fundamentalist told me, "When we get calls for administration to the sick, they often ask for us to send a silenced elder."

44. Telephone interview with Terry Emerick.

45. This was done in April 1991. The church's new name is "The Restoration Church of Jesus Christ of Latter Day Saints."

46. Before we laugh at Walton, though, we should recall that there is historical precedent for prophets doing time. And in the civil rights movement, going to jail was a badge of honor, just as for the fundamentalists it is an honor to have been silenced.

47. See, for example, the revelations published in the March and May 1987 issues of *The Voice*, a publication of the Church of Jesus Christ, Zion's Branch, 108 South Pleasant, Independence, Missouri.

48. Lundgren made national news in January 1990. His career was tracked in most newspapers. See especially the coverage in *Cleveland Plain Dealer*, *Kansas City Star*, and *News-Herald* (Willoughby, Ohio).

49. Paul Wenske, "Iowa group waits for Armageddon," *Kansas City Star* (9 April 1990): A-1, 6; Larry Fruhling, "Separatist group embarks on spiritual quest," *Des Moines Register* (4 February

1990): 1, 5A; Larry Fruhling, "Rumors fly as clan eyes doomsday," *Des Moines Register* (1 April 1990): 1, 3B.

50. On Strang, see William D. Russell, "King James Strang: Joseph Smith's Successor?" in F. Mark McKiernan, Alma R. Blair, and Paul M. Edwards, eds., *The Restoration Movement: Essays in Mormon History* (Lawrence, Kansas: Coronado Press, 1973), 231-256.

Chapter 5

The Politics of Dissent and the Reorganized Church

---

by Donald J. Breckon

Introduction

Previous chapters have reviewed the historical process of the Reorganized Church, arguing that it arose as a dissenting movement with strong traditions of local and individual autonomy. These traditions have made it more likely that dissident movements would emerge from it over time. Many of these movements, however, might have been coopted into the larger organization through a better means of bringing issues to the surface and resolving them peacefully. This is an inherently political process, one that cannot be escaped and must be understood by the membership and the leadership both. This chapter deals with the political process within the Reorganization, pointing out issues and procedures of merit and concern and offering methodologies for the more effective management of the politics of dissent.

The Nature of Politics

Politics is often associated with government, but need not be, at least with municipal, state, or national government. Politics is involved in all aspects of life, including religious organizations. In fact, politics and personalities are two factors that permeate most aspects of life. People must be effective in understanding and working with both if they are to be successful in nearly any enterprise that requires the involvement of more than one person.

Politics is about governing, about winning and holding control, regardless of the organization. Oft-quoted folklore has it that "politics is the art of compromise," and certainly there is an element of truth in the statement. Compromise is often important in winning and maintaining control, especially in a democracy.

Politics, in this author's opinion, is more about power, and especially about the balance of power than about any other theme to which it might be applied. The root word in Greek for police and politics is the same, hence it is about control. Power in and of itself is neutral. Power is the ability to produce an effect, to make things happen. Power, of course, can be used to block actions, wherein the greater influence will determine the outcome. Power is the ability to be influential, to make a difference. Hence, it is not bad to seek power, or to use it, or to strive to maintain it. Indeed, it is part of the original scriptural charge to humankind to "have dominion" over creation. Seeking and using power for positive outcomes is closely aligned with stewardship and, of course, with education. In fact, Pittacus said in 569 B.C. that "The measure of [humankind] is what [they] do with power."

Power can be used and abused, and has been throughout the centuries. "Power always has to be kept in check," said Senator William Proxmire. That is so because "power corrupts," as Senator Adlai Stevenson said. However, Stevenson went on to say, "The lack of power corrupts absolutely." "Power corrupts the few while weakness corrupts the many," wrote Eric Hoffer. "Those in power want only to perpetuate it," said Justice William Douglas, although it is probably also true that those without power want only to obtain it. In a sense, a major appeal of religion to the masses is the potential to be supplied with divine power. "Power undirected by high purpose spells calamity, and high purpose by itself is utterly useless if the power to put it into effect is lacking," remarked Theodore Roosevelt.[1]

Power can be possessed but not expressed; that is, people can choose to use power or not use power to induce or block change. One real tragedy in life is that people feel powerless and act powerless. But when they are united with others of like mind, they are very powerful.

Power can be shared! The essential difference between a dictator and the president of the United States is the locus of control. The power of the president is enormous, but there are checks and balances in the legislative and judicial branches of government that dictators do not have to deal with, along with the prospect of the president needing to be reelected periodically.

Power can be based in expertise, influence, money, social standing, or in numbers. Power struggles are inevitable. Therefore, "an understanding of the nature of power and of where and in what degree it exists is an important ingredient...in planned change."[2]

Politics and Power in the Reorganized Church

The ultimate source of power in most religions is, of course, God. As stated earlier, power can be shared, and God gave humanity agency and delegated power to them. Yet in all religions throughout time, some people possessed more power than others, and in most religious groups power struggles existed. Accordingly, people in several hundred varieties of religious tradition worship the same God because groups won or lost a power struggle.

Priesthood was, among other things, a divine designation of power, and the offices of priesthood circumscribed the power delegated. Some religions delegated power to the people, again in varying decrees. Many religions today practice various forms of theocratic-democracy; however, the Reorganized Church is unique in describing itself in such terms. The concept retains some of the power of God but shares that power with people, through priesthood, and through common consent of the membership. Common consent, of course, does not mean unanimity on all issues. Such is an impossible goal. Instead it is the involvement of all members in the policy-making process and the basic ideal that once an issue is decided all members will allow it to be implemented, even if another decision was preferred.

The democratic portion of theocratic governance allows all members to have the right to vote at local and regional or stake gatherings, and provides for representatives of the local jurisdictions to participate in the decision-making process at the church's World Conferences. Representation provides the basis for many political battles within the church, as individuals vote their conscience on issues before these policy-making bodies. Typically their conscience often represents the consensus of the geographical areas they represent, or the ideological position commonly held by members of their group, be it based on gender, ethnicity, or national origin.

Power struggles and political battles are not unique to conferences. They occasionally occur within and between quorums, with both winners and losers emerging from the process. Prominent church leaders sometimes become losers, and have occasionally left the church voluntarily, while others have remained in the church, bitter and virtually powerless. The political process is never pretty, and in the process there must always be winners and losers, regardless of the honorable intentions of both sides of any particular issue.

Dissent and Political Power

The term "dissent" has developed a negative connotation over the years, especially when applied to people seeking to influence policy within the Reorganized Church. This is unfortunate, because many positives can arise out of the political process. The negativity associated with the term arises from the fact that those described as dissenters disagree with decisions and positions of the church's leadership who were placed there by divine designation, or with the decision of the majority of the movement in a democratic process through conference action. Of course, dissent can take many forms: withdrawal, inactive status, withholding of financial and other types of support, disruptive behavior, or a myriad of other means of publicly expressing dissatisfaction with the status quo. It also can take the form of working within the system to change the leadership and policies, or it can take the form of movement outside the organization to recreate a new institution modeled on the ideals of those in dissent.

Dissent, as with power, is a neutral term. Dissent is generally considered good by those supporting the dissident position, as with Martin Luther and others who dissented against the Catholic church and formed the Protestant traditions, or as with Joseph Smith, Jr., and the Latter Day Saints who dissented against all organized religions. Certainly, however, the Catholics did not support the Protestants' dissent and believed those people in error. Likewise, organized religious groups in western New York in the late 1820s did not believe Joseph Smith and his followers were acting appropriately in establishing a new church. The approach toward the issue, it seems, is carefully conditioned by which side of the fence the individual observer is standing.

There is nothing new about these issues, and members of the Reorganized Church must understand that dissent, power, politics, and personalities have been at the very heart of organized religion since the beginning of recorded history. These issues were responsible for the Old Testament struggles between Cain and Abel, Joseph and his eleven brothers, Israel and the priests of Baal, Moses and the Egyptian Pharaoh. In the Book of Mormon, dissent, power, politics, and personalities were involved in Lehi leaving Jerusalem, in the tension between Nephi and Laman, and subsequently between the Nephites and Lamanites. In the New Testament the themes of dissent, power, politics, and personalities were responsible for the ongoing battle between the Jewish Christians in Jerusalem and Paul's gentile Christians over the fundamental direction of the movement. Early Latter Day Saints dealt with the same themes and sought to overcome various divisive issues arising in the church between 1830 and 1844.

The experience of the Reorganized Church is neither better nor worse than any of these historic controversies. The political process is a natural part of any religious institution, as it is a part of any secular organization. It is the means whereby issues are raised, discussed, and resolved. It is the only way to accomplish anything worthwhile, and while it is a sometimes difficult process, the organization, the gospel, the leadership, and the members are better off when a variety of opinions and a wide-open political process are operating. The best policy, with the widest support, derives from the open and above-board process.

In this environment the dissenting tradition is not just a valuable one, it is absolutely critical to making good policy. It is important for the church's membership to recognize that dissent is a normal part of most organizations, and the key issue is how dissent is perceived and handled. This involves power and politics; it involves influence and control; it involves the balance between the theocratic and democratic elements of church governance; and it involves the personalities of those in power and the personalities of the dissidents. Much that is good in the church occurred because of dissent and wisely used political power and because those in power accommodated the demands of those dissenting. Many changes that are approved by a large majority of voters and are widely supported at present—such as the ordination of women—were once advocated by dissident individuals considered at the time to be liberals, radicals, nonconformists, or worse. If those individuals had been forced outside the movement rather than allowed to make a place for themselves within it, the Reorganization might have been even more tardy in its realization of the importance of women in the ministry of the church and not yet have extended priesthood to them. Indeed, if power is effectively used, much good will occur. However, even if power is wisely used, there frequently will be differences of opinion; the political process is never neat and tidy. What is wise and appropriate use of power will always be a matter of perspective. Regardless, politics and power will be called into play by both the power structure and the dissidents, and both should have access to it. Usually the church emerges stronger as a result of the interplay of these forces.

Unity of purpose instead of uniformity of belief is an oft-stated, admirable goal. However, in a religion based on revelation, people often believe God is on their side, or they are on God's side; therefore, they operate under the divine imperative to demand capitulation rather than compromise. People with such beliefs are capable of much evil, as for example in the burning of witches or of tarring and feathering Mormons. It is the type of mentality on which the Catholic Inquisition of the Middle Ages and the Haun's Mill massacre were built.

To the extent that democracy is the free exchange of ideas and the orderly selection of the best for implementation, many people have been dissidents at one time or another, and likewise have been critical of dissidents at other times. As Jesus Christ advised the scribes and

Pharisees, it is usually best to be careful not to cast stones at dissidents or at the power structure, and instead, choose "inclusive" rather than "exclusive" strategies for bringing about change.

An Organization Perspective

Any organization looks different to those at the top of its power structure than to those at the bottom. Both perspectives are equally valid to the extent that they are based on experience. Priorities for action will differ from person to person, based on their perception. The following illustration is designed to help people sense that the view of a community from the top down is very different from the view from the bottom up.

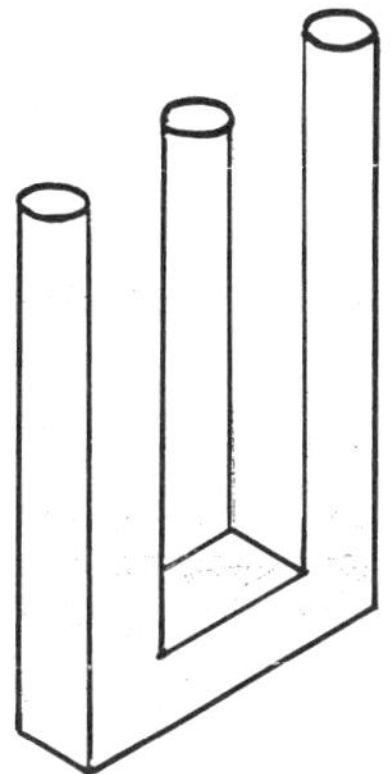

NOTE: Cover the bottom half of the diagram and view the exposed part of this diagram. Then cover the top part of the diagram and view the exposed part at the bottom. This illusion demonstrates the well known fact that a church looks different when viewed from a position of powerlessness at the bottom.

This being the case, it is important to look at the politics of dissent from both points of view. Having established that dissent, power, and politics are normal parts of all organizations, including religious groups, and that any or all of this can either be the cause of much good or of much evil, it is appropriate to explore this application in the Reorganized Church.

The Politics of Dissent from the Top Down

Certainly the administration of the church was centralized in the First Presidency during the 1920s, under the leadership of President Frederick M. Smith. Kenneth R. Mullikin has written of this process:

> From this point forward Smith enjoyed almost unchallenged power within the church. Administratively he controlled all quorums, councils, and territories; he appointed missionaries, department heads, stake and district presidents, and pastors in the Independence Stake. He could allocate or withhold finances during the inter-Conference period, and he was editor-in-chief of all church publications. He exercised profound legislative strength by initiating legislation through his dominance of the Joint Council, presenting revelations in which the prophetic voice was accepted or rejected by a majority, and chairing Conference meetings in which he controlled the debate as parliamentarian. Finally, in a judicial respect, Smith presided over the Standing High Council, the court of high appeal in the church.[3]

As indicated earlier, power is possessed but not always expressed. More recent church presidents have such power, but they have not always used it in similar ways.

Experience has established that the control of resources is an important way to deal with dissent. The First Presidency and the Presiding Bishopric control the budget and can direct resources to or withhold resources from any recalcitrant. If, for example, a group believes more emphasis should be placed on social issues, officials can choose to designate both fiscal and human resources to address that problem. Conversely, if individuals or divisions within the church power structure dissent too strongly, their budgets can be cut, division personnel can be reduced, personnel changes can be made, and the base of support for the opposition can be neutralized, all presumably for other legitimate reasons. Of course, dissident church leaders can be reassigned somewhere where they will be offset, or strong leaders can be reassigned to an area where a dissident membership needs to be brought under control. From a personnel management point of view, this is good management in that the issue for administrators is matching personnel with the needs of the area. Loyalty to administrative superiors is a trait that is almost always valued in subordinates. Sometimes dissidents are promoted or led to believe they will be promoted if they become more of a team player and thus are coopted. These approaches have happened at all levels of church hierarchy.

Control of the agenda is another effective tool in dealing with dissent. In the largest sense, the church's agenda for change is controlled by the power structure who, by use of long-range planning committees, establishment of task forces, or simply by proposing changes, themselves determine what changes will be seriously considered.

On the theocratic side of the theocratic-democracy, the prophet in no small measure determines what topics to pray about for guidance, and, of course, what language to use to convey divine intent, as well as when to convey it and, as with the Temple and the ordination of women, when to implement the divine message. The human element in divine guidance should not be underestimated. Of course, World Conference ratification is one check on the use of such power, albeit a relatively ineffective one. The Reorganized Church is generally accustomed to accepting the revelations to the church as if the human element of the prophet is not a factor. It follows, therefore, that major controversial changes such as ordaining women or building the Temple would be directed through revelation. So, to the extent that there is a human element in revelation, revelation can be used to override human resolutions.[4] That fact is not intended to imply that it has always been used in that manner, but the potential exists.

The church hierarchy also controls the agenda of World Conference, as well as stake and regional conferences. The power to decide what receives conference consideration is an important aspect of administrative power. Political expertise will often dictate placing a controversial issue near the end of a long agenda where, with the hour late, the conferees tired and probably a little bored, only brief consideration occurs before it is approved. Anticipating every contingency and having strategies in place, should they arise, is another tool that can be used to influence the outcome of business sessions. In essence, only one side of the issue, that supported by the church hierarchy, is well organized and led to present its case. Opposing forces, in most instances, have insufficiently prepared to make persuasive cases and have not the leadership with the knowledge or ability to usher proposed ideas through the institutional structure to gain its approval in conference.

Control of the agenda also relates to personal influence. Well-timed statements from apostles have swayed many Conference decisions. Likewise, the strong personality of a stake president can deter a group from bringing a matter forward for consideration by the stake or World Conference. Conversely, the persuasive powers of a stake president are often responsible for an issue moving forward.

After analyzing revelations and resolutions on the Word of Wisdom, for instance, it seems clear that the church by resolution went much further in imposing restrictions on priesthood and members than God ever intended, at least as indicated by original revelation to the church.[5] Some of this was personality oriented; Joseph Smith III and many other members of the nineteenth-century Reorganization were adamant prohibitionists and their savvy and position in the church hierarchy enabled them to secure acceptance of strict interpretations against the use of liquor.[6] A similar process was at work in the twentieth century in the manner in which the church hierarchy moved the membership gradually over a period of years toward outright rejection of the early Mormon concept of baptism for the dead.[7]

Control of the conference agenda is also critical in declaring items out of order, or asking for tabling or referring matters to committees for further study. Controversial items that presiding officials want "killed" can often be effectively handled using this political strategy. Similarly, limiting time for introduction of new matters, controlling who gets the floor to speak to an issue, and how long they are permitted to speak are important control measures that can be used if necessary. Of course, these items are appropriately used for other reasons as well.

Control of information to the church is also an important political consideration within the institution. Joseph Smith III recognized this clearly, and early in the Reorganization he had the First Presidency appointed as editors-in-chief of church publications. The right to control what information goes out to the church and how it is phrased is an important aspect of directing the church along lines deemed most important. For those with alternative positions seeking to change the church's direction, it can be an especially frustrating development to find that there is no outlet for the presentation of their ideas. In many instances dissidents have set up their own publications and established their own distribution networks, but this has ever been a shadow, for the mainstream membership have been largely untouched by such actions. As a result, efforts to change church directions from within in this manner are largely ineffective.[8]

Remembering that power in this arena is possessed but not always expressed, the First Presidency can—but certainly does not always—use that power to control what news is announced, what editorial stances will be published, and what articles will be published. Articles on topics of importance to the church leadership can be solicited from writers known to be favorable to the administration. Controversial articles can be edited so as to be suitable, or they can be rejected outright.[9]

The publication and distribution of task force reports and Christian education materials is yet another way that information can be controlled. In a real sense the leadership can largely control what issues are discussed by the membership through these media. During the 1960s a group of young, well-educated liberals entered church employment to write church school materials. They proceeded to replace many of the traditional Restoration values with more liberal, Protestant conceptions about fundamental religious questions. A protest arose among the Saints because they realized, far better than perhaps many in leadership positions did, that the new materials would redirect the thought processes of the church's youth along lines that many members thought inappropriate.[10]

From the perspective of the church hierarchy, what control is inherent in the institutional structure is needed to accomplish the mission of the church and the spreading of the gospel. Some methods must exist, therefore, to get the overarching majority of the church's membership moving pretty much in the same direction. It is a benevolent institution, therefore, one which uses this authority to accomplish good. In most instances, such control has been used appropriately for the greater good of the Saints although dissidents who were left by the side in any controversy may feel differently. The key point, however, is that power is neutral and can be used appropriately for the furtherance of objectives deemed worthwhile.

The Politics of Dissent from the Bottom

The church as a theocratic-democracy does provide significant opportunity for the membership to make a difference. While members may feel powerless at times, in fact, they are not. Certainly "politicians need to stay in touch with their constituents and be aware of constituent priorities!"[11] Groups can coalesce on a variety of issues at almost any time to make themselves heard

within the institutions in which they hold memberships.

Almost by definition, the church was not intended to
be a pure democracy where the membership makes all
the decisions. A theocratic-democracy clearly indicates
that God is in charge and that those who represent God
in the church hierarchy have the balance of power on
their side. However, if leaders get too far in front—or
behind or sideways—of their people, they cease to be
leaders who are taken seriously. Readiness to act and
readiness to follow should be a basic component of all
leadership decisions. Apostle Paul said, "I have fed you
with milk, and not with meat; for hitherto ye were not
able to receive it, neither yet now are ye able."[12]

Be that as it may, common consent implies at least
endorsement of leadership position. Yet agency and
stewardship concepts require individuals to act responsibly on personal understandings. An understanding of
power and politics, then, is an important component of
personal stewardship of God-given abilities.

If an individual or a small group wishes to challenge
the power structure, that is, to dissent from an official
position, the question is how to do it effectively. Individuals are apt to feel powerless, and they may in fact
be powerless. The political question that needs to be
asked is, "How can power be amassed?" Or stated
differently, "How can enough power be gained to force
the power structure to seriously consider and hopefully
adopt all or part of our position?" Such groups:

> Should remember that (1) larger numbers are power; (2)
> coalitions are power; (3) a unified position is power; (4)
> members who are in credible positions are power; (5)
> knowledge is power; (6) voting is power; and (7) money
> is power.[13]

The above mentioned principles of power are applicable at the congregational, region or stake, or World Church level.

The concept of "large numbers as power" or "strength in numbers" is time tested and cannot be ignored. If a position is valid enough that large numbers of people espouse it, it will be taken more seriously than if such is not the case. Those who dissent from official positions would do well to seek support, to organize in a variety of ways, and to communicate that message to the majority of the church and all of the leadership.

If, for example, people wanted the church to establish a strong or different position on an issue, it is important to assess the amount of support that exists for that position. Talking about the issue, increasing understanding of the various aspects of the issues, and increasing discontent for the status quo are all effective ways to do this.

The concept of "coalitions are power" suggests that discontent and action must have a broad base of support. People of like mind in other jurisdictions should not only be asked to support your point of view but to organize others as a group to work with your group. An effective networking approach has developed in a variety of other common institutions similar to the national political party structures, and similar strategies can be developed using the same principles.

The concept of "a unified position is power" is the antithesis of "divide and conquer." A focused-action plan, with a priority or two that all will support, is important when challenging the power structure of any institution. Dissidents should not allow themselves to be perceived as "disagreeing or fighting among themselves." This gives the institutional leadership the opportunity to dismiss the dissidents summarily as "they don't know what they want."

The concept of "members who are in credible positions is power" applies because of the value of experience, expertise, and reputation to any reform effort. If people known to have good judgment and who are in positions of influence in other circles of power are involved, a reformation program must be taken more seriously than if it only involves people who are largely unknown.

It is especially important to have well-known, highly respected people in leadership, spokesperson roles in such attempts. Carefully selecting the person to represent the group as spokesperson in public meetings may be the most critical decision of a dissenting effort. Care must be taken not to select a professional "rebel," who, while once credible, has lost credibility by being against everything.

To say that "knowledge is power" is a truism, yet it is a key to changing an organization along lines wanted by a dissenting group. Change agents must know the issues inside and out. They must articulate a strong case, one that is logical and well documented. They must also thoroughly understand the position they are proposing to change, including its history and nature, as well as that of the proponents of status quo and the negative effect of changing status quo. They must thoroughly understand all sides of the issue.

It is also important for dissident groups to understand the decision-making process within the organization they seek to change, especially the opportunities and appropriate timing of actions to achieve the desired results. Moreover, it is critical to anticipate how those presiding will react and to have contingency plans ready. Certainly effective presiders will have done like-wise, and the outcome may be determined by who is best prepared rather than who is right.

The concept of "voting is power" is just as important in religious politics as secular politics. Many a congregational or stake decision has been made because some group made a concrete effort to get out the favorable vote. At the World Conference level it is necessary to get the right people to be delegates. Of course, those can be countermanded by the power structure, as in 1988 when Blue Valley Stake was disorganized, in part so it could not send a dissident delegation to World Conference, but these extreme actions are improper and, happily, rare. More often, members are free to choose, and political organization at the local level can go far toward making their cases, as well as gaining their passage by practicing some common political tactics.

Finally, the concept of "money is power" applies because any change movement costs money. Flyers, newsletters, travel costs, telephone calls, and postage all cost money. If the dissenters are wealthy enough or the group is large enough, the large sums expended in presenting its case can yield positive results. Every movement needs to be adequately financed.

The Ethics of Dissent

Dissenting from the "party line" of church leadership often produces growth, increases understanding, and precipitates change. This is almost always a positive development. Again, it should be remembered that unity of purpose is more important than uniformity of belief. Dissent is not always good or always bad, nor is controlling dissent. While right and wrong are difficult to circumscribe, ethical standards need to be remembered and applied.

> Decisions on an individual or a group basis such as when laws or policies are formulated are most ethical when they produce
> - The greatest good for the most people (good motives and good results).
> - Justice (fair and impartially administered).
> - Utilitarianism (practical enough so it can work in foreseeable circumstances.[14]
>
> Generally speaking, behavior can be considered ethical or good if it
> - Increases trust among people.
> - Promotes integrity and decreases deceit in relationships.
> - Dissolves barriers between people.
> - Increases cooperative attitudes.
> - Enhances self-respect.
> - Does not exploit others.
> - Eliminates confusion and allows individuals to move toward love of others.[15]

These standards can be effectively applied to dissent and especially toward power politics within religious organizations. The greatest good for the most people suggests that dissent should not be based in selfish motives but must be directed by the best interests of the church. Justice and fairness suggest that the dirty political tricks, lies, half-truths, and other such items are always out of place in religious organizations. Kindness, honesty, and humility are qualities that should characterize even power politics in a church setting. Utilitarianism or pragmatism suggests that the outcome of any contentious issue must be workable for the organization and its membership and that it will not create major new problems.

Increasing trust, promoting integrity, dissolving barriers, increasing cooperative attitudes, enhancing self-respect, decreasing the exploitation of others, and eliminating confusion are all desirable aspects of power, politics, and dissent when applied to any setting, but which are imperatives to a Christian setting. These attributes should characterize the behavior of power brokers, at either the top or the bottom on the organizational structure.

The problem becomes more complex, however, when a situation is deemed serious enough to warrant disruptive dissent. Certainly the laws permitting women to vote or the more recent civil rights movement required disruptive behavior, at least in the minds of those dissenting. The greatest good for the most people can sometimes justify civil disobedience, conceivably, but not normally, even in religious organizations.

When the Protestant reformers believed the Catholic church was in apostasy, the ends were believed to justify the means. To the extent that fundamentalist branches today believe the Reorganized Church is in apostasy, any tactics can be justified, starting with the least disruptive and escalating to media strategies, pickets, lawsuits, and violence. While everyone would prefer that such tactics not occur, they can be justified at least to the satisfaction of those undertaking them. Of course, the institution also uses political tactics to deal with each stage of the opposition, preferably (from an institutional point of view) anticipating each stage of the escalating power struggle. Ideally, ways should be found to accommodate some of the demands of the dissidents, so as to resolve the power struggle in a manner that both sides can live with if not fully endorse. Such is not always possible. The recent struggle with the fundamentalists resulted in no winners because no common ground could be found, and separation—perceived by many to be irrevocable—has occurred, to the detriment of the parent church and the dissidents.

I believe the power structure of the Reorganized Church attempted to accommodate many of the dissidents' demands and did so in kindly and compassionate ways. However, while much was done, more could have been tried. While hindsight is always better than foresight, strategies other than those used might have been more effective. Most dissident groups refused consistently to work for change from within, over a period of time deciding to separate and move on a path that would result in separation while simultaneously creating discord and disruptions in the parent church. While there is enough blame to go around, the dissidents seem to have decided relatively early that the situation was serious enough to warrant a "demand everything and secede if we don't get it" strategy. This prompted an equally adamant position on the part of the hierarchy, to everyone's detriment. It would have been preferable to have one stable religious organization rather than at least two marginal organizations.

A Concluding Point of View

Politics, power, personalities, and dissent are very much part and parcel of religious organizations as well as all others. If used responsibly by those perceived to be both the powerful and the powerless, the organization will benefit. If used irresponsibly, the organization will be damaged, perhaps irrecoverably.

A logical conclusion about the responsible use of power politics in the church can best be caught up in the following scriptures:

Though I speak with the tongues of men and of angels,...though I have the gift of prophecy, and understand all mysteries, and all knowledge; and though I have all faith, so that I could remove mountains,...and though I bestow all my goods to feed the poor, and though I give my body to be burned, and have not charity, it profiteth me nothing.[16]

No one can assist in this work except he [or she] shall be humble and full of love, having faith, hope, and charity, being temperate in all things.[17]

In the final analysis I must conclude that politics and power are inherent in all human activities and that all who use them should be temperate and characterized by humility and love.

Notes

1. Lawrence J. Peter, *Peter's Quotations: Ideas for Our Time* (New York: Bantam Books, 1977), 413-414, 416.

2. Donald J. Breckon, et al., *Community Health Education: Settings, Roles, and Skills* (Rockville, Maryland: Aspen Publications, 1989), 132.

3. See Kenneth R. Mullikin, "The Supreme Directional Control Controversy: Theocracy Versus Democracy in the Reorganized Church, 1915-1925," in chapter 3 of this book, with reference to endnote 45.

4. Roger D. Launius, "Joseph Smith III and the Quest for a Centralized Organization, 1860-1873," in Maurice L. Draper and A. Bruce Lindgren, eds., *Restoration Studies II* (Independence, Missouri: Herald Publishing House, 1983), 104.

5. Donald J. Breckon, "The Church's Position on Alcohol, Tobacco, and Drugs: A Critical Analysis," *Saints Herald* 120 (September 1973): 26-28, 44.

6. Paul Shupe, "Indulging in Temperance: Prohibition and Political Activism in the RLDS Church," *Journal of Mormon History* 10 (1983): 21-33.

7. Roger D. Launius, "An Ambivalent Rejection: Baptism for the Dead and the Reorganized Church Experience," *Dialogue: A Journal of Mormon Thought* 23 (Summer 1990): 61-84.

8. A present-day example is the publishing activities of the fundamentalist dissenters. Several periodicals and pamphlets have been printed, but while they do have an effect they do not reach anything approaching the majority of the far-flung membership. In terms of changing the direction of the mainline church, therefore, these activities are ineffective.

9. I have had articles rejected for publication in the *Saints Herald*, for instance, with the statement that, "The church isn't ready for that issue now!"

10. William J. Knapp, "Professionalizing Religious Education in the Church: The 'New Curriculum' Controversy," *The John Whitmer Historical Association Journal* 2 (1982): 47-59.

11. Robert Patton and William Cissell, *Community Organization: Traditional Principles and Modern Applications* (Johnson City, Tennessee: Latchpin Press, 1990), 144.

12. I Corinthians 3:2.

13. Breckon, et al., *Community Health Education*, 136.

14. Donald J. Breckon, *Matters of Life and Death* (Independence, Missouri: Herald Publishing House, 1987), 25.

15. Ibid., 24.

16. I Corinthians 13:1-3.

17. Doctrine and Covenants 11:4b (Independence, Missouri: Herald Publishing House, 1970 ed.).

Chapter 6

The Sociology of Dissent and the Reorganized Church

by Maurice L. Draper

Introduction

The networking and interrelationships of any organization reveal that issues of agreement and disagreement, authority and rebellion are present. This chapter describes and offers some aspects of this socialization process, especially concerning dissent and control, as it relates in general to religious movements and in particular to the Reorganized Church. The intent is to raise the consciousness of individuals concerning the nature of this process and to prescribe some means for using it to the best advantage of the membership and the institution.

Social Change

Social change is a pervasive theme in social science theory and research. Virtually everything in the social milieu is in the process of change, although social theorists have not universally agreed on the amount and perception of change. In years past, social scientists have been taunted by other observers of the social scene about an inclination to emphasize the structural, orderly, repetitive, and predictive aspects of society. Many researchers have emphasized these features of society to the neglect of its more dynamic processes.[1]

Such criticism is not altogether justified, however, especially in view of the intense interest in recent years in the processes of change, both of society in general and in its institutions. Some of the classic textbooks place considerable emphasis on the social processes in human interaction: competition and cooperation, conflict and accommodation. More recently scholars, communications media personnel, and the general public have all become concerned about the nature and rate of social change. Industrial and commercial organizations have produced in overwhelming numbers manuals on promoting and managing change. Social scientists have rewritten the textbooks and produced new ones emphasizing the tensions between change and continuity. Entire courses and training programs in universities and business organizations are devoted to the processes and problems of social change.

Religion is not exempt. Organized religion, through the interaction of its structures with other institutions, both affects and is affected by the change process in society at large. Technological development in the realms of communication and transportation have conquered the distance between nations and cultures. One of the results is that the reciprocal influence of religion and other social institutions is more powerful in world-wide terms than ever before in human history.

Factors in Social Change

Social change involves many social processes. Sociologist Richard T. LaPiere identified five fundamental categories: social progress; reformism; various aspects of determinism; cyclical theories; and the social process of assimilation, social lag, cultural acceleration, and asocial elements. He emphasized social change as contrary to the "normal" stability of society.[2] In contrast, W. Loyd Warner adopted the opposite view, that "the nature of our collectivity is such that change is built into it and is an essential part of it; that to be what it is at any one moment in time, this society must continually change and become something else."[3]

Whether stability or change is the "normal" state of society is scarcely debated at the present time. Change has been pervasive, and at an increasing rate, throughout the twentieth century. The issue now attracting the attention of researchers, as well as that of the general public, is the rate of change. The troubling questions now are concerned with the tolerance level of individual persons, managing change purposefully, and coping with the consequences of change.

The rapid rate of social change in modern times gives new force to challenges to human relationships at a high level of intensity. It is doubtful these challenges are new in the sense that earlier generations may not have faced them. There is little doubt, however, that the human spirit today experiences the incredible effects of individual exposure to new data, new mobility, and new relationships with cultures formerly unknown. In my opinion, the greatest threat to human life in the future is not the population explosion and the food shortage projected by Malthusian theorists. It is, rather, the overwhelming effect of the flood of data and the increasingly complex interaction and intense stimulation produced by the information technology of the age. Like the inexperienced swimmer at an ocean beach with an unusually rough surf, we are tossed about and rolled over by powerful wave after wave. We are buried in data and new experiences. We can scarcely react to one new idea or relationship until others are upon us.

This is a serious problem for us even when dealing with mechanical and physical processes. It is no less a problem in our cultural relationships: politics, economics, art, education, and religion. Rather than debating the normalcy of social change, we need to be focusing our attention on the management of change. We need to be evaluating the social factors that balance change with sufficient stability so the change process itself has some meaning. Change in society at large and in social institutions is inevitable. The question confronting us is whether or not such change can be constructive.

Sociology addresses, among other things, the study of change and the processes of competition, conflict, and accommodation. Is it possible that society's future is bound up with the lessons that we need to learn, both as individuals and in organizations, about accepting change as inevitable and how to be enriched by the process of accommodation rather than destroyed by conflict?

Dissent in Organizations

Organizations are sometimes classified as "closed" or "open" structures. A closed organization has little direct interaction with its social environment. An open organization involves significant interaction, usually as a deliberately chosen policy by its leaders and members. In the modern world there are few closed organizations, in fact, though there may be some whose members and leaders attempt to avoid such interaction and to shield themselves from the consequences of that which does occur.

Commercial and industrial organizations are obviously in the open category. The reason for their existence is to interact with the larger society in the process of producing goods and services that are desired by the public and which will produce economic gain for the members of the organization. Most such organizations have a bureaucratic structure, with lines of authority and accountability. Some have a modified bureaucratic form, especially those that are perceived as cooperatives and partnerships. It is interesting to note, however, that even such participatory kinds of structures, intended to be more democratic than the traditional bureaucracy is perceived to be, usually require some kind of executive office to administer decisions and attend to the day-to-day functions.

In recent years a growing number of organizational consultants have prophesied the decline and ultimate disappearance of bureaucracy. The basic dimensions of the bureaucratic form are

1. A division of labor based on functional specialization.
2. A well-defined hierarchy of authority.
3. A system of rules covering the rights and duties of employees.
4. A system of procedures for dealing with work situations.

5. Impersonality of interpersonal relationships.
6. Promotion and selection based on technical competence.

Warren G. Bennis offers a description of the "flaws and problems in the bureaucratic model."[4] We have all experienced them: bosses without technical competence and underlings with it; arbitrary and zany rules; an underworld (or informal) organization that subverts or even replaces the formal apparatus; confusion and conflict among roles; and cruel treatment of subordinates, based not on rational or legal grounds but on inhumane grounds.[5]

At first glance this seems like a persuasive argument for the elimination of all bureaucratic organizations. But before we fall into that trap, let us note that every one of the criticisms is aimed at faulty application of the principles involved rather than at the principles themselves. This is a description of incompetence and inhumane attitudes on the part of the persons involved. It is further interesting to note that the solutions offered by Bennis, widely supported by other management and organization consultants, focus sharply on the development of skills, competence, values, and attitudes by all the members of organizations. The solutions offered are related to the quality of the persons, almost without exception.

I am not arguing for the retention of bureaucratic forms nor for the substitution of other forms for bureaucracy. No doubt there are better ways of organizing human resources for our mutual benefit than we have yet developed. It is important to consider, however, the basic question of the quality of the people. Unless we do so, no form of organization will be ultimately satisfactory. Bennis is among those who promote the idea of organizational change through planning, participation by all of the persons affected by decisions, sharing of information through educational and communications programs, and the cultivation of a professional attitude on the part of all concerned. These are all fundamentally related to the kind of people who make up an organization.

Because personal qualities are so elemental in human social relationships, factors of dissent in organizations are inevitably associated with these personal qualities. Structural factors play a role, but social structures exist and are sustained by persons having a value system that nourishes them.

The inherent purpose of an organization has significant implications for its structure. If an organization is established for the explicit purpose of realizing specified objectives, it is expected to be governed by the criterion of efficiency. An organization so governed has been defined as a bureaucracy. Neither the will of the majority nor the personal choice of a ruler or a ruling clique reigns supreme, but the rational judgment of experts. Sociologist Peter Blau observed:

> But if men organize in order to ascertain the ideas that prevail among them and then to agree on common objectives, their purpose requires that the basic principle which governs their action is freedom of dissent. ... To assure that the majority viewpoint remains supreme, a limitation has to be imposed on the majority itself. It must not stifle the opposition of any minority, however small its numbers or extreme its view, for unless dissenting voices can be heard today, tomorrow's decisions will not be democratic ones.[6]

It is well to keep in mind that many religious organizations are more or less bureaucratic, ranging from authoritative hierarchies to decentralized, autonomous, local congregations.

Dissent in Religious Organizations

Sociological studies of religion include, among other things, analysis of its forms of organization. No single organization is a "pure type," but scholars have developed categories that help us understand the similarities and differences among religious bodies. They identify the national church, the sect, the denomination, and the cult as major types. The theoretical formulation of these categories has been debated, rejected, refined, and promoted. Without entering into this debate, let us note that the concept has been extremely useful to those who want to understand the social aspects of human religious experience and activity.

Sects frequently have their origin in dissent within established churches or denominations. The dissent may result from different causes. There may be difference of doctrinal belief. Sometimes there is dissatisfaction with the organization's structure and leadership practices. Dissent has developed over political issues, as when the Civil War produced the "North" and "South" divisions of some Protestant denominations in the United States.

Dissent occurs in both authoritative bureaucratic organizations and in those that take pride in their democratic practices. It is expressed in varying degrees of intensity. It ranges from efforts at reform from within to outright rebellion and the creation of independent competitive groups with their own internal structure and formal leadership. Dissent from within may be intended to retain traditional forms and procedures in opposition to new ones. It may also be aimed at reform intended to free the organization from outmoded traditions and procedures. Thus, it may be undertaken both by priestly traditionalists or by prophetic visionaries of a "new age."

Some religious bodies are more tolerant of dissent than others, having developed an institutional procedure for accommodating the dissenters. There are many individual holy orders, for example, in Roman Catholicism, each having a special purpose and related program of action. If an attitude of exclusive validity were to characterize such bodies, the result would be highly divisive, with each claiming to be representative of the true ministries of the Christian gospel. On the other hand, religious groups having a congregational type of organization have been known to split into separate bodies over disputes about ministerial leadership styles or even personality conflicts.

Not only are there organizational factors in dissent within religious bodies, there are also disagreements over theological issues and programs of action. For example, in those that are more sectlike, some members may believe that the body is too withdrawn from society and that they need to adopt some programs of social action. In other instances, movement in that direction arouses the ire of those who are inclined to withdrawal from the world. In bodies that emphasize literal interpretation of infallible scriptures, any hint that they are subject to circumstantial interpretation leads to conflict.

Dissent within the Reorganization

Every instance of dissent has its unique aspects. No doubt the principles that apply to social organizations and religious bodies in general also apply to the Reorganized Church in both its bureaucratic and its democratic aspects. Some specific and unique characteristics of the Reorganized Church in this respect deserve our attention.

Dissent appeared in the church in the earliest period of its existence. When Joseph Smith, Jr., presented his prophetic utterances to the church, a group of elders in autumn 1831 challenged his inspiration and the language of his revelations. At that time Joseph acknowledged their concern. He might have reacted vigorously against it on the basis of his sense of divine call. Instead, he invited the group to search out what they considered to be the document that is "even the least that is among them," and then to select "him that is the most wise among you" to make an effort to "make one like unto it."[7] The group selected William E. McLellin, who failed in his attempt. Joseph's invitation to the dissenters no doubt prevented the development of a more serious rift.

Indeed, there were other occasions, the most dramatic one being in 1844. Certain practices that developed in Nauvoo resulted in active conflict. Among the dissenters was William Law, who had been ordained on 19 January 1841 as a counselor to Joseph and a member of the First Presidency. Some of the developments in Nauvoo were abhorrent to him. In the course of his opposition to them, he was expelled from the church on 18 April 1844. He joined with his brother, Wilson, and others in publishing a newspaper, the *Expositor*, attacking the church leadership and the practices they opposed. The *Expositor* printing office was then destroyed by action of the city council. These dramatic events were part of the public unrest that led to Joseph's death only a few weeks later.[8]

There have been other occasions of dissent also after the Reorganization was effected. Some of them led to disaffection, withdrawal, and expulsions. Others were resolved by conference actions, including approval of documents presented by the president of the church as inspired counsel. An example of the latter is in the action of the General Conference in April 1887 at Kirtland, Ohio. Differences had developed over several matters of sacramental procedure and the question of which day of the week should be recognized as the Sabbath. Looking back on the situation, we may think that some aspects of the situation were trivial, and they may even seem humorous to us. From the perspective of one hundred years later, we may wonder why these were issues of disagreement.

One issue concerned the frequency of administration and the liturgical procedure for the Lord's Supper. Should it be administered every week or once a month? Should the prayers of consecration over the bread and wine be offered before the bread is broken and the wine is poured or afterward? Are these such profound questions that they require the inspired Word of God to answer them? However trivial this may seem to later generations, they were important issues at the time. They were settled (at least in a formal sense) when the Conference adopted the prophet's counsel. The prophetic word was that the question of frequency was unimportant, providing the people participate in "sincerity of heart and purity of purpose." Also, either procedure for the consecration is valid and contention over the matter should be avoided.[9]

Another question at the time had to do with instrumental music in worship services. This question was not limited to the Reorganized Church. At least one other denomination had formally adopted the practice of altogether avoiding the use of instruments in worship. The debate crossed denominational lines and became a concern of the Saints. The prophet's response to this was a compromise. Singing in the spirit of joy is acceptable with God, whereas, "song with grievous sadness in them that sing and bitterness of spirit in them that hear is not pleasing to God." Furthermore, to avoid intruding on the feelings of the tender and sad among them, they should refrain from using instruments in prayer and testimony services. Otherwise, all kinds are acceptable including organs, brass, and string instruments.[10] The reference to string instruments is especially interesting, since many people of that day regarded violins as "instruments of the devil" because they were used for public entertainment and dancing.

At other times dissent arose over administrative procedures and official roles. It was a sad occasion when Jason W. Briggs and Zenos H. Gurley, Jr., two prominent figures in the process of reorganization after the martyrdom of Joseph and Hyrum Smith in 1844, withdrew from the Reorganized Church in 1885.[11] Briggs said it was because of differences "in the interpretation put upon certain lines of policy and doctrine; and while others were allowed to discuss those lines of policy, I was not permitted to do so. ... It was simply a matter of discussion through the columns of the *Herald* that caused my withdrawal."[12]

Another period of dissent occurred during the administration of President Frederick M. Smith, also over matters of church government.[13] There were philosophical factors, but these had to do more with role definitions than with doctrinal questions. From the beginning of his tenure, President Smith had been promoting a procedure for the assignments of the apostles that would change their role from administrators of organized field jurisdictions to that of field development and church extension. His perception of the apostolic ministry was that they should be under the immediate supervision of the First Presidency, to be sent to new fields for mission development. On occasion they might be assigned to administrative functions, but these would be ad hoc assignments rather than those with indefinite terms.

Members of the apostolic council had been accustomed to being in the "administrative line," with field administrators reporting to them. Some of them saw President F. M. Smith's proposal as a limitation on their official functions and their personal ministry. Their opposition to the proposed change in assignment policy led President Smith to submit his resignation to the Conference in April 1919. Before action was taken, however, the apostles in quorum session adopted a conciliatory statement and requested President Smith to withdraw his resignation, which he did.

The problem did not go away, however, and in 1925 the Conference adopted a statement on church government submitted by President Smith defining the role of the First Presidency as the administrative authority. The issue was similar in some ways to that which led to the withdrawal of Briggs and Gurley in 1885. One apostle, T. W. Williams, and several members of the Quorums of Seventy left the church in protest after the 1925 Conference action. More recently, there have been differences over the composition of the World Conference (1964), missionary work among tribal people involved in polygamous marriages (1972), content of the religious education curriculum (1960s), and the ministerial roles of women (1984). Some of these issues have been debated in theological terms, but frequently the focus has been not so much on fundamental doctrines as on organizational structure and program decisions. For example, in the debate over missionary work among polygamous people, the question for the church leadership was not that the marriage doctrine of monogamy should be changed, but about the procedure to be used in transforming the polygamous culture into a monogamous one. Opponents did not see it in that light, and they accused the church leadership of abandoning a cherished doctrine.

One result of dissent in the Reorganized Church is the emergence of "splinter groups," especially in recent years. In 1925 some dissenting members transferred their membership to the Church of Christ (Temple Lot). Others may have united with various existing churches beyond the boundaries of the Restoration movement. Still others may have simply dropped out without any transfer of membership or activity with any group. Some of them, however, formed a separate congregation in Independence, Missouri, under the leadership of the former apostle, Thomas W. Williams. They built a small gray stucco chapel on the south side of Kansas Street. This small congregation continued to meet for several years, but Williams, himself, shortly moved to Los Angeles where he was elected as a member of the city council and became famous in the area as a public orator at ceremonial events. The congregation eventually dissolved. The property was used for some time for educational and social activities, finally being sold to the Reorganized Church as part of the site for the Independence Temple.

Some persons were disaffected by the reorganization of the World Conference in 1964, in which the ministerial body of the elders in the Melchisedec priesthood was dropped from the ex-officio category of Conference members. No organized groups developed from this action. The same is true of those who were troubled by the broadening of the religious education curriculum during the 1960s. It is fair to assume, however, that those who were most deeply troubled by these issues did not forget them. When the ordination of women was approved in 1984, according to the statements of some of those who oppose it, this was the "straw that broke the camel's back."

A group of persons whose opposition had developed over the missions to polygamous tribes, religious education, and Conference reorganization had been publishing for some years material attacking the church leadership over these issues. Such material was widely distributed by its publishers, fanning the flames of dissent among troubled members who had not yet broken their ties with the church. When the ordination of women was approved, some of these members undertook active opposition. When they failed to respond to the church leaders' efforts to reconcile their relationships (even if unity of belief was not possible), they became subject to the church's disciplinary procedures. From among them several independent congregations were organized in the area of Independence, Missouri, and elsewhere.

Dissent as an Inherent Aspect of the Reorganized Church

In popular usage the term "dissent" has taken on a harsh meaning. The dictionary meaning is nonjudgmental: "v. 1. to differ in opinion: disagree. 2. to withhold approval or assent. n. 1. disagreement. 2. religious nonconformity."[14]

In the sense of these definitions, dissent is inherent in the Reorganized Church. Three fundamental doctrines and related practices in the church contribute to this condition. The first is the belief in contemporary divine revelation. The second is the doctrine of common consent. The third is the doctrine of individual agency. The interaction of these doctrines, especially based on a radical interpretation of their meaning, leads inevitably to the probability of dissent. Exercised within the limits emerging from their moderate interaction, dissent is desirable. Exercised beyond those limits, without the balancing effect of such interaction, dissent becomes more than difference of opinion and leads to conflict and rebellion.

Belief in revelation accompanied by a conviction that the prophetic human instrument is infallible is one of the characteristics of a religious cult. Carried to extremes this has been known to cause incredible human tragedies. The mass suicide/murder situation in Jonestown is a dramatic example in recent years. Other forms of bizarre behavior are also encouraged by a claim to infallible divine direction: yielding to the self-proclaimed leader one's right to personal decision-making; giving up one's property and earnings to the leader; withdrawal from society; purification sacrifices of animals and even humans in sacramental rituals.

Belief in revelation accompanied by the practice of common consent, however, denies the idea of human infallibility in the process. If revelation concerns anyone other than the individual receiving it, those others have both a right and duty to explore its meaning for them. Perception of truth, even by revelation, involves the human mind. Its expression, therefore, is less than perfect and absolute. When explored by those to whom it is addressed, it is subject to acceptance or rejection.

By definition of the doctrine of revelation it is possible that the prophet may have valid insights not shared by others at the time. The message, therefore, may sometimes be rejected. If this happens, it raises the further question of the nature of subsequent relationships. Shall those differing in opinion take their leave from each other? Or, shall they search for the overriding values that they share and allow their further mutual experience to resolve the issue in dispute?

The doctrine of common consent implies the latter. It aims at procedures by which mutual understanding can be achieved. One aspect of these procedures is patience and good will, in which spirit common understanding is sought in prayer, study, and mutual faith.[15] If radical views are held about revelation to the exclusion of the process of common consent, dissent becomes more than difference of opinion and is rebellion.

Emphasis on individual agency also influences the nature of dissent. When the American political principle of personal freedom is radically interpreted, social responsibility disappears. Similarly, when the theological principle of agency is abused, the sense of community is destroyed. Frequently even the term used to identify the principle contributes to its abuse. The word "agency" is confused with the philosophical term "free will" and the result is a combined term that distorts the meaning of both of the others: "free agency." This phrase has an inherent contradiction. "Freedom," in the absolute sense, means without restraint of any kind. "Agency," on the other hand, implies a contingent relationship. An agent is one who acts and represents another. No action is free from the conditions in which the action occurs, and anyone who represents another has some responsibility toward that principal party.

"Free agency" is really nonexistent by definition. Human behavior is always subject to the conditions of human existence, including the social relationships. For those who believe in the religious doctrine of agency, the actor is never free from responsibility to seek to know and respond to the divine will. There are, therefore, restraints on the exercise of human agency. Individuals are not morally free to behave as though they are responsible only to God because of an infallible perception. They are part of human society and subject to the principles of human relationships, both in general and in the various organizations and groups to which they belong.

Because the Reorganized Church teaches these three principles enthusiastically, and individuals are prone to radical interpretations of them, dissent is inherent in the church.

Response by the Church to Dissent

As the church leadership and its Conferences act by the bureaucratic principle of efficiency in its more radical aspects, the organization's response to dissent is a sharp and legally correct discipline. When the dissent is radical and threatens the well-being of church members or the organization itself, such response also carries with it a high degree of moral quality.When dissent is milder, the church's response is likely to be more tolerant in the hope that the issues will not become divisive.

As the church leadership and its Conferences act by the principle of reconciliation, it undertakes ministries of interpretation, encouragement, and acceptance of differences of opinion. Even when dissent assumes offensive forms, the church should follow the procedure on reconciliation described in Doctrine and Covenants 95:7. This document was presented as inspired instruction to the church at a time of great stress in 1833, when its members were subject to mob violence and loss of property. It provides that when offenses occur and the offender demonstrates a spirit of repentance, forgiveness is to be extended again and again. (The revelation says "until seventy times seven.") When offenses occur and the offender does not repent, even then forgiveness is to be extended three times. It is not until the fourth offense, without repentance, that disciplinary action is justified.

The reason for this tolerance is clear upon reflection. In the first instance it is possible that the offense was unintentional. In the second instance it may be that a forgiving attitude will then stimulate the spirit of repentance in the offender. In the third instance the offended party is, at the very least, refusing to act impulsively or out of the spirit of vengeance. In the fourth instance it may be assumed that the offenses are deliberate, that the offender is not likely to respond to ministries of reconciliation, and that the fact of the offense is well established by the evidence. Given these principles and procedures, the response of the church to dissent is in the spirit of reconciliation, even when it results in discipline.

Dissent is inherent in the Reorganized Church, but so also are the procedures for response to dissent. The factors that seem to encourage dissent need to be kept in balance—revelation, explored in the process of common consent by persons who recognize social responsibility as well as individual rights. When radical interpretations destroy the balance, dissent is negative and destructive. When they are kept in balance, dissent can be wholesome and productive.

Notes

1. John F. Cuber, *Sociology: A Synopsis of Principles* (New York: Appleton-Century-Crofts, 1968), 557.
2. Richard T. LaPiere, *Social Change* (New York: McGraw-Hill, 1965), chapter 1.
3. W. Loyd Warner, *The Corporation in the Emergent American Society* (New York: Harper and Brothers, 1962), 3.
4. Warren G. Bennis, *Changing Organizations* (New York: McGraw-Hill, 1966), 5.
5. Ibid.
6. Peter Blau, *Bureaucracy in Modern Society* (New York: Random House, 1956), 106-107.
7. Doctrine and Covenants 67:2b-c (Independence, Missouri: Herald Publishing House, 1978 ed.).
8. Dallin H. Oaks, "The Suppression of the *Nauvoo Expositor*," *Utah Law Review* 9 (Winter 1966): 862-903.
9. Doctrine and Covenants 119:5.
10. Doctrine and Covenants 119:6.
11. See Alma R. Blair, "The Tradition of Dissent—Jason W. Briggs," in Maurice L. Draper and Clare D. Vlahos, eds., *Restoration Studies I* (Independence, Missouri: Herald Publishing House, 1980), 146-161, and Clare D. Vlahos, "The Challenge to Centralized Power: Zenus [sic] H. Gurley, Jr., and the Prophet Office," *Courage: A Journal of History, Thought and Action* 1 (March 1971): 141-158.
12. Jason W. Briggs, "Testimony in the Temple Lot Suit," *Complainant's Abstract of Pleading and Evidence* (Lamoni, Iowa:Herald Publishing House, 1893), 400. See chapter 1 by Roger D. Launius in this volume for information about the issues over which the dissent occurred.
13. On the Supreme Directional Control controversy, see Paul M. Edwards, "Theocratic-Democracy: Philosopher-King in the Reorganization," in F. Mark McKiernan, Alma R. Blair, and Paul M. Edwards, eds., *The Restoration Movement: Essays in Mormon History* (Lawrence, Kansas: Coronado Press, 1973), 341-357; Larry E. Hunt, *F. M. Smith: Saint as Reformer*, 2 vols. (Independence, Missouri: Herald Publishing House, 1982); and Paul M.

Edwards, *The Chief: An Administrative Biography of Fred M. Smith* (Independence, Missouri: Herald Publishing House, 1988).
14. *Webster's II, New Riverside Dictionary*, 1984.
15. Doctrine and Covenants 25:1b; 27:4c.

Chapter 7

Dissent Among Dissenters: Theological Dimensions of Dissent in the Reorganization

---

by Larry W. Conrad

Introduction: Dissent Among Dissenters

The April 1970 Saints' Herald offered a unique and revealing glimpse into the nature, character, and development of dissent in the Reorganization. The cover photograph showed W. Wallace Smith receiving a copy of the Herald Publishing House reprint edition of the 1830 Book of Mormon. W. Wallace Smith presided over the Reorganized Church at a time when it expanded its missionary outreach across the world and also opened itself to the currents of Protestant theology at a rate unparalleled in its history. At the same time, church leaders sought to recognize and reevaluate the church's ties to its Mormon origins.

199

The same issue of the *Herald* contained an article by four young men who had recently confronted the history of the Nauvoo era while serving as guides at the church's historic sites there. Like many other Reorganization members of the 1960s and 1970s, an encounter with the church's history had forced a personal review of their theology. In "Baptism for the Dead: A Scriptural Perspective," the authors extended the long-standing Reorganization desire to revise early Mormonism's approach toward that doctrine. They admitted that Joseph Smith, Jr., taught the doctrine, but concluded that the practice was a "clear departure from basic Restoration concepts fundamental to Joseph's revelatory works prior to this doctrine."[1]

The Reorganization's experiment in revising and redefining Mormon origins is also reflected in actions at the April 1970 World Conference. On a date no less significant than 6 April 1970, the Conference recommended a continuation of studies on changing the name of the church. The next day, the Conference authorized major revisions in the format of the Doctrine and Covenants, removing Sections 107, 109, and 110 on baptism for the dead to a newly created historical appendix. Section 113, written in the aftermath of the assassinations of 1844 and suggesting that Joseph Smith "has done more (save Jesus only) for the salvation of men in this world, than any other man that ever lived in it," was also removed from the book's main body and relegated to the historical appendix.[2]

Twenty years later the World Conference decided to publish the Doctrine and Covenants without the historical appendix. And, in 1990, concerned that the church had betrayed its heritage, an estimated 15 percent, according to one source, of all Reorganization members in worship on Sunday morning met in dissenting congregations. In 1988-1989 alone, 1,200 Reorganization priesthood were silenced or otherwise released from office.[3] The divisions within the church today are exceeded in severity only by the schisms that resulted from the assassinations of Joseph Smith, Jr., and Hyrum Smith in 1844 and the Supreme Directional Control controversy of the 1920s.[4]

The dissent and division present today stem in large measure from the changes of the past forty years that were reflected well in the April 1970 *Saints' Herald* and World Conference. The post-1950 era constitutes what may rightly be called a Reorganized Church reformation. In this period, Reorganization progressives emerged to engage in the steady dismantling of what had been a traditional Reorganized Church consensus. They challenged the belief that the Inspired Version of the Bible is a superior work of correcting and restoring the scriptural text; questioned the antiquity of the gospel as understood and practiced in the Reorganization; argued against the presentation of the gospel as a set of specific principles; asserted that the Reorganized Church is not the only true church with authority to administer the sacraments; rejected the view that the Reorganization serves as the penultimate restoration of the New Testament church; undermined belief in the historicity of the Book of Mormon; questioned the propositional character of revelation; softened traditional teachings on the ancient apostasy and the gospel's restoration; deemphasized the gathering to Zion and the second coming of Jesus Christ; instituted educational and other requirements for priesthood; advocated ordination of women; and challenged millennial ideals.[5] Despite the claims of some progressives that the church has not changed, this reformation has struck at the very core and essence of the Reorganized Church's origins and reasons for existence since the 1850s.[6] What has happened, in short, has been the substantive breakdown of the religious consensus that has guided the organization since near its founding.

Although the current crisis in the church can be discussed in terms of recent developments, it is but the culmination of tensions building for more than a century: the clash between the desire to remain faithful to the stories, symbols, and events of early Mormonism, on the one hand, and the yearning for respectability among and hence openness to Protestants on the other. These tensions were held in creative balance under Joseph Smith III whose gentle pragmatism balanced a diverse band of Mormon dissenters. The tensions erupted during the centralization of power and reinterpretation of the tradition under Frederick M. Smith, eased under Israel A. Smith, and resurfaced under W. Wallace Smith in the reformation just defined. During this recent reformation period the 1880s-1950s Reorganized Church theological synthesis collapsed. The failure to convincingly blend the symbols, stories, and events of the Reorganization's tradition with an influx of Protestant ideas has created a theological vacuum. No creative theological giants have moved in to fill the void for the institutional church. The most significant theological work of the Reorganized Church during this reformation was *Exploring the Faith*, and it was written by a committee, a telling sign of the fragmentation of Reorganization theology.

As Alma R. Blair and Clare D. Vlahos have perceptively noted, the Reorganization has sought to be a form of moderate Mormonism.[7] My thesis is that the theological basis for dissent in the Reorganization is found in this tension between trying to remain faithful to the church's origins in Mormonism while also remaining open to the influences of the wider Protestant community. In this essay I will examine three major theological issues which tend to spawn dissent in the Reorganized Church: authority, the nature of theological and salvific truth, and the church's scriptures and history. An exploration of the ways two contemporary streams of Reorganization thought approach these issues will further illumine the character of dissent in the Reorganization and the depth of the theological crisis facing the church's leaders and theologians. Finally, I will discuss the contributions of dissent to the development of Reorganized Church theologies for the close of the twentieth century.

The Necessity of Dissent

Before examining the issues spawning dissent in the Reorganization, a preliminary consideration is required concerning the identification and expression of dissent. First, in its purest form religious dissent becomes necessary when the individual believes the integrity of the gospel and the self are at stake. To dissent is not merely to hold certain beliefs, but involves the decision to confess those beliefs publicly against the beliefs of others because one comes to believe that the essential core of the gospel is at stake. Dissent, then, in its purest form, is a centered act of faith, necessitated and demanded by the integrity of the gospel and the self, but undertaken for the good of the whole community. Dissent may or may not lead to institutional censure, but depending on the issues involved and the relative

203

weight they are assigned by the individual and the church's hierarchy such might happen.

A second factor involves identifying which person or group is in dissent, and there are a couple of distinct ways to approach the issue in the context of the Reorganized Church. Dissent may be defined as dissent from the respected tradition. By this standard the current leadership in the church is in dissent, its theology having gone beyond the realm of reinterpretation of the tradition and toward effecting radical change. While the Reorganization's First Presidency would probably not agree that radical change has taken place, too much evidence to the contrary is present for such an assertion to be persuasive.[8] At the April 1974 World Conference, as only one of many examples that could be cited, Clifford A. Cole, then president of the Quorum of Twelve Apostles, conceded that the church had been radically changing and that it must continue to do so to ensure the fulfillment of its role in the world. He asserted:

> We doubt that we have a plan, or an institution, or a social order to offer the world. And if we did have, it would only be a few years until that contribution would be outdated and unable to meet the needs of the time. If the Saints had successfully established a Zionic community in Missouri in the 1830s, it would have little importance to offer the world today *unless* it had changed radically from the Zion the early Saints envisioned.[9]

This bespeaks the sense of radical change that touches at the very heart of the Reorganization.

By another standard, and this is the issue that will be considered in detail here, dissent may be defined as dissent from the institution, particularly the teaching and polity of the church as defined by the First Presidency. By this standard current fundamentalist leaders would be classified as in dissent. They have rebelled from the hierarchy in ways unacceptable to Reorganization leaders and have pressed the rebellion as far as possible because their interpretion of the gospel demands it. It was such a commitment to ideals that led to the creation of the Reorganized Church.

Dissent and the Issues

The first major issue that spawns dissent in the church, as might be expected from the previous discussion, is authority. The Restoration movement arose in the midst of a crisis of authority and sought to identify, support, and establish a new authority to resolve the unanswered questions of the day. In heralding the coming of a new foundation for Christian faith, the beginning of Mormonism was a decisive and ringing dissent against all existing churches and theologies.[10] In the Restoration scheme of things, if one accepts the church's authority, a sacred canopy is constructed in which and under which one lives. This canopy gives history, indeed the universe, coherence, meaning, and purpose. To enter the church is to enter a new world, which becomes the world. To leave the church, or to seriously weigh the possibility of leaving it, either because one may have found truth outside it or because one thinks the truth is not in it, is to lapse toward the chaos of nothingness.

In a movement founded on authority, especially exclusive authority, the question inevitably arises: Where is this authority located within the church? Historically, two opposing theological options have surfaced in the movement. The first, a more democratic option that finds support among Protestants but which has a distinctive form in the Restoration, locates the authority in the lower levels of the organization. Supportive of this option, Section 17 of the Book of Doctrine and Covenants authorizes the elders to "conduct the meetings as they are led by the Holy Ghost."[11] Elders, priests, teachers, and deacons are to be "ordained by the power of the Holy Ghost *which is in the one who ordains him*" [emphasis added].[12] In a movement that values the return of apostolic authority and the spiritual experiences of the New Testament era churches, this is a grant of potentially great latitude and freedom to local levels of the church. Ministerial authority is not dependent on the level of theological or secular education, and in this tradition authority is often equated with competence. With such a localization of exclusive, restoration-based authority, differences in levels of authority are more clearly differences in degree, not kind. Combined with the hierarchical way of thinking, it is a short step from thinking that one is *an* authority to thinking that one is *the* authority. This becomes more likely when one is inclined to believe that the leadership is losing its authority by not teaching the doctrines and ways as previously taught.

The democratic option, based on selected passages and experiences, achieved its institutional form in the early days of the Reorganization, propelled by historical necessity in the absence of respected, centralized authority, and was later supported by Joseph Smith III.[13] The more democratic localization of authority has been opposed by a stronger tradition, more rooted in Mormonism, of elevating the prophetic office and the concentration of authority in the president. In response to the Hiram Page incident, for instance, Section 27 of the Doctrine and Covenants established Joseph Smith, Jr., as the exclusive recipient for the church's revelations and commandments.[14]

The Supreme Directional Control controversy of the 1920s formalized and clearly established the concentration of authority and power in the prophetic office for the Reorganization. The dominant option of the Reorganized Church's structure can be seen in administrative policies governing calls to the priesthood, silences, and reinstatements after excommunication or expulsion. All reinforce the location of authority in the First Presidency. The exclusive power to present documents to Conferences for reception or removal of canonical status further reinforces the power of the Presidency.[15] The lack of a polity with clear separation of legislative, executive, and judicial powers, combined with the concentration of authority in the First Presidency and the historical distance from exercise of more democratic options, has spawned dissent and even schism by tending to preempt dialogue and restrict diversity.

In addition to authority, a second issue spawning dissent in the church is the question of the location of theological and salvific truth. Closely related to the issue of authority, this issue encompasses not only who has the authority to define what the church teaches is true but also whether salvific truth is confined to the Reorganization. Founded on the concept that the ancient priesthood had been restored to Mormonism after having been lost in the apostasy, the church has traditionally claimed that it alone possesses the authority and truth necessary for salvation. While this is clearly established in Sections 1 and 20 of the Doctrine and Covenants, the concept of the prisonhouse and Section 76 attempt to soften the teaching about the church's exclusive authority by offering the opportunity to hear the gospel in the afterlife. Thus, traditional teaching avoids confining most of the world's peoples, including non-Christians, to eternal damnation.

The importance of this question, however, has increased greatly during the Reorganized Church reformation as many concluded that traditional teachings about exclusive claims to authority and theological and salvific truth were naïve or in some critiques considered just plain wrong. For many still dazed by the last forty years of reformation, the question is no longer: Is the Reorganized Church the only true church? Rather, the question now is: Is the Reorganization a true church? What, if any, are the Reorganized Church's distinctive claims to truth?

Third, since the beginning of the movement, the very history of the church itself has spawned dissent. The founding events of Mormonism continue to evoke dissent, from the Mormons who leave to join fundamentalist Protestant sects to the historiographical debates over the "New Mormon History."[16] The early Reorganization formed to dissent from Nauvoo Mormonism and existing splinter groups and sought a more moderate expression of Mormonism. Early Reorganized Church leaders, such as Isaac Sheen and William Marks, dissented from the authoritarian style of Nauvoo Mormonism as well as elements of an evolving theology, especially the practice of polygamy.[17]

In recent years Jan Shipps and others have sought to bypass the prophet versus fraud dichotomy in historical research and to legitimate the study of Mormonism as a new religious tradition.[18] But this approach is difficult for a movement like the Reorganization, which has failed to confront much of its history and has wrestled with the tensions between Mormon origins and distinctives and openness to the Protestant mainstream. From the debates over polygamy and plurality of gods in the early years of the church to current debates on the First Vision, the church's history has been the source of much dissent. The debate has been equally intense over the scriptures which emerged from that history. The content, manner of reception of some sections of the Doctrine and Covenants, and doctrinal authority of the book itself have all been questioned, from the Briggs/Gurley controversy of the 1880s to the 1970 and 1990 World Conferences.[19]

The Book of Mormon has spawned dissent as well, from all who denounced the "gold Bible" at its publication to debates over its historicity within the Restoration churches in recent decades.[20] Reorganized Church fundamentalists decry the attitudes of the church's leaders toward the book, for example, at least since the leadership's willingness to tolerate criticism of the Book of Mormon's historicity in the "Position Papers." Seeking a middle ground, William D. Russell responds to the results of historical research by outlining a view of the book as inspired, canonical fiction, but still as a second witness for Jesus Christ.[21]

The Issues and Two Contemporary Streams of Thought

Characteristic tensions of the recent church reached their pinnacle during the Reorganization's reformation and have been manifest in the dichotomies relating to the three sensitive issues spawning dissent in the context of two major streams of theological thought. The first major stream, that of Reorganized Church fundamentalism, has taken a variety of forms, encompassing such diverse persons as Barney Fuller, Lee Abramson, Vern Elefson, and Richard Price. The most systematic exposition of Reorganized Church fundamentalism has been offered by Richard Price, whose *Saints at the Crossroads* and subsequent writings held inviolate three basic claims:

> (1) that Jesus Christ founded a specific church organization during the apostolic era and that this church, as foretold in scripture, lost the authority required to represent Christ and administer His sacraments. This apostasy was reversed with the coming of the latter-day light as God restored the true church and its priesthood authority through Joseph Smith, Jr. Subsequent to the splintering of the early Mormon movement in 1844, the Reorganization has served as the only true and authoritative remnant of the Restoration;
>
> (2) that the church's teachings have been based on the deposit of revelations received through Joseph Smith, Jr., and his successors, as well as the Inspired Version and the Book of Mormon;
>
> and (3) that the primary mission of the church is to establish the city of Zion in Independence, Missouri, in preparation for the second coming and millennial reign of Christ.

Of all streams of theological thought, fundamentalism, in the form espoused by Price, best expresses the 1880s-1950s synthesis of Reorganized Church thought that has now broken down within the mainstream church organization.[22]

The other stream, at another end of the Reorganized Church's theological spectrum, represents a transliteration of present-day Protestant thought into Reorganization attitudes. While fundamentalism has its roots in Mormon origins, this stream has roots in the Reorganization's traditional openness to Protestantism. Persons in this stream, a stream which developed rapidly in the 1960s, have attempted to practice theological disciplines in a mainstream Protestant mode. Often educated in Protestant seminaries, they try to express Protestant ideas in Reorganized Church terms and settings.[23] While not all Reorganized Church theological writing at the World Church level reflects this perspective, Protestant theology influences the writings of World Church leadership to a degree unprecedented in the Reorganization. The 1990 World Conference sermon by Wallace B. Smith, for example, has a remarkably Protestant tone with little reference to traditional Reorganized Church teaching, concepts, stories, events, or heroes.[24]

At the turn of the century, dissent usually came from the persons most open to Protestantism and other non-Reorganized Church influences because the leadership more closely allied itself with fundamentalist tendencies. In the last thirty years, however, dissent most often has come from fundamentalists because the leadership allies itself with more Protestant streams. Nevertheless, during the Reorganized Church's reformation, dissent has come from all parts of the spectrum as the debate has raged over the identity and destiny of the organization.

At this point, it is important to recognize that dissent means more than holding certain beliefs. Being in either of the two streams discussed here does not automatically place one in dissent from the institution. If a fundamentalist works enough on an area such as authority and gives the issue enough relative weight, she or he is likely to conclude that the current leadership has strayed far enough on this issue that the gospel itself is now at stake. Therefore, it is decision time, then action time, and the integrity of the gospel and of the individual fundamentalist demand that she or he dissent in a public manner. At the other end of the spectrum, liberal writers may devote much time to the development of a Reorganized Church christology, but christology does not in itself spawn dissent in the church. The Book of Mormon does, however, and the more scholars work on Book of Mormon issues, the greater the possibility of dissent. In fact, if research does not confirm traditional church teachings, scholars could decide that the church's position on the Book of Mormon is so flawed that the integrity of the gospel demands dissent forthrightly and overtly. Dissent need not lead to withdrawal, silence, excommunication, or expulsion, but could do so depending on how important the issues appear to the dissenter and to the hierarchy.

In the context of the Reorganization's reformation, new forms of dissent have developed which begin with the tensions between Mormon origins and Protestant thought but which have now evolved to the point that the tensions have collapsed. For the dissent to remain identifiable with the Reorganization, the dissenter must retain the difficult tension between Mormonism and Protestantism, a tension so integral to the church's character and development.[25] Persons from the fundamentalist end of the spectrum, given their belief in the basic Restoration story and their leanings toward a centralized religious structure on the issue of authority, seem most likely to organize their dissent. If they make a formal break with the institutional church, they are likely to form separate organizations and branches. Persons dissenting from the Protestant end of the spectrum seldom organize a new group, perhaps because they have been disillusioned by the Reorganized Church's tradition and prefer to discard it. They are more likely to move toward a more pluralistic mainline Christian church or even to drift away from institutional forms of Christianity. Unless one wants to become completely Protestant, however, persons in the Protestant transliteration scheme, having found a hearing in the hierarchy, will likely remain in the church.

Having outlined the three major issues spawning dissent, as well as two streams of contemporary Reorganization thought, how do the two streams approach the issues most likely to spawn dissent? With respect to authority, the fundamentalists accept the church's dispensationalist approach to salvation history and therefore claim an exclusive authority. They tend to have a mixed view of authority, however, locating authority in individuals and congregations, the more democratic view of the early Reorganized Church, and yet defining the church as being in apostasy when its prophet succumbs to false doctrine, a more authoritarian Mormon view. For the fundamentalists, to be without a prophet is to be without the very office which stands between them and the darkness of medieval apostasy or the tentativeness of the pre-1860 Reorganization. If the prophet is in apostasy, the church has regressed to the 1840s and is in a theological and constitutional crisis. To be without a prophet permanently, the fundamentalist dissenters must radically rethink their theology.

Like the leaders of the early Reorganization, they must question the authority of persons ordained in the established church and the authority of persons affiliated with any splinter groups prior to finding the Reorganization. For Price and other dissenting fundamentalists, the established church is viewed as having departed from the original doctrines of the faith, a departure symbolized in their minds by an apostate prophet and a hierarchy intent on changing the church by imposing heretical views on an unsuspecting but loyal membership. The dissenting fundamentalists' attitudes toward the established church and their separation from it is strikingly similar to early Reorganized Church attitudes toward Brigham Young and the Mormon church in Utah. For Price and other dissenters, like early Reorganization members, the theological controversies swirl around distinctively Latter Day Saint claims. The "new Reorganization" of present-day fundamentalist dissenters finds its basis in existing and developing branches gradually forming a loose confederation, held together by a shared history and searching for a form of unity. Their writings detail hierarchical excesses and explain what they conceive of as the original beliefs of the church. *Restoration Voice* and *Vision* magazines function as *The True Latter Day Saints' Herald*, providing a forum for expression of the movement's emerging beliefs and a communication link for the scattered people and branches.

As dispensationalists, they must wrestle with many questions: When did the prophet(s) fall? How much Reorganization teaching do we accept? Has the established church been rejected? Those without patience to wait will look for one "mighty and strong" and seek a new organization and the filling of the leading quorums. Those with patience, like Price and his supporters, wait and struggle with the theological and historical questions. The dispensationalist theological evaluation effectively reinforces the dissenters' ties in faith with a particular historical community at the same time that the reevaluation distances the dissenters from the contemporary expression of this particular historical community. The essentially revisionist attitude toward the church's history and tradition, present from the foundation of the Reorganization, is thus curiously and profoundly preserved even among the dissenting fundamentalists of the Reorganized Church reformation. It is precisely this grounding in a heritage and tie to particular symbols, stories, and events that gives the fundamentalists their strength and appeal. This close tie to the heritage is virtually nonexistent among Reorganization members transliterating Protestant thought; this lack is their Achilles' heel.

The complexity of the fundamentalist attitude toward authority is revealed, however, in its tendency to adopt a high view of the prophetic office but to seek a more democratic polity. Advocating the more gentle democracy of Joseph Smith III, fundamentalists favor locating authority in individuals and congregations. Taking this approach on questions of priesthood authority, they also reflect this preference in their attitudes toward personal religious experience. Reorganized Church fundamentalism is singularly experiential, accepting at face value the full measure of the gifts of the Spirit. They look to the confirming evidence of the burning in the bosom and the Spirit's witness to the truth of the Book of Mormon.[26] The church's divine commission and authority is not merely rationally held and apprehended but confirmed in the heart through the personal testimony and witness of the Spirit as guide, guard, and healer.

For fundamentalists the issues of authority and salvific truth are intertwined. The fundamentalist perspective on theological truth is guided by the Doctrine and Covenants dictum that the elders of the church have not been sent out to be taught but to teach.[27] The fundamentalist assumption has generally been that the church has nothing to learn. That is, the church knows all it needs to know and has no need for education in the biblical and theological disciplines. The ability to proof text from a traditional Reorganized Church perspective is deemed sufficient. Confusing authority with competence, the church is understood to possess exclusive authority to represent God and likewise an exclusive claim to teaching the truths necessary for salvation. They assert that the fullness of the gospel may be found only in the Reorganized Church.

Consistent application of the fundamentalist position necessitates belief in exclusive male priesthood authority, the rebaptism of all previously baptized non-Reorganized Church Christians desiring to join the church, a Restoration-based curriculum, and close Communion. Given these beliefs, it is hardly surprising that many arguments of Reorganized Church fundamentalists are directed against non-Reorganization Christians and those Reorganized Church leaders thought to be most sympathetic toward Protestantism. In the fundamentalist view the church was organized with an authority and truth not found among Protestants, a light bursting forth in ways unprecedented in the Protestant Reformation. A leading fundamentalist charge against Reorganization leaders is that church officials are ecumenical and moving toward membership in the National Council of Churches, that they are using materials prepared by Protestant churches, that they are attending Protestant seminaries, and that they are actively substituting Protestantism for the Restoration. Reorganized Church officials, they lament, revise Reorganization theology in light of Protestant theology and thereby deny the exclusive authority and truth of the Restoration movement preserved in the Reorganization.[28]

If the Reorganized Church possesses exclusive authority and truth, fundamentalists argue, then similar exalted status will be granted to the church's history and its distinctive canon. The fundamentalists study church history, the Inspired Version, the Book of Mormon, and the Doctrine and Covenants with reverence. The first four volumes of the official church history guide their understanding of the church's founding and nineteenth-century development. The Book of Mormon and Doctrine and Covenants are read with a status placing them equal to the Bible. The Reorganization's revisionist history, such as that which traces the teaching or practice or knowledge of polygamy to Joseph Smith, Jr., is unacceptable. The history of the early Reorganization movement helps guide the fundamentalist dissenters in their moves toward new forms of organization.[29]

The relativization and corresponding devaluation of the distinctive Reorganized Church tradition and history is perhaps the reformation's most painful blow to fundamentalists. It is no coincidence that fundamentalist editions of the "Position Papers" place this quotation from the essay, "The Nature of the Church," on the cover: "Nor can we affirm today that this is 'the only true and living church upon the face of the whole earth with which ... the Lord (is) well pleased' (D.&C. 1:5)." In traditional Reorganized Church fashion, the three books are defended against any who would minimize their authority by questioning the accuracy of the Inspired Version or historicity of the Book of Mormon.

The truth of the Doctrine and Covenants is also defended, but certain sections have been excluded from the fundamentalist version of the canon due to apostasy.

Reorganized Church fundamentalists differ little in their attitudes toward authority, salvific truth, church history, and scripture from what the Reorganized Church stood for during much of the 1880s-1950s consensus. Indeed, to read fundamentalist literature is almost like being placed in a time warp, as if the last forty years of history had not occurred. As an example, fundamentalist Edith Scott recently attacked the notion that no one has seen the first person of the Trinity by proof texting from the three books and church history and denounced justification by grace through faith as "fabricated by Martin Luther and promulgated by others in the Reformation."[30] Protestant thought has been caricatured to the point that Protestants would not recognize it, then declared insufficient and in need of the fullness of the gospel. Merva Bird, however, in one of her articles, revealed that even Reorganized Church fundamentalists are open, in a limited way, to Protestantism. With Protestant fundamentalists Bird expressed fear of the New Age movement, one world political order and religion, the United Nations, the pope, and the peace movement. Using Revelation 13 and 17, she was clearly influenced by American apocalyptic fundamentalism, as well as early Mormon millennial expectations.[31]

At the other end of the theological spectrum, persons transliterating Protestant thought are less likely to be in dissent because their approach to theology is much more widely supported by the leadership and bureaucracy than fundamentalism. If this group dissents, it is more likely to do so because it sees no need to retain Reorganized Church symbols and prefers a fuller Protestant form uninhibited by the constraints of the Restoration. With respect to authority this stream rejects exclusive Reorganized Church claims to authority. The absolute claims to authority at the foundation of the movement have been relativized and the Reorganization's creation has been placed on the level of the Protestant Reformation. This stream completely rejects the claim that the Restoration movement is the only authoritative expression of Christian faith. As the Department of Religious Education explained in an October 1967 position paper:

> Thus we affirm that God does call the priesthood to his work and commissions them, but their call does not invalidate the call of others.
>
> We also affirm that we have received the grace of God through the sacraments, and ministrations of the priesthood, but that such channels are not the exclusive channels.
>
> We also affirm that through the institution we know we have encountered the Christ and have been called to authentic discipleship, but that such an experience does not invalidate the similar experience of others in differing churches.[32]

This side of the Reorganization denies exclusive possession of authority and theological and salvific truth.

Attempting to secure the church more firmly in the mainstream of the Christian tradition, progressives generally gave more weight to the authority of the Protestant tradition than to the Reorganization's unique tradition. They gave full expression to the non-Mormon pole of the search for an identity, the openness to mainstream American Protestantism. Disillusioned with the Reorganized Church's tradition, many came to question important theological issues. Reflecting the Reorganization's traditional inferiority complex, they appealed to Protestant theology for help in correcting the perceived errors and excesses plaguing the tradition.[33]

Because the progressives concluded that the church's claims to authority were not exclusive, neither were its claims to theological and salvific truth. Not the only true church, the Reorganization nevertheless remained a true church, at least to some degree. Curiously, while embracing a more liberal theology, progressive attitudes toward authority are also mixed. Tending toward theological creativity as well as individualistic and perhaps even idiosyncratic approaches to theology, too many progressives have been hesitant to allow dissent from the church's fundamentalists. While the fundamentalists tend to favor the localization of authority in individuals and congregations, particularly in light of the present crisis, progressives tend to support this approach only when the subject is theological innovation, not when the subject is institutional polity or fundamentalism.

In recent times, while the fundamentalists advocated the gentle pragmatism and democracy of Joseph Smith III and the localization of authority in persons and congregations, progressives favored a strong, centralized leadership with nearly complete authority vested in the First Presidency. While democratic tendencies and willingness to allow dissent have occasionally been personal choices, the approach of the institution has been toward quelling protest to the reformation. Political power, and who controls it, has something to do with this crisis, but the fundamental issues still revolve around theology and how it is taught within the Reorganized Church. It cannot be denied that it has been the progressives who have forcefully exercised political power in the enforcement of theological conceptions in agreement with the church's leadership. Never before has the church created special membership categories for dissenters and never before has its leaders suspended operations of entire stakes because local members rebelled against the hierarchy.[34] Administrative silencing of priesthood and expulsion of church members have been used more extensively than at any other period in the Reorganization's past.[35] Richard Price expressed the fundamentalist position on this issue when he wrote that one can be a progressive and not believe in the historicity of the Book of Mormon and still be in the hierarchy. Yet one cannot be a fundamentalist and oppose Section 156 and remain in the hierarchy or sometimes even in the priesthood.[36]

Progressive attitudes toward tradition and polity within the Reorganization have often led to alienation by the progressives from the larger church, even for those who remained a part of it. Those progressives who remain have found authority in the liberating truth of the crucified and risen Christ, experienced in the transformed and transforming body of all who receive Christ as Lord by grace through faith. Freed from the church's traditions, progressive Reorganization members have found new life in the Christ of grace and claim the wider Christian community with its rich tradition and history. In doing so, however, they may distance themselves from the very community they long to serve. Indeed, they may find themselves estranged from the very community that was established with the primary purpose of founding a community. Lacking acceptance in this community, progressives may:

1. remain in the church, often at high levels, but continue their efforts to reinterpret Reorganized Church symbols in ways more compatible with Protestant thought;

2. exercise hierarchical power to continue to reform the church and reestablish its unity; or

3. completely leave the Reorganized Church.

Any of these options may further isolate them from many members of the church, certainly it isolates them from the fundamentalists.

Dissent and the Loss of a Distinctive Reorganized Church Tension

As long as both the progressives and fundamentalists maintain the tension between Mormonism and Protestantism, regardless of where they might sit on the scale between the two, they can be considered people within the tradition of the Reorganized Church. On both the progressive and fundamentalist sides, however, a uniquely disturbing development has taken place in recent years when radicals of both sides abandon the traditional tensions. When these defining tensions collapse for persons on either end of the spectrum, they have moved beyond the bounds of the Reorganized tradition and dissent loses its distinctive Reorganization character. The consequences, in some cases, have been bizarre and tragic.

On the fundamentalist side, not new to Mormonism but to the Reorganization, a radical form has developed cultlike tendencies. The most significant example of this overthrow of tradition was the cult led by Jeffrey Lundgren. Completely bypassing the moderate Mormon tradition of the Reorganization, which has tempered the movement through its relationship with Protestantism, Lundgren looked toward the darker aspects of the charismatic era of 1830-1844 for a model. Carrying this approach to extremes unfathomable by Reorganization members of all stripes, Lundgren's efforts unraveled following several tragic events. This form, not to be confused with other forms of fundamentalism that preserve the distinctively Reorganization tensions, seemed to emerge in the destabilized situation in the Reorganized Church where theological confusion has reigned. This theological vacuum has simply been too much to bear for some persons raised with traditional Reorganization views of church history and exclusive claims to theological and salvific truth.

As some fundamentalists have moved beyond Price-styled fundamentalism, some progressives have moved beyond the transliteration of Protestant thought. The revisionist nature of the Reorganization, its openness to non-Mormon influences, the lack of an exegetical tradition, and other factors, have led some to push beyond the limits of the Reorganization and even beyond the bounds of Christianity. Some RLDS progressives are attracted to humanism, process philosophy revised to exclude God, agnosticism, and non-Christian forms of feminism. Unlike the fundamentalists, dissenting progressives are not likely to organize if they leave the church, perhaps because their dissent, unlike fundamentalist dissent, is against the Mormon aspects of the church and in favor of and perhaps beyond the Protestant aspects. The Protestant aspects to which they are attracted already exist in institutional forms elsewhere and there is no need to organize a new form.

Although the forms just mentioned differ vastly, they were energized within the Reorganization by the tensions between Mormon and Protestant theological conceptions. This represented a creative dynamic which, while still imperfect and lacking rigorous criticism, was nonetheless a sustaining element that intrigued and propelled the movement's constituents. The severe strain in the tension during the period of reformation, including its collapse for many, led to a profound search for a new and unifying theological foundation. The results of the search thus far have been confusion and dissent.

Dissent and the Hierarchy

The tensions between the church's desire to remain rooted in Mormonism and yet to remain open to Protestant thought may also be seen in the prophetic office and its response to dissenters. The First Presidency itself has, through history, alternated between an authoritarian style of leadership and the more democratic, congregational option borrowed from Protestantism. Joseph Smith III, Israel A. Smith, and W. Wallace Smith generally embodied the democratic tendencies and usually tolerated more diversity within the church than Frederick M. Smith and Wallace B. Smith. The progressives have generally supported, or at least acquiesced in the location of authority within the church in the First Presidency. The location of authority in the church in the Presidency has resulted, in some eras, with a correspondingly broad exercise of administrative powers. The usual response in recent decades is that dissenters must restrict their expressions of dissent to the appropriate legislative forums or meetings with individual church officials. To do otherwise is regarded as "compromising of the First Presidency's responsibility to lead."[37]

Nowhere is the concentration of power in the Presidency more evident with respect to dissent than in the editorial policy of the First Presidency. Based on WCR 386 and sections of the Doctrine and Covenants, the Presidency stated that when its members were "ordained and sustained in their office by action of the World Conference, they are automatically granted wide powers of discretion in order to administer, discipline, regulate, and keep in order the affairs of the Church of Jesus Christ."[38] The First Presidency extended its role as editors-in-chief of all church publications to mean:

> There certainly must be opportunity to express dissent and dissatisfaction and this should be done directly with the officer or officers involved. The First Presidency are willing to give a hearing to responsible criticism. *Members do not have a right, however, to directly circularize the church with a point of view or style which conflicts with the program emphasis being presented to the church* [emphasis added].[39]

Thus the forums for public, wide-ranging dialogue do not exist within the institutional church, a direct consequence of the church's ecclesiology.

Dissenters desiring to debate and influence others are in conflict with the editorial policy of the First Presidency the moment they begin to publish and circulate their positions. In this statement, not only are doctrinal questions off limits but also are opposing ideas for church programs and style. The editorial policy of the First Presidency forbids the sending of dissenting materials across jurisdictional lines, a policy grounded in the theology of the authority of the Presidency and prophetic office.

The Standing High Council's statement, "The Ethics of Dissent," affirms the value of dissent but offers limited opportunities for its expression. The Standing High Council, nominated and chaired by the First Presidency, recently quoted with favor a 1985 policy statement by the First Presidency that offers five general principles for sharing information across jurisdictional lines. The material, even though distributed by an individual member of the church, must:

> 1. be distributed through the appropriate branch-level channels;
> 2. be sent with the knowledge and authority of the presiding elder;
> 3. contain the author's name;
> 4. deal with issues and not personalities; and
> 5. *be subjected to the editorial review of the First Presidency*" [emphasis added].[40]

The Presidency's editorial policy and the Standing High Council's statement show little sign of being balanced by the democratic option with respect to authority on which the Reorganization was founded. In this policy the authority of individuals and congregations is almost totally neglected.

The Reorganization's Reformation, Dissent, and Future

The last forty years in the Reorganization have been filled with excitement, and often turmoil, as the old has given way to the new. The provincial character of midwestern Mormonism, once a major strength, proved to be a major weakness when D. Blair Jensen and Charles D. Neff went in mission to the Orient. Neff discovered that all the church's tracts describing how the Reorganized Church differed from other Christian churches were useless in a nation where only 3 percent of the population claimed to be Christian.[41] At such an historic moment the church could have followed the Utah Mormon model of reshaping their converts rather than their church, but the long-standing Reorganized Church wariness of Mormon origins gave way to the traditional Reorganized Church openness to Protestants. The church's leaders decided to move toward cooperation with other denominations, to teach basic Christian faith, and to become an inclusive world church. Missionary activity in the Third World, combined with the coming of the first generation of seminary-educated Reorganized Church members and other American cultural shifts, led to a decisive turn toward mainstream Protestant Christianity. Church leaders chose reevaluation and revision of traditional Reorganized Church views of history and theology, opting for greater openness to Protestant influences over and against Restoration distinctives and Mormon origins. The way was opened for a radical, fundamental revision and reshaping of the church. The genie was out of the bottle.[42]

Dissenters from the right complain, often justifiably, that the church's foundation has been whisked out from under them. Dissenters from the left complain, often justifiably, that the changes have come much too slowly and been much too timid. Few on the right or the left recognize the extent to which the conflict in which they participate is rooted so deeply in the theological foundations of the Reorganization. Both sides are heirs to a tradition founded by persons of widely differing backgrounds who, in their dissent, sought to steer between the Scylla of excessively authoritarian, speculative Nauvoo Mormonism and the Charybdis of rigidly creedal, congregational Protestant sectarianism. As Clare D. Vlahos observed, "The early Reorganization waited, caught somewhere in between, neither gentile nor Mormon."[43]

No longer content to wait, the Reorganized Church of the current reformation era has sought to reshape its future, to be a "moderate Mormonism" more moderate than Mormon through a reevaluation of its history and theology at an unprecedented rate and depth. The desire to be faithful to its heritage and Mormon origins and also to be open to Protestant influences reached a point of climactic crisis in the reformation era. If these two tendencies, on a collision course from the beginning, are fundamentally incompatible, what, if anything, can keep the church together? Is hierarchical power the only force that can hold it together? Can hierarchical power without a lineal descendant of Joseph Smith, Jr., in a church with such otherwise loose ties to early Mormonism, hold the elements together? If hierarchical power is the only basis for the church's unity, to what end is the church held together?

At the risk of redundancy, I must again insist that the roots of the problems surfacing in the Reorganized Church reformation are theological. When the problems are of this nature, wide-ranging dialogue that seeks the wisdom and guidance of the Spirit is absolutely essential. To be a Reorganized Church member is to live with the tension, to choose *both* Mormon origins *and* Protestant openness. To choose *either* Mormon origins *or* openness to Protestant or non-Restoration thought is to abandon the Reorganization. With greater tolerance and widening of the limits of pluralism, much of the dissent that now takes place outside the church could take place within the church. A church that does not have room for both Geoffrey F. Spencer and Richard Price is too small, both figuratively and literally.

Disillusioned with traditional Reorganization beliefs and confronted with new religious and cultural systems in non-Western missions, the first generation of seminary-educated Reorganized Church theologians chose to respond to the shattering of the movement's theological world by fundamentally reshaping the church.[44] While the church has moved in the direction of mainstream Christianity, it has done so at great price, even at the expense of appreciating the enduring value of the church's origin and tradition. Much of the non-fundamentalist Reorganization theological writing sounds fresh and new, but also tentative, ambivalent, and lacking a sense of roots and heritage. The rise of fundamentalist dissent may be attributed to the theological confusion at the World Church level, the lack of forums for dialogue and debate within the church, and the progressives' unwillingness to grant the fundamentalists the latitude to disagree.

Long on criticism and short on constructive solutions, the progressives have grown weary of their own reformation and remain unable to convincingly blend Reorganized Church symbols and stories with those of the wider Christian community. Contemporary Reorganization theology is paralyzed, still mired in the collapse of the 1880s-1950s synthesis and unable to move forward. The best approach for all sides in this time of reformation and dissent would be to look once again at the stories of the tradition and to reread the stories of the Christian faith. The texts of the faith have stories to tell which could bring a saving message. The value of dissent is that it can contribute to a fresh, more responsible hearing of the stories and to a more faithful interpretation of the Christian tradition in the context of the Reorganization. As Edwin Scott Gaustead, alluding to Reinhold Niebuhr, suggests: "Consent makes democracy possible; dissent makes democracy meaningful."[45]

The current disarray in Reorganization theology is itself spawning dissent. Having hurriedly placed new wine in old wineskins, the church now struggles to find its center and itself. The confusion is most evident in the current church program and the priesthood. In pursuit of its primary program objective, the Reorganized Church, which never had a theology of temples, now devotes nearly all of its resources toward completion of a massive temple project in Independence, Missouri. Why? In the rush to ordain women without first considering the theological implications, the Reorganized Church failed to seize a fundamental opportunity to reinvigorate the entire priesthood through a careful review of the hierarchical structure and division of labor. Why? In the midst of this theological crisis, Reorganization thinkers, like Martha in the Gospel of Luke, have been busy about many things but not with far-reaching and constructive attempts to develop Reorganized Church theologies that could guide the church into the third millennium.

Theologically the greatest strength of the Reorganized Church is its openness to the revelation of God in Jesus Christ, with an openness to truth from the Christian community beyond its borders. It is this openness to the revelation of God in Christ that has enabled the church to advance in reformation, relativize the place of Joseph Smith, Jr., and free the tradition from the excesses of Mormonism.

Theologically the greatest weakness of the church has been the tendency to elevate ecclesiology above all else. The church is at its best when ecclesiology is subordinated to Christology, at its worst when Christology is subordinated to ecclesiology. In other words, the church errs when it takes itself too seriously and becomes an idol. Much of the turmoil in the Reorganization today, on the right and on the left, stems from mistaking the church for an end rather than a means. The church could heal and advance theologically and missionally, even now, if all sides of the polarization recognized that Christ alone is the head of the church. The Spirit is greater than the church's leaders, greater than the church's dissenters, even greater than the church. As Paul admonished the fractious church at Corinth, the church is on a perilous path when it begins to place the purity of doctrine ahead of the primacy of love.[46]

The most pressing theological need in the church is to articulate a compelling, comprehensive theological vision that creatively and faithfully integrates Reorganization symbols and stories with the wider Christian tradition in the modern context. To discern this vision, *all* voices, including dissenting voices, must be heard. As Gaustead explains:

> In the first century, amidst a plethora of fresh dissent, the sober counsel was "Test everything; hold fast what is good." It is sober counsel for every century, and every generation. Dissent neither conducts the examination nor controls the results: it only insures throughout history that testing will take place.[47]

Too narrowly defining the limits for dissent within the church robs the church of the opportunity to dialogue in ways necessary to discern the Spirit's vision for the church.

Such a vision, faithful to the church's past and its future, could once again free the church to attract and retain its youth. The church needs youth who, in pursuit of the theological disciplines (including biblical studies, systematic theology, and church history) are willing to commit their lives in Christian service through the institutional church. If the church is faithful to the best of its heritage, it will be willing to receive and listen to all who come to it humbly in faith, hope, and love, saying: "I have come here not to be dictated by any man or set of men. I have come in obedience to a power not my own, and I shall be dictated by the power that sent me."[48]

Notes

1. Harry J. Ashenhurst, Bruce Graham, Bob Mesle, and Dale Tripp, "Baptism for the Dead: A Scriptural Perspective," *Saints' Herald* 117 (April 1970): 22-23, 25.

2. World Conference Resolution (WCR) 1077 and 1080. For a discussion of the Reorganization's reinterpretation of early Mormonism using as an example baptism for the dead, see Roger D. Launius, "An Ambivalent Rejection: Baptism for the Dead and the Reorganized Church Experience," *Dialogue: A Journal of Mormon Thought* 23 (Summer 1990): 61-84.

3. "Reorganized LDS Church in Turmoil After Split in Faith," *Salt Lake Tribune* (9 July 1990): B7. According to the "Membership Census Report," (12/31/88 and 12/31/89) "Church Membership Report—1988 and 1989," Office of Membership Records, in *1990 World Conference Reports*, page 110, there were 1,242 priesthood silenced or released during this period.

4. On these crises, see D. Michael Quinn, "The Mormon Succession Crisis of 1844," *Brigham Young University Studies* 16 (Winter 1976): 187-233; Roger D. Launius, *Joseph Smith III: Pragmatic-Prophet* (Urbana: University of Illinois Press, 1988), 30-51; Paul M. Edwards, "Theocratic-Democracy: Philosopher-King in the Reorganization," in F. Mark McKiernan, Alma R. Blair, and Paul M. Edwards, eds., *The Restoration Movement: Essays in Mormon History* (Lawrence, Kansas: Coronado Press, 1973), 341-357; Larry E. Hunt, *F. M. Smith: Saint as Reformer*, 2 vols. (Indepen-

dence, Missouri: Herald Publishing House, 1982); and the chapter by Ken R. Mullikin in this book.

5. Howard J. Booth, "Recent Shifts in Restoration Thought," in Maurice L. Draper and Clare D. Vlahos, eds., *Restoration Studies I* (Independence, Missouri: Herald Publishing House, 1980), 162-175. For further evidence of these changes, compare *The Position Papers* (Independence, Missouri: Cumorah Books, 1975) or *Exploring the Faith* (Independence, Missouri: Herald Publishing House, 1970; 1987, edited by Alan D. Tyree), with William H. Kelley, *Presidency and Priesthood: The Apostasy, Reformation, and Restoration* (Lamoni, Iowa: Herald Publishing House, 1908) and Joseph F. Luff, *The Old Jerusalem Gospel* (Lamoni, Iowa: Herald Publishing House, 1903).

6. Alan D. Tyree, a counselor in the Reorganization's First Presidency, claimed recently that the church had not changed. See *The Kansas City Star* (6 April 1990). This assessment cannot be supported by the historical evidence, especially in light of so many written and oral statements by high church officials to the contrary. The remarks in written and oral form from such individuals as Apostle Geoffrey F. Spencer on the validity of disjunctive revelation clearly mandates radical departures from the past. The First Presidency's official statement in the *Saints Herald*, "The Nature of New Revelation" (1 February 1984), paved the way for an acceptance of women's ordination, made possible by revelation to the church at the April 1984 World Conference. To claim that the reformation has not touched the core of the Reorganization is to misunderstand both the reforms and the traditional consensus.

7. Alma R. Blair, "Reorganized Church of Jesus Christ of Latter Day Saints: Moderate Mormonism," in McKiernan, Blair, and Edwards, eds., *The Restoration Movement*, 207-230; Clare D. Vlahos, "Moderation as a Theological Principle in the Thought of Joseph Smith III," *The John Whitmer Historical Association Journal* 1 (1981): 3-11.

8. See Roger Yarrington's editorial in the *Saints Herald* 137 (September 1990): 356, 362.

9. Clifford A. Cole, "The Cause of Zion: Today and Tomorrow," Part I, *Saints Herald* 121 (August 1974): 486-489, 508; Part II, 121 (September 1974): 558-561, 570; quote from 558.

10. This issue is too well accepted to be debated. For discussions of this subject please refer to these works: Marvin S. Hill, *Quest for Refuge: The Mormon Flight from American Pluralism* (Salt Lake City, Utah: Signature Books, 1989); Dan Vogel, *Religious Seekers and the Advent of Mormonism* (Salt Lake City, Utah: Signature Books, 1989); Richard L. Bushman, *Joseph Smith and the Be-*

ginnings of Mormonism (Urbana: University of Illinois Press, 1984); Klaus J. Hansen, *Mormonism and American Culture* (Chicago: University of Chicago Press, 1981).

11. Doctrine and Covenants 17:9 (Independence, Missouri: Herald Publishing House, 1970 ed.).

12. Ibid., 17:12b.

13. Early sections of the Doctrine and Covenants by Joseph Smith III focus on local concerns and organization to a much greater degree than later sections. Section 117:12 encourages strong local organizations within the church. Section 118:1c declines to fill the leading quorums, with preference toward filling the quorums of elders, priests, teachers, and deacons. Section 119:4 cautions the elders to be more accepting and less fearful of new persons coming into the church. Section 119:8b embraces the ministry of all. Section 120 talks more of branches and districts and, though calling for local officials to respect general ones cautions the latter: "In matters of personal importance and conduct arising in branches and districts, the authorities of those branches and districts should be authorized and permitted to settle them; the traveling councils taking cognizance of those only in which the law and usages of the church are involved, and the general interests of the church are concerned" (120:7a-b).

14. See as examples, Doctrine and Covenants 27:2. Numerous other Doctrine and Covenants passages support and enhance the localization of authority in the president: 43:1-2; 68:2c; 99:6, 9-10; 104:4, 42; 107:39; 122:2a; 133:2b; 134:6b; 148:10b; 149:6a; 149A;4; 156:4, 9.

15. See the *Church Administrator's Handbook* (Independence, Missouri: Herald Publishing House, 1987 ed.), 6-7, 19, 21-22, 28, 40, 59, 66.

16. The literature on this subject is already massive and growing daily. Some of the more significant include Marvin S. Hill, "The Historiography of Mormonism," *Church History* 28 (December 1959): 418-426; Leonard J. Arrington, "Scholarly Studies of Mormonism in the Twentieth Century," *Dialogue: A Journal of Mormon Thought* 1 (Spring 1966): 15-32; Robert Bruce Flanders, "Writing on the Mormon Past," *Dialogue: A Journal of Mormon Thought* 1 (Autumn 1966): 47-61; Rodman W. Paul, "The Mormons as a Theme in Western Historical Writing," *Journal of American History* 54 (December 1967): 511-523; Thomas G. Alexander and James B. Allen, "The Mormons in the Mountain West: A Selected Bibliography," *Arizona and the West* 9 (Winter 1967): 365-384; Leonard J. Arrington, "The Search for Truth and Meaning in Mormon History," *Dialogue: A Journal of Mormon Thought* 3 (Summer 1968): 56-66; Moses Rischin, "The New

Mormon History," *The American West* 5 (March 1969): 49; Richard L. Bushman, "Faithful History," *Brigham Young University Studies* 9 (Winter 1969): 11-25; Robert A. Rees, "'Truth is the Daughter of Time': Notes Toward an Imaginative History," *Utah Historical Quarterly* 39 (Autumn 1971): 15-22; Richard D. Poll, "God and Man in History," *Dialogue: A Journal of Mormon Thought* 7 (Spring 1972): 101-109; Robert Bruce Flanders, "Some Reflections on the New Mormon History," *Dialogue: A Journal of Mormon Thought* 9 (Spring 1974): 34-42; Thomas G. Alexander, "Toward the New Mormon History: An Examination of the Literature on the Latter-day Saints in the Far West," in Michael P. Malone, ed., *Historians and the American West* (Lincoln:University of Nebraska Press, 1983), 344-368; Thomas G. Alexander, "Historiography and the New Mormon History: A Historian's Perspective," *Dialogue: A Journal of Mormon Thought* 19 (Fall 1986): 25-50; Paul M. Edwards, "The New Mormon History," *Saints Herald* 133 (November 1986): 472-474, 480; Marvin S. Hill, "The 'New Mormon History' Reassessed in Light of Recent Books on Joseph Smith and Mormon Origins," *Dialogue: A Journal of Mormon Thought* 21 (Fall 1988): 115-127; Richard P. Howard, "New Currents in Mormon History," *Saints Herald* 135 (November 1988): 483-484, 486; Roger D. Launius, "Whither Reorganization Historiography?" *The John Whitmer Historical Association Journal* 10 (1990): 24-37; Louis Midgley, "The Challenge of Historical Consciousness: Mormon History and the Encounter with Secular Modernity," in John M. Lundquist and Stephen D. Ricks, eds., *By Study and Also By Faith: Essays in Honor of Hugh Nibley on the Occasion of His Eightieth Birthday, March 27, 1990* (Salt Lake City, Utah: Deseret Book, 1990), 2: 502-551; Martin E. Marty, "Two Integrities: An Address to the Crisis in Mormon Historiography," *Journal of Mormon History* 10 (1983): 3-19; Louis Midgley, "Faith and History," in Robert L. Millett, ed., *"To Be Learned Is Good, If..."* (Salt Lake City, Utah: Bookcraft, 1987), 1-8.

17. Launius, *Joseph Smith III*, 77-96.
18. Jan Shipps, *Mormonism: The Story of a New Religious Tradition* (Urbana: University of Illinois Press, 1985).
19. See on this subject, Alma R. Blair, "Reorganized Church of Jesus Christ of Latter Day Saints: Moderate Mormonism," in McKiernan, Blair, and Edwards, eds., *The Restoration Movement*, 207-230; Alma R. Blair, "The Tradition of Dissent—Jason W. Briggs," in Draper and Vlahos, eds., *Restoration Studies I*, 146-161; Clare D. Vlahos, "The Challenge to Centralized Power: Zenus [sic] H. Gurley, Jr., and the Prophet Office," *Courage: A Journal of History, Thought and Action* 1 (March 1971): 141-158.

235

20. On this questioning of the Book of Mormon's historicity, see Wayne Ham, "Problems in Interpreting the Book of Mormon as History," *Courage: A Journal of History, Thought and Action* 1 (September 1970): 15-22.

21. See William D. Russell, "The Historicity of the Book of Mormon and the Use of the Sermon on the Mount in III Nephi," in Maurice L. Draper and A. Bruce Lindgren, eds., *Restoration Studies II* (Independence, Missouri: Herald Publishing House, 1983), 193-200.

22. Richard Price, *Saints at the Crossroads* (Independence, Missouri: Cumorah Books, 1975), and numerous other publications. For a greater list see the materials cited in William D. Russell, "The Fundamentalist Schism, 1958-Present" chapter 4 in this book.

23. A few examples of works firmly in this stream include but are not limited to: Peter A. Judd and Clifford A. Cole, *Distinctives: Yesterday and Today* (Independence, Missouri: Herald Publishing House, 1983); Peter A. Judd and A. Bruce Lindgren, *An Introduction to the Saints Church* (Independence, Missouri: Herald Publishing House, 1976); Department of Religious Education, "The Nature of the Gospel" and "The Nature of the Church" in *The Position Papers* (Independence, Missouri: Cumorah Books, n.d); C. Robert Mesle, *Fire in My Bones* (Independence, Missouri: Herald Publishing House, 1984); C. Robert Mesle, *The Bible as Story and Struggle* (Independence, Missouri: Herald Publishing House, 1989). As a specific example, Geoffrey F. Spencer has related Paul Tillich's "Protestant Principle" to the Reorganization by noting Tillich's contribution and then fashioning what Spencer called a "Restoration Principle." See Geoffrey F. Spencer, "Revelation and the Restoration Principle," in Draper and Lindgren, eds., *Restoration Studies II*, 186-192. For a more detailed account and critique of these two contemporary streams of Reorganization thought in the context of the church's reformation, see my article coauthored with Paul Shupe, "An RLDS Reformation? Construing the Task of RLDS Theology," *Dialogue: A Journal of Mormon Thought* 18 (Summer 1985): 92-103.

24. Wallace B. Smith, "Witnessing of God's Saving Grace," World Conference Sermon, *Saints Herald* 137 (May 1990): 181-184.

25. Many historians have commented on the tightrope walked by the Reorganization between Mormonism and Protestantism. See on this issue, Clare D. Vlahos, "Images of Orthodoxy: Self-Identity in Early Reorganization Apologetics," in Draper and Vlahos, eds., *Restoration Studies I* 176-186.

26. Doctrine and Covenants 9:3c; Book of Mormon, Moroni 10:3-5.

27. Doctrine and Covenants 43:4b.

28. This charge can be found in many fundamentalist writings. See especially Price, *Saints at the Crossroads, Decision Time* (Independence, Missouri: Cumorah Books, 1975), and *Action Time* (Independence, Missouri: Price Publishing, 1984).

29. See Price, *Decision Time*; Richard Price and Larry Harlacher, *Restoration Branches Movement: Pamphlet #1 — Forming of Restoration Branches* (Independence, Missouri: Price Publishing, 1986).

30. Edith Scott, "The Restoration Gospel Versus Protestant Theology," *Restoration Voice* #71 (May/June 1990): 6-7.

31. Merva Bird, "Decade of Destiny," Ibid. #71 (May/June 1990): 9-11.

32. Department of Religious Education, "The Nature of the Church," *The Position Papers*, 54.

33. This statement has been supported by numerous citations to theological and historical and organization works published by Reorganization thinkers previously. See especially the writings of Clifford A. Cole, Geoffrey F. Spencer, C. Robert Mesle, Peter A. Judd, Charles D. Neff, Joe A. Serig, and Wayne A. Ham. In addition, review the sociological study by former apostle and member of the First Presidency, Maurice L. Draper, "Sect-Denomination-Church Transition and Leadership in the Reorganized Church of Jesus Christ of Latter Day Saints," M.A. Thesis, Kansas University, 1964.

34. Both of these actions have taken place since the 1984 decision to ordain women. The *Guidelines for Priesthood* (Independence, Missouri: Herald Publishing House, 1985), created special categories for priesthood holders who were not performing properly. In the 1986-1987 period both Central Missouri and Blue Valley stakes, near Independence, Missouri, were "suspended" and operated as something other than a stake. These actions were unprecedented.

35. The silencing of priesthood has been more common than the church's leadership would like to admit. Few silencings took place in the early controversies of the 1960s and 1970s. The best work on this subject is William J. Knapp, "Professionalizing Religious Education in the Church: The 'New Curriculum' Controversy," *The John Whitmer Historical Association Journal* 2 (1982): 47-59. I am aware of no silencings or expulsions of progressives during this crisis. Nor were the progressives ever placed in special membership categories to deny their voting privileges. Progressives were usually allowed to create individual liberal congregations where they could worship in ways they wished without fundamentalist interference. Examples included, but are not limited to, the Oland Mission in Lamoni Stake, the Santa Fe Stake Mission, and Walnut Gardens in Blue

Valley Stake. In contrast, since the 1984 decision to ordain women hundreds of fundamentalist priesthood have been silenced and eight expelled from the church for failure to support the new policy. In 1980, for example, seventy-seven priesthood members were silenced (out of a total active priesthood of 18,578). By contrast, in 1989, 501 priesthood were silenced or released out of nearly 20,727 priesthood. Source: *World Conference 1982 Report*, page 150 and "Membership Census Report," (12/31/88 and 12/31/89) "Church Membership Report—1988 and 1989," Office of Membership Records, in *1990 World Conference Reports*, page 110.

36. Richard Price, audiotape of his session with stake president regarding possibility of Price's silencing (April 1985).

37. First Presidency, "Coping with Conflicting Messages," First Presidency Meeting Papers (January 1979), 7.

38. Ibid., 6.

39. Ibid., 7.

40. Standing High Council, "The Ethics of Dissent," *Saints Herald* 135 (April 1988): 141-146.

41. Clifford A. Cole, "The World Church: Our Mission in the 1980s," *Commission* (September 1979): 42.

42. This action did not, I would repeat, make inevitable the Reorganization's swerve toward greater identification with Protestantism. Other churches have moved into the same mission areas without losing their distinctive sectarian attributes, notably the Mormons and Jehovah's Witnesses. After all, Mormon converts from non-Christian religions in Korea celebrate something as uniquely American as Utah Pioneer Day and the Fourth of July. Moreover, much of the fermentation taking place in Reorganized Church intellectual circles that led to greater co-opting of mainline Protestant ideas were promulgated by people relatively unconcerned with non-Western missionary activities. Their background and interests arose from their non-Reorganization education and broader look at the religious milieu rather than a desire for missionary activity beyond the boundaries of Western civilization.

43. Vlahos, "Images of Orthodoxy," 184.

44. Once again, for evidence see my earlier notes on the writings of Cole, Neff, Spencer, Mesle, et al.

45. Edwin Scott Gaustead, *Dissent in American Religion* (Chicago: University of Chicago Press, 1973), 2.

46. I Corinthians 12 and 13.

47. Gaustead, *Dissent in American Religion*, 154.

48. Joseph Smith III, at the age of twenty-seven, upon coming to the Amboy Conference of the Reorganization to be received as its

president on 6 April 1860, as quoted in Launius, *Joseph Smith III: Pragmatic Prophet*, 117.

Chapter 8

Ethics and Dissent in Mormonism: A Personal Essay

by Paul M. Edwards

During the majority of my church life I have been a dissenter, my dissent ranging from slight discomfort over procedures to open rebellion as legalistic interpretations and prejudices became social legislation. Usually I have been in the minority and, with select company, have stood in isolated grandeur in priesthood quorums and church assemblies. For a variety of reasons I have remained with the movement, taking as my clue those significant persons who, following their own conscience, have also remained. Because of this decision, it has been expected I would accept without undue confrontation or gyrations the will of the majority.

Personally I have difficulty with any form of government that limits my right to express myself as I wish. Intellectually I prefer to live in the United States over other countries (with the possible exception of Great Britain in April). Emotionally, however, I find considerable problem with practical democracy. Such democracy is basically government by a large committee. And a committee, as you know, is an organization where everyone gives up what they passionately believe so they can dispassionately agree about something none of them believe.

Recently the Reorganized Church accepted a document that anticipated women's participation in the priesthood.[1] I found myself voting in agreement with the majority on this issue. Naïvely I expected that the opposing minorities would abide by that decision in the same quiet and unobtrusive manner expected of me when I was in the minority. I anticipated that after an initial outburst they would remove themselves to a place of quiet, deal with their frustration, gird up their loins, and live in the presence of majority consciousness. But, alas, that has not been the case. These persons identified as the opposing minority feel the truth has been violated, and action taken, because of misdirected and thus probably unprophetic leaders. The majority was declared *wrong* by virtue of having been *seen* as wrong.

These dissenters concluded that majority opinion is not valid when the body of religious truth is denied. They maintain that if the majority does not rescind its action, traditionalists will find it necessary to leave and begin a new church—or more accurately, reestablish a restored reorganized restoration of the reformation. The church, they contend, has betrayed the prescriptive "constitution" of the movement and thus has violated the contract they made with the church.[2] In some real cases they are correct.

Admittedly, over the years, the point of my dissent has been to change the church. I have endeavored to make it what I would consider theologically valid and socially responsible. Granted, my purpose was not to retain its tradition, but to alter it. On the other hand, current dissenters see themselves as preserving the tradition, as actually defending the church. And if we recognize their prescriptive contract then they are probably correct. It becomes my responsibility, I would think, to accept the existence of truths unaffected by the majority, or to leave. I am not sure I see the point, or even the future, of dissenting against a universal truth if I have accepted it.

If, however, the church is what the majority considers it to be, as led by whatever spirit we acknowledge, then the role of the dissenters is to call us to our task and, hopefully, to alter the church if they can do so by their pressure. The question boils down to whether the rule of the majority is a legitimate part of the constitutional structure of Reorganized Church governance or a left-over concept of wilderness America that is fun to talk about but totally alien to the movement. The second aspect of the question is to ask if dissent is valid once the constitutional nature of the church is understood.

The traditionalists' mind in this case is a mechanism operating on credulity. They consolidate a reliance on the unquestioned and unalterable wisdom of the past — a wisdom existent by virtue of simply being past. It is a proposal to substitute memory for reality, assuming that concepts of the past can deal more acceptably with today than can the understandings of the present.

It sounds a little harsh but I believe this tradition is the result of an increasing general cowardliness through which persons have lost some of the personal courage required to face life as a living, changing, adjusting reality. They are reluctant to rely on their personal valor to cope with the difficulties of their lives, seeking instead a reality dependent more on recall than intelligence.

In the middle of these opposing views of the church, what is the role of the dissenter within Mormonism? Obviously I am in favor of open dissent. Time prevents me waxing eloquent on my reasons for this or recreating the tortured path that led me to these conclusions. But I will begin my comment by recognizing that one of the most insidious things about institutional actions is the denial of the fact that error is most often something which is in itself true. The opposite of truth is not falsity but often just another truth. What is seen as error is often something misplaced in time or space, as dirt is simply earth in the wrong place.

Ethics is based on assumptions about the nature of reality. These assumptions give ethics their universal nature; that is the difference between ethics and codes, like the Kaiwanian Code of Ethics. For most of us ethics are identified only when they are broken; that is, we do not tend to know when something is ethical, only when something is unethical.

The wood-carvers of Silver Dollar City, near Branson, Missouri, have a standard answer when asked how they can carve such beautiful animals from wood. "Well, if you want to carve a dog," they say, "just take a block of wood and chip away everything that doesn't look like a dog." Dissent in an institution is much like this. The question of dissent concerns what is being chipped away as well as what is the vision of the final product. There is a strong tendency by some to preserve the unfinished block of wood; others, dissenters, continue to chip away feeling that each and every cut gets them closer to the final product. The definition of ethics in the movement depends on whether the "reality" of God's purpose is seen in the *process* of carving or in the *completion* of the sculpture. Questions arise about the ultimate intention of the carver and the essential nature of the dog.

It is my tendency to assume that dissent is ethical because I do not know, nor can I envision, the ultimate purposes of the block of wood. I feel dissent is essential to the final success. This assumes, of course, that I know what a dog looks like and that the block is not already a perfectly formed dog. It also assumes our cuts are not destroying the block's existing beauty or reality. And it assumes the purpose of involvement lies more in the carving than it does with the product.

The traditionalists do not concur with my assumptions. They see the block as containing the essential dog. The product does not need to be changed or altered. The process of chipping is necessary to cut away that which is not the "true dog," but it is also dangerous, for it can only disturb or even destroy the beauty of the wood. To chip on the already acceptable is unethical.

In his essay, *On Liberty*, John Stuart Mill argues against the unbridled tyranny of the majority. He admits that the distinction between the will of the majority and a universally valid truth is difficult if not impossible to make. But he sees dissent as the best, if not only, manner in which men and women can challenge the rampaging assertions of the majority. But what right does a minority have to challenge the majority?

If the existing body can maintain its order internally, controlling the pressure to change, then the presence of dissenters is usually acceptable and they are even allowed to propose change. Unlike pure democratic governance, however, change in the religious institution—particularly in a self-preserved system—is not only revolution, it is heresy. A wide variety of beliefs and practices can be tolerated within a large body, but a smaller group must retain conformity to preserve the purity of the group's practices and beliefs. But in neither of these cases can the variety of beliefs affect the core of believers who maintain the tradition, for these persons control the institution. If the core is altered the institution collapses.

Religious pluralism is not really the question. Many dissenters, as well as academic liberals, are confused about this. Pluralism is only possible with ideas secondary to the core beliefs of the institution. The question is this: How much deviation from standard belief can we demand from those who maintain the movement? The power of those who direct is not challenged by the varied beliefs but rather by those persons who, because they are capable of altering beliefs, pull power and authority away from those selected to yield it.

Frederick Sontag has told us that "those who preside over orthodox institutions would not have it so, since part of their success lies in the claim to be the 'authorized version.'"[3]

*   *   *

Institutional Mormonism, of either the Latter-day Saint or Reorganized Church variation, is not constitutionally adaptable to dissent. It seems to follow then that dissent cannot be ethical. By its own nature dissent weakens the power the church was constitutionally designed to strengthen. Without this power the church would not be what the majority of the members want it to be. If the power is effectively challenged, or the essential nature changed, the movement becomes something the majority did not join and do not want it to be.

There are several ways to identify dissent as constitutionally outside Mormonism. This fundamental exclusion at the same time suggests that for the majority in institutional Mormonism, dissent is unethical.

First, there can be no real dissent within the group because the leadership reflects—and the consent of the people authorizes—the General Will of the body. This Rosseauian and Burkean assumption suggests how the institutional church acknowledges truth and identifies the General Will (World Conference) as prescriptive. We adopt a legalistical view of Mosiah 13:35, "It is not common that the voice of the people desires anything contrary to that which is right; but it is common for the lesser part of the people to desire that which is not right." The prescriptivists believe "right" has emerged out of generations of trial and error and the corrective influence of time. The same concept, applied to the concept of corruption, would suggest a majority of sinners would be more sinful than a minority, and this would affect the decisions of those sinners when they vote. Apparently this is not recognized as the case.

The essence of the General Will is love. This love, defined politically by Burke and Calhoun and philosophically by Plato and Aristotle, reflects the relationship between a person's passionate *concern* for and involvement with another (even an institution) and the *duty* espoused by this concern. The metaphysical assumptions of the contemporary Mormon movement indicate that love is individual; it emerges out of the agency of persons caused by their creation from nothing

(Reorganized Church) or preexisting souls (Latter-day Saints). Thus, love is not a matter of ownership. The interesting point here is that to a large measure members in good standing believe love for the institution requires an obedience that acknowledges contractual love as ownership.

In the Mormon tradition, then, we can suggest that dissent is related to love; that is, one does not dissent if one really loves the institution. The arguments against dissent tend to revolve around the assumption that personal feelings must bow below that of the church, that no disagreement be allowed to harm the church. Dissent is not considered then, nor can it be dealt with, as evidence of a love greater than that expressed by obedience or ownership.

There is a second way in which dissent lies outside the legal assumptions of the movement. The members have been sold on the idea they have a right to answers, a point of view which implies that there are answers. Thus, leaders must respond to every question with an answer rather than acknowledging the impact of the questions. For many dissenters, of course, to question *is* the answer; and, as Meda, they appeal for "one moment of bewilderment to save us all." Institutional Mormonism lies on the edge of the great cosmological razor. On the one hand, members force the leaders into being managers, decision makers, and problem solvers; and on the other hand, we demand full expression of our personal agency.

Trying to balance this, the president of the movement is defined as the responder to attacks on the managers, and managers become executors of a system rather than directors of inquiry. The role of the prophet falls more to articulation of the General Will rather than to invoking paths of righteousness or making judgments about our faults. Prophetic pronouncements are weighed against the winds of time and the contracts of prescriptions.

Dissent is limited in yet a third way in the member's tendency to confuse power and authority. Power is the ability to take control and to obligate others to you; authority is the right to do so. The theological grounds of Mormonism suggest that authority lies with the body by general acceptance (Latter-day Saints) and common consent (Reorganized Church). But power begins at the top with the authority being delegated; thus, people tend to assume that power is authority and thus consent to power.

The significance of this lies in Mormonism's failure to provide theologically and historically for its middle class. The Catholic church failed to recognize its political vulnerability during the decay of feudalism, and it came apart at the weakest link when pressured. Mormonism appears to share something of the same problem. The movement has not produced a theology or a history (or a political science) that reflects the growth of a nonaligned class.

This class is not so much economic or family oriented (even though in both the Reorganization and LDS organizations these are important). Rather, it consists of persons who are tasting both power and influence—as well as professional acceptance and understanding—outside the church. Thus, they are increasingly aware of their own authority by virtue of knowledge and ability, while at the same time more aware of their lack of power within the institution. This group includes the intellectuals (and closet skeptics) as well as those faithful to the tradition but not necessarily to the doctrine.

It also includes persons who have come to believe their opinions reflect an honest minority. These persons considered themselves challenged—and usually blocked—by those who control the majority and who are conservatives (prescriptivists) of the Edmund Burke variety. They feel excluded from power because they are neither rich enough (in terms of holding authority) nor poor enough (willing to trade obedience for protection).

* * *

Mormon governance did not emerge full-blown from some preconceived plan. It grew pragmatically in reaction to needs. It started with an institutional aristocracy and grew up around it. This aristocracy, the priesthood, is one of tradition: an interrelation of duty and freedom. The interrelation operates, at least in the Reorganized Church, via call and ordination. The process identifies God's selection in the call and the need for institutional loyalty, obedience, and standardization in the ordination. God calls you to a work, but it is the church that authorizes you to do it.

In the prescriptive view the divine plan for humankind is worked out in history. For the Reorganized Church history is transcendentally directed and immanently rewarded; for the Latter-day Saints history is immanently directed and transcendently rewarded. In either case the plan becomes the contract and the contract is prescriptively unfolding. This view recognizes the people as the source of authority but suggests no essential nature to the membership other than their General Will. What makes a good legislative body, apparently, does not depend on who is sending persons to confer, but who are the persons sent. The purpose of representatives is not to reflect local points of view or

250

causes, but to send capable people to speak as they wish about the General Church.

The legislative duty is not necessarily to mirror the public mind or to mold the church by balancing local views, but rather to provide a collective moral/spiritual fulfillment that emerges as the result of their sameness. The majority rules only when consistent with the moral absolutes which exist independently and which come together in community. The public is called together to provide consent—a consent based on their public liberty. In this case, as with Burke, liberty means the right to accumulate the rewards of belonging to the social condition.

The hierarchy of authority reflects an aristocracy that controls paternalistically. This hierarchy has two important characteristics: It is not a closed hierarchy, nor can the mass select its members. The aristocracy is not denied to the people, nor is it totally out of reach of the most humble citizen. Any man or woman can aspire to this authority—at least in the Reorganized Church—recognizing the criteria for belonging are loyalty, dedication, and willingness to pay the costs. The aristocracy is self-perpetuating. Replacement occurs when one or more of the leaders—themselves of the aristocracy—select, groom, and eventually identify new members and leaders. The authority is thus self-perpetuating, giving it an institutional immortality.

Within the system the prescriptivists accept the Burkean view that "All men (and women) have equal rights, but not to equal things." This version of Orwell's "All the Pigs" story identifies common consent as the "presumed consent of every rational creature that they are in unison with the predisposed order of things." That is, they have voted correctly. One gives consent by accepting the proper order of things as established by a society of moral peers through the passing of time. Liberty, it then follows, is the freedom to receive the fruits of moral men's decision, to belong to a community in which order and the "correct manner of things" occurs. Freedom is expressed in society, not individually: We are free when we are properly within the group whose General (collective) Will is being fulfilled.

Mormonism began as a faith that expressed a growing recognition of human free will. It seemed to glory in the "efficacy of human effort versus the awful sovereignty of God which Calvinism had stressed." As the West revolted against the denial of human freedom, "Mormonism made the meaningfulness of human striving a part of its basic belief."[4] However, this concept was not fundamental; and as the system responded to pragmatically developed criteria, the idea changed. Human freedom and the exercise of agency were found to be excellent attributes for the development of an emerging religion, but it did not speak well for institutional orthodoxy.

In today's Mormonism responsive action has been limited and the degree of agency restricted. And, while there is a significant amount of complaining, there really is not a great deal of dissent—more evidence of dissenters than of varieties of dissent. For the Reorganized Church there is considerable smoke for a fairly small fire; for the Mormons not even much smoke. Reorganized Church dissenters will stay longer in the structure, but in the final analysis they will find the need to be outside.

The real ethical question, I believe, lies not in dissent, however, but in the failure of dissent. The pressure to become a part of the comfortable, the unchallenged, and the mediocre. The disparity simply reflects the easy process of abandoning the ethics of Plato for those of Aristotle. Aristotle's assumption that the state is most effectively served by the middle ground was based on the avoidance of extremes. It assumes that the exaggeration of human feelings produces an outcome of extremes, ignoring the fact that some virtues such as courage and kindness do not decrease in value as they increase in intensity. Plato, on the other hand, called for the implications of passion, asking men and women to allow themselves to be extremists in the name of participation. Persons cannot speak or act calmly about that which calls forth their total passion. This distinction between the ethics of passion and that of mediocrity explains why Plato's followers built cathedrals and Aristotle's built manor houses.[5]

The more popular middle-of-the-road responses to the central ideas of our time leave us driving one additional nail into the coffins of Mormon dissent. As dutiful followers not only of the church but of the social fads of our civilization, we seek to manage the behavior of the church and in so doing leave behind the passionate source of our dissent. Caught between our discomfort and the desire to let the professional do it, we further weaken our assertion of concern by accepting professional bureaucracy's tempting offer to "Let us do that for you." One must recognize the "loneliness that accompanies independence and the uneasiness that accompanies freedom," as Thornton Wilder put it. The danger that we face is compounded by this loneliness which threatens us. Our fear is not just that the church will somehow force us to conform to it but that we will be easily molded by the environment. In adapting to the institution's willingness to make decisions one learns to conform and to actually prefer to let the institutional church be the master of one's religious expression. It was Supreme Court Justice Louis Brandeis who warned, "The irresistible is often only that which is not resisted."[6]

If Mormonism wants freedom of expression and really counts on the support of free minds, then a relationship based on something other than obedience must be created. The movement must, as English philosopher Bertrand Russell has suggested, establish a morality that reflects initiative not submission, one that reflects hope rather than fear, and one that concentrates on things that must somehow be done rather than things that must of necessity be left undone.[7]

But if such a change happened, it might necessarily be the end of the movement—perhaps not the end of the institution but of the community. If the Mormon movement is defined by its tradition and its prescription, then to stand in dissent is to want it to be that which it is not. To loyal members it would appear that dissent is disloyal, disloyal to the movement that existed when we made a contract. Thus it is unethical for us to attempt to change the contract made with the General Will, for such a change violates the promise made as prescriptions of the past extend to the present and the future.

I personally believe dissent is good because I do not want Mormonism—or any other institution—running loose upon the world unchecked. But my opinion, if acted on, is a violation of my part of the prescription, a violation of the expectation of my association and a violation of the source of my authority. Mine would be a disloyalty compounded, it would seem, because I have access to the highest authority, the most significant insights, and the most important pulpits. *If* the prescriptive view of Mormonism is correct then I am a spokesman—not for myself nor some contingency, certainly not for some particular current body but for the movement itself—for the prescriptive truths of two centuries. If not, then I am unlawfully accepting the authority and the community it grants me.

The situation is much like the one Socrates faced when he was imprisoned for crimes against the state. When offered the chance to escape, he refused and eventually accepted his drink of hemlock. His reasons lay in his acceptance of the protection of the state, his enforcement of laws that protected him, his willing use of the advantages of the court system to rid the streets of thugs and the assemblies of traitors. He had not seen fit to challenge the power of the system when it worked as he wanted; and now, when that same power exercised in the same way, turned against him, he had no ethical option but to submit.

The minds of our members have yielded in almost ritualistic sacrifice to the prescriptive value of the system. We are prone to assume that a consistent belief, a steady understanding, an obedient heart, and a loyal mind are essential to the proper understanding of what is right. Thus, what emerges from any conflicts is the eventual death of one of these positions since these cannot be multiple positions. It would be my hope that there might be a new understanding of value and thus of a new assumption on which to build our value and ethic systems. But that hope lies outside the tradition.

There is some confusion in the minds of the members between contracts and covenants. Leadership expects, with some justification, that the people will abide by the covenant. The distinction has something to do with implied and direct obligations. There are those who see their relationship as a set contract based on a set of assumptions made at a given time. "The church is just not the same as it was in 1830" they say; but what they mean is, "It is not the same as I understood 1830 to be when I was baptized in 1960." They see their joining as a contract, and their loyalty is to that contract.

The covenant thesis is one of shared value in which the obligation is to mutually held assumptions, goals, and expectations. When the conditions under which the covenant is made are altered by time or events it does not breach the covenant, nor does it mean that one is limited by what it was. It means only that the mutual goals and expectations are still being pursued. If most marriages were covenants rather than contracts, marriages would work better.

Going back to the wood-carvers as dissenters, I would suggest we look at this block of wood and realize that it is not yet a dog—not a perfect dog in the block or in the mind of the carver. Cutting away may well produce a more aesthetic dog. And thus, in the confrontation between views, we might find a tension that sustains the two rather than destroys them. Like McDonald's great golden arch, the two halves sustain the total. Such a belief is tied up in Plato's love and Christians' belief and rationalists' dialectic. It assumes a lesson to be learned and is built on the idea that we do not look at positions to find what discernible value they have, but to see what lies beyond them, within them, envisioning what can be constructed from them.

That is my preference. But honesty requires me to acknowledge the prescriptive movement's concerns about the behavior of the dissenter.

Notes

1. Doctrine and Covenants 156 (Independence, Missouri: Herald Publishing House, 1990 ed.).

2. This point has been made repeatedly by fundamentalist dissenters and documented *ad nauseum* in the lectures and essays of William D. Russell. See his article in this collection, "The Fundamentalist Schism, 1958-Present," for a discussion of the arguments.

3. Frederick Sontag, *International Journal of Philosophy of Religion* 14 (1983): 189.

4. Ibid., 162.

5. Richard M. Weaver, *Ideas Have Consequences* (Chicago: Phoenix Books, 1948): 119.

6. Harold Dodds, *The Importance of Being an Individual* (New York: Harper Torchbooks, 1959): 53.

7. Bertrand Russell, *Principles of Social Reconstruction* (London: Allen and Unwin, 1916), 204.

Chapter 9

Dissent and the Future of the Church

---

by W. B. "Pat" Spillman

Introduction

Even if the legends are true, it was still not a "media event" in those days. When the monk clad in a coarse woolen cassock approached the entrance of the castle church at Wittenberg, Germany, at noon on 31 October 1517 and nailed a card to the church door it may well have gone without immediate notice. The doors of the church were the parish bulletin board. Notices of weddings, burials, special masses, and other church events frequently could be found there. But it was no ordinary notice the monk tacked up that day; nor was he an ordinary monk.

The cleric, Martin Luther, was a professor of theology at the University of Wittenberg. A thoughtful and reflective man, Luther was already a well-known and respected teacher in central Germany by the time he was in his early thirties. Basically a conservative, dedicated scholar, Luther was at first amazed, then scandalized by the wealth and power of the Roman Catholic church when he first visited Rome as a young man.

During the Middle Ages, the Roman Catholic church, as the single universal institution in Western Europe, sought to influence all aspects of community life. From politics and economics to manners and morals, the church exhorted the populace and demanded adherence to its dictates on the pain of death of both body and soul. However, while its moral and spiritual influence was unrivaled, it exercised its political and economic control unevenly, depending heavily on the support of secular lords for enforcement. Moreover, even as the church influenced the surrounding society, the church's interaction with the secular world increasingly laid secular methods and values on the religious institution. It was, therefore, with a combination of both sadness and outrage that Luther watched the secular aspects of the church overwhelm the spiritual.

The notice Luther posted on the door of the castle church was a challenge to formally debate a series of ninety-five propositions dealing with the current practice of selling indulgences, a means by which persons could obtain forgiveness for sins by making a special penance offering to the church. But Luther's complaint about the uncanonical and promiscuous sale of indulgences was only part of his concern for the church. Like many dissenters of the past, Luther believed the Roman Catholic church had become too worldly and was guilty of accommodating with the secular culture. Luther had a good point. The more ubiquitous the Roman Catholic church became in European society, the less difference there was between church life and other aspects of the community. Making church and the rest of society one was indeed the church's objective. But instead of the society becoming like the church, the church increasingly took on the secular characteristics of European life.

Though it was certainly not Luther's intent to create a rival church, he quickly discovered that his theological disagreements with church leaders tapped into a deep vein of popular discontent with papal control over all aspects of life. The social and political conditions of central Europe were ripe for revolt. Many lords wanted relief from burdensome papal strictures and financial appeals while tens of thousands of peasants longed for freedom from the oppression of the nobility and church hierarchy alike. While he may have been surprised at the extent of the revolution he sparked, Luther nevertheless took full advantage of his newfound popularity. Using Johannes Gutenburg's recently invented movable-type printing press to disseminate his ideas about church reform throughout Europe, he became one of the first print propagandists of the modern world.

As one might expect, the church quickly determined that Luther was potentially a dangerous voice and sought to silence him. After an ecclesiastical court predictably found him guilty of heresy and expelled him, Luther found refuge in the court of a powerful German lord where he continued his attack on what he charged were the radical departures of the church from its traditional theology and mission. Inevitably, both nobles and commoners, each for their own reasons, looked to Luther for leadership in what came to be the beginning of an entirely new branch of Christianity: Protestantism.

This is an old and familiar story to students of religious history. It also has the echo of current events to many observers of the contemporary scene in the Reorganized Church of Jesus Christ of Latter Day Saints. While one would not want to press the analogy too far (contemporary print propagandist and professional dissenter Richard Price is no Martin Luther, for example), there are instructive parallels between the events of the Protestant Reformation and dissents of the past few decades in the Reorganized Church.

The Reorganization and a
Shift of Paradigms

The Roman Catholic church went through what we today would term a major "paradigm shift" between the early centuries of the Christian movement and the sixteenth century. The term "paradigm" refers, among other things, to a model or an accepted standard. Sociologists have invested the term with special meaning when they apply it to social theory. A social paradigm, according to Fritjof Capra's representative definition, is a "constellation of concepts, values, perceptions and practices shared by a community, which forms a particular vision of reality that is the basis of the way the community organizes itself."[1]

By this definition, then, a paradigm shift is a significant change in the way people perceive reality, a major alteration in what is accepted as a standard or accepted way of thinking or doing things. The world of 1500 was radically different from that of the Roman Empire in which Christianity emerged a millennium and a half earlier. So was the church. From a tiny, embattled sect of Judaism in the first century, the Roman Catholic church of the Reformation era had become wealthy almost beyond calculation, with power and influence that called kings and emperors to account all across Europe. Doctrines and practices that enabled the Roman Catholic church to survive and prosper in the hostile environment of a pagan empire gradually metamorphosed into beliefs and traditions supportive of its authority in a society which depended on the church as the single unifying institution in a fragmented world.

Martin Luther and other sixteenth-century reformers were undoubtedly uncomfortable with the realities they perceived in their world. They did not accept the values of the secular world, and because of that, they therefore vigorously opposed what they believed were unjustified changes in the church's original character and mission.

The Reorganized Church underwent a similar, though far less extensive, paradigm shift in a much shorter period of time. Despite its relative brevity, the Reorganization's transition provoked reactions quite familiar to students of the Reformation. Scholars have documented well the theological and administrative rifts in the Reorganized Church that led to its major incidents of dissent.[2] Like sixteenth-century dissenters who saw changes in Roman Catholic doctrine and practice destructive of the church's original nature, contemporary Reorganization fundamentalists fervently believe the leadership of the organization has strayed far from the narrow path of orthodoxy. Richard Price, self-appointed strategist of the fundamentalist cause, stated the basic premise of the most recent fundamentalist discontent succinctly: "When Christ restored His Church, He established it with unchangeable laws and doctrines, making it exactly as He wanted it. Any change from those basic laws and doctrines is apostasy."[3]

In a world of dynamic change affecting virtually all of its institutions including churches, most would agree that avoiding *all* change is impossible. Therefore, Price's definition of apostasy allows him to cry "heresy" at the slightest alteration of practice, policy, or doctrinal interpretation. Although Price's view is no doubt extreme and stated more for its propaganda effect than for serious analysis, it does represent the essence of the ultraconservative belief present in most churches or, at a higher level of abstraction, in religions. Because *someone* will always find *any* change heretical, one may conclude that perceptions of apostasy in religious institutions are inevitable. So also is schism. As sociologists Rodney Stark and William Bainbridge point out:

> Among the most common events in the history of religions is schism—a group of disgruntled members breaks away from a religious organization in order to found a new organization. When such groups leave, they rarely do so quietly or amicably. Instead, they justify their departure in severe denunciations of their parent body. "The church has betrayed its holy mission on earth." "It has become worldly and sinful." Indeed, the departing sect claims that it, not the parent body, embodies continuity with the original faith. The sect is not a *new* church, but the restored original. The parent body is the "new" religion—a sinful perversion of the original legacy.[4]

Rhetoric notwithstanding, even the most rigid Reorganization fundamentalists would probably not oppose *all* change; rather, the heart of the theological discord between fundamentalists and church leaders is in the *nature and extent of change* and how those changes come about. Fundamentalists charge that over the past two decades church leaders deliberately and radically altered essential doctrines including concepts of priesthood, the sacrament of the Lord's Supper, belief in the Book of Mormon, and the nature of the body as the "only true church" of Christ. Church leaders defended themselves, claiming that while changes have come, they have been peripheral to the central doctrines and traditions of the faith. The essential core beliefs remain the same. As *Saints Herald* editor Roger Yarrington explained, "The church has changed, is changing, but not its central beliefs which, when addressed to a changing world, are still vital and are still being taught, believed, and lived."[5]

The most recent dissents hinge on what people regard as the central beliefs of the church. Wide differences in the basic assumptions of current church leaders and those of various fundamentalist factions exist. For fundamentalists, doctrines involving such topics as scriptural literalism, concepts of Zion, the value (or threat) of working with other religious bodies, and the role of prophecy are *basic* beliefs which are not subject to rational debate. While church leaders have been willing to critically examine these topics, fundamentalists insist they are God-given doctrines, the truth or falsity of which is not open to question.

Perhaps the most troubling concern for many fundamentalists is what they feel is the gradual loss of the most unique aspects of Reorganization theology and practice, or to put it another way, the fear that church leaders are "changing the Church into a completely different denomination."[6] In the nineteenth century and for the first half of the twentieth, the theological glue which held the church together was a commitment to premillennialism and the belief that God truly cared which church one joined. The church's primary appeal was in its sense of destiny and community. To Latter Day Saints, the church was composed of God's chosen people who, if faithful, would inherit the greatest rewards in heaven; the church was organized according to God's plan, using God's only authorized priesthood, and was building God's community (Zion), which would usher in Christ's return and the millennial reign. This is essentially what the fundamentalists call the "Old Jerusalem Gospel." It was this message, with minor variations, that the church promoted from its birth in 1830 through the 1950s.

During the church's first century of existence there was little internal theological argument over the validity of this rather exclusivist message. Major Reorganized Church schisms before 1960 were largely the result of administrative disagreements, not theological ones. To be sure, the Smith-Gurley affair of the 1880s had theological overtones (regarding interpretation of the scriptures), but the crux of the issue was the *power* of the First Presidency to determine orthodoxy, not its theological position, per se.[7] Despite its limited concern, the conflict led some of the church's most important leaders away from the organization they helped found. A generation later, the highly publicized Supreme Directional Control controversy of the 1920s was administrative to its core. The issue in this case was who had the authority to direct the work in the field, the First Presidency or the Quorum of Twelve Apostles. Though the question was also narrow, emotions were even more heated and perhaps one-third of the church departed the fold by the time it was over.[8]

In spite of the massive defection, the church remained essentially true to its exclusivist self-concept for at least the next generation. Frederick M. Smith was not a religious liberal. Politically he was a "Progressive," a movement that crossed traditional party lines and called for reform of various aspects of U.S. political, social, and economic life. Administratively he was a "Mugwump," a nonderogatory term applied to those convinced of the efficacy of professionalism and rational bureaucracy as a way of meeting the challenges of modern society.[9] But theologically Smith differed little from his father, whose hope he shared that the Reorganized Church would eventually build Zion, the community of righteousness which would usher in the millennium. Both Fred M. and his younger brother and successor, Israel A. Smith, strongly believed the church was God's chosen institution. Indeed, Israel Smith was one of the church's historically great apologists. His 1952 pamphlet, *The Return*, was characteristic of his legalistic defense of the church's legitimacy over the Mormons.

As traditional as the Smith brothers were, however, both were instrumental in initiating a major paradigm shift, eventually resulting in the dissents of the 1980s, when they set in motion policies that eventually helped diminish the church's historic sense of theological uniqueness. Fred M. encouraged the use of the tools of modern behavioral science and management theory in church work. His emphasis on education, training, and professionalism undermined the naïve pietism on which the church often depended in its earliest years. When the church had few opportunities for ministerial education, reliance on the Holy Spirit instead of "book learning" became a necessity for many. By the late nineteenth century, however, many Reorganization conservatives made reliance on "inspiration" rather than formal education a mark of pride. In this regard, they were not unlike conservatives of the larger Christian community who reacted to the biblical-criticism movement of the latter 1800s with an exaggerated biblical literalism and disdain for the "teachings of men," which they saw as threatening the basis of their faith. The largely rural Reorganized Church population tended to sympathize with the conservative approach, and lack of formal education became, for some Saints at least, a virtue rather than an impediment or unavoidable circumstance. For the most conservative Reorganization members, faithfulness and education were at opposite ends of a mutually exclusive continuum; the more one had of one, the less of the other. Preparation of any kind was to be avoided; spontaneity opened the door to inspiration.

Israel A. Smith built on Fred M.'s encouragement of education and its implications for professionalism. The church under Israel promoted the Department of Religious Education's plans to broaden the preparation and depth of its full-time staff and church school teachers in the field. Near the end of Israel's life, in a move reminiscent of the church's Kirtland and Nauvoo educational activities, the church ambitiously created the School of the Restoration, the prototype of today's Temple School, to provide specialized leadership training for ministry.

By themselves the efforts of the Department of Religious Education and the School of the Restoration did not represent an immediate threat to the church's historic sectarianism. However, the administration of Israel's successor and a third son of Joseph III, W. Wallace Smith, accelerated the trend toward expecting greater expertise and professionalism from its full-time ministers and looked increasingly to secular institutions and seminaries of other faiths to obtain the required training. In the early 1960s the Department of Religious Education began employing young seminary-trained executives, and the church began requiring that its appointee field ministers have at least two years of college work before their church employment.

The seminary and secular institutional training had a significant and perhaps unplanned effect. Partly as a result of pressure brought by the church's small but influential seminary-trained staff, many of the church's traditional doctrines came under greater critical scrutiny. A church-sponsored survey conducted in the late 1960s confirmed what many conservatives feared about the implications of secular and seminary education when it revealed that

> ...there is a very clear difference between appointees in general and those persons in the church who are seminarians or who hold a seminary degree. Generally the B.D. [bachelor of divinity] and seminarians are more liberal in theological orientation and overall perspective. They tend to be more critic[al] of the institutional church, see a greater need for education, particularly of appointees, and are more ecumenically oriented.[10]

Unfortunately, many of the church's most conservative members believed that to even *consider* questioning the basic tenets of the faith, much less to debate them, was apostasy. Fundamentalist Saints generally shared the conservative Christian belief that what one believes is as important as what one does, and God *knows* what one believes. Those who act or believe wrongly imperil their souls; if they share their wrong views, they imperil the souls of others. It is, therefore, vital to maintain orthodoxy and eradicate even the most embryonic heresy as quickly and thoroughly as possible.

If fundamentalists were uneasy as church doctrines were reexamined in the late 1950s and early 1960s, they were in for much greater discomfort as the decade of the 1960s progressed. For a variety of reasons the church began to deemphasize its most unique aspects and stress those more characteristic of "orthodox" Christian denominations. It particularly played down its historic "one true church" claim. In part, this resulted from the church's missionary work in the Third World and other non-Christian cultures. Church leaders sent into those areas in the post World War II years quickly discovered that traditional Reorganization "true church" missionary techniques were meaningless in societies where people did not know Christ at all. It was a waste of time trying to convince people who did not yet know who Jesus Christ was, much less what a church was, that the Reorganized Church faith was the true successor to the original Restoration movement.[11] In its attempt to bring ministry to both body and soul in its new missions, the church found itself walking a path trod by many other Christian organizations and found cooperation in some cases was more efficacious than competition. In Joint Council seminars held in the late 1960s, in which theologian Paul Jones and historian Carl Bangs from the liberal Methodist seminary, St. Paul School of Theology in Kansas City, took the lead, church leaders addressed unfamiliar problems posed by having to define the church's theology in terms understandable to persons as yet unexposed to Christian concepts.[12] Jones and Bangs helped the Presidency and Twelve identify the most basic elements of the Restoration faith. In so doing, they pointed out how the Restoration fit into the larger Christian mosaic.

Among the more notable changes emerging from the church's reexamination of its theology in the seminars was a much greater acceptance of ecumenism than before. Early in the administration of Wallace B. Smith, the First Presidency held a series of meetings for its appointee and executive staff in which a new stance toward authority and the church's relationships with other Christian bodies was clearly identified. In one presentation the First Presidency clearly abandoned the historic Reorganized Church assertion that it had the sole authority to minister in Christ's stead in this world:

> An unfortunate and erroneous concept about the nature of authority is that only one organized church institution at a time may have authority to represent God. It is the testimony of the Reorganized Church of Jesus Christ of Latter Day Saints that we have been called of God to accomplish the divine purpose in God's world. When we make this assertion it does not necessarily follow that no other person or institution has spiritual authority. ... If the other person or institution is blessed as we are with the authority of the Holy Spirit, we rejoice with them in the work of God among us, and pray with them that the Lord of the harvest may send even more laborers into the ripening vineyard. ... Many of our members have borne witness of the presence of the Holy Spirit blessing their efforts to share the meaning of God's ever present revelation in the world within the context of ecumenical fellowships. The church may be missing an important dimension of its unique calling unless it shares its light fully with other Christians who are committed to similar goals.[13]

Such a shift in emphasis could not help but be viewed with alarm by those Latter Day Saints rooted in the tradition of the Restoration and holding fast to the distinctiveness and legitimacy of the Reorganization.

The Reorganized Church's Demographic Shift

As disjunctive as the church's reexamination of its doctrine may have seemed to some people, a more subtle but perhaps equally powerful paradigm shift was occurring as a result of the church's increasing and perhaps unconscious accommodation to the standards and values of the United States' middle class. The latter half of the twentieth century marked a period of gradual transition of the church from a largely rural and working-class constituency to a more white collar, urban, middle-class membership. This change in the makeup of the Reorganization, coupled with the church's traditional openness to trends in the surrounding culture, ensured that the complexion of the movement would also change, and it did so appreciably in the 1960s and 1970s.

From the time of Rigdon's "Family" in Kirtland, Ohio, in the 1830s through the remainder of the nineteenth century, the Latter Day Saint movement particularly appealed to the poor and working classes of America and, later, of Europe. Indeed, many problems of the early organization were due to an insupportable influx of poverty-stricken converts who expected to improve their physical as well as spiritual lives through affiliation with the church.[14]

Although more stable under Joseph Smith III's cautious leadership and the absence of mass migrations of immigrants and dispossessed families, the early Reorganization was still a movement of people of humble means. The church budget was always precariously lean, even well into the twentieth century. F. Henry Edwards blamed the paucity of income, in part, on the lack of sufficient financial resources among the church's membership:

> Because the church was poor, proselyting was chiefly among the poor. Local missionary enterprises were almost never adequately financed, and in many urban situations the best housing that could be secured was a home, an upper room, or a storefront. Hundreds of honest, thrifty, and industrious but poor people joined the church but, with few exceptions, neither their resources, their education, nor their experience elsewhere qualified them to manage the business of the church as a means to freedom and power.[15]

In the early years of the Reorganization most church leaders were far from well-off financially. Joseph Smith III, for example, received little or no income from the church in his early years as prophet except for a modest stipend earned as working editor of the *Saints' Herald*. Living under the burden of perpetual financial stress, at one point he seriously considered selling the Kirtland Temple, which he had personal title to, and applying the proceeds to his personal debts.[16]

Early Reorganized Church missionaries often went into the field virtually penniless, "without purse or scrip" as they described it then. The families left behind often had to fend for themselves. If they were fortunate enough to live near relatives or other church members, missionary dependents received help with their farms and other economic needs. Attempting to overcome the hardships imposed by such a policy, the church tried to help by providing small family allowances whenever it could, but these seldom were anything more than a small supplement to what the family could produce for itself. Perhaps the Spartan existence the missionaries and their families endured seemed tolerable because many other members of the church and the missionary prospects with whom they worked were not markedly better off. Concepts of poverty and wealth are always relative to those with whom comparisons are being made.

The church continued to maintain its modest image well into the 1950s. Even if they could afford to do otherwise, its leaders were expected to live frugally. For example, many appointee ministers did not have automobiles. Among those who did, basic transportation was all they got; only those in cold climates were allowed heaters. Many children of appointee families up through the 1950s testify to receiving (sometimes gratefully, sometimes with resentment) food and used clothing from other church members. To emphasize its thrifty use of contributors' tithing, and perhaps as a deterrent to those who might try to benefit financially at the church's expense, the church published leaders' official (elder's) expense and family allowances in the *Conference Daily Bulletin* until 1958. Not even the general officers, including the First Presidency, were immune from such publicity.

During the 1960s, however, the church began making significant efforts toward providing more substantial support for its leadership and their families. As rising contributions permitted, the church gradually improved its appointee family allowances and instituted attractive fringe benefits such as fully equipped church automobiles, total medical care, college tuition reimbursement for dependents, and a relatively generous retirement plan. In 1973 it initiated a policy of tying appointee family compensation to a level close to the median income figures put out by the United States Bureau of Labor Statistics. The effect of these actions was to place the standard of living of appointee families squarely into the American middle class. Moreover, if the wife was employed, an increasing likelihood of modern life, her earnings were considered on top of the husband's church allowances, giving many appointee families a family income well into upper-middle-class standards.

Another change in appointment policy accelerated this trend. During much of the church's history, appointee ministers came into church service in their early adulthood. Before the 1960s it was common for appointees to begin church work in their twenties, occasionally even in their late teens. For all practical purposes, many of these men had little career experience or personal resources other than what they received from full-time church work. However, increasingly in the 1970s and 1980s, the church appointed men in their thirties and forties after they had already developed a career in other areas of life. Many families coming into appointment during this period already had considerable financial resources to augment their church incomes. The result of all this was to put the church's appointee leaders in a position of substantial financial health, with a concomitant stake in maintaining stability and respectability within the surrounding society.

Church leaders were not alone in transitioning into the middle and upper middle class during the latter half of the twentieth century and, indeed, probably would not have been able to do so without similar changes among the church's population. Although the Presiding Bishopric does not keep statistics that would allow one to document a demonstrable growth in median income of the church's general membership over time, a Commission on Education study in the late 1960s revealed that 56.65 percent of church families surveyed had a gross income of $8,000 or more (43.63 percent had incomes over $10,000).[17] The comparable median family income for the United States in 1970 was $8,734.[18] While this single survey statistic does not necessarily prove the point, even in the absence of statistical confirmation one would merely have to observe locations of Reorganization churches and survey the vehicles in church parking lots to conclude that the church in North America is no longer constituted largely of lower and working class families. While it is true that church program budgets during the latter 1980s were lean, the institution nevertheless demonstrated considerable wealth. In the early part of the twentieth century most Reorganized Church branches met in rented quarters or in members' homes. Eighty years later nearly all branches had their own facilities, many worth hundreds of thousands of dollars. The Temple project in Independence is undoubtedly a measure of the church's aggregate affluence. Within the space of two years, a church with fewer than 51,000 contributing members raised more than $40 million toward a project expected to cost at least $75 million before its completion.[19] This is not the accomplishment of a people of modest means.

The more wealth one has, the less likely one is to promote policies that may threaten it; the more integrated one is within society, the less motivation one has to radically alter it. As the church and its leaders moved securely into the North American middle class, it quite naturally began to see tension and apartness from society as potentially damaging to its newly acquired status. The church found itself with an increasing interest in maintaining stability and peace with the surrounding culture. In short, the church experienced a paradigm shift in the way it regarded its mission and role in society. As it once saw its mission and destiny apart from, and in many respects, inimical to society as a whole, the church in the latter twentieth century began to see the benefits of cooperation and increased accommodation to societal standards and demands.

From Sect to Denomination

Ironically the paradigm shift that reduced tensions with society and brought church leaders, and indeed much of the church, to a greater identification with the larger Christian community and North American society, unfortunately produced greater internal tensions in the church. At least some of the most recent internal tensions and resulting dissent stems from the very respectability the church has earned as it has evolved theologically and socially from what might be called a sect to a denomination. Although definitions of such terms as sect, denomination, and church are debated among sociologists, there is general agreement that sects represent relatively small religious groups sharing beliefs and practices in relative contradistinction to the majority of society. Among the many typologies differentiating sects from other religious bodies, one of the more useful was proposed by sociologist Glenn M. Vernon in the early 1960s. Vernon distinguished between sects and denominations using a number of indicators. Table 1 following categorizes the distinctions:

Table 1*

CHARACTERISTIC	SECT	DENOMINATION
Size	Small	Large
Relationship with other religious groups	Rejects—feels that the sect alone has the "truth"	Accepts other denominations and is able to work in harmony with them
Wealth (church property, buildings, salary of clergy, income of members)	Limited	Extensive
Religious services	Emotional emphasis—try to recapture conversion thrill; informal; extensive congregational participation	Intellectual emphasis; concern with teaching; formal, limited congregational participation
Clergy	Unspecialized; little if any professional training; frequently part-time	Specialized; professionally trained; full-time
Doctrines	Literal interpretation of scriptures; emphasis upon other-worldly rewards	Liberal interpretation of scriptures; emphasis upon this-worldly rewards
Membership requirements	Conversion experience; emotional commitment	Born into group or ritualistic requirements; intellectual commitment
Relationship with secular world	"At war" with the secular world which is defined as being "evil"	Endorses prevailing culture and social organization
Social class of members	Mainly lower class	Mainly middle class

---

*Glenn M. Vernon, *Sociology of Religion* (New York: McGraw-Hill Book Co., 1962), 174.

Even a cursory knowledge of Latter Day Saint history would lead one to conclude that according to Vernon's typology, the Reorganized Church *began* as a sect. As Vernon and others have pointed out, one key feature of a sect is its tension with the "prevailing culture." Where denominations have largely made peace with society and share its values, sects tend to attract people who, for one reason or another, do not feel part of the larger society around them. Sects often reject conventional religious and secular practices and adopt modes of belief and behavior that clearly set them apart from the predominant culture. As pioneer sociologists Robert Park and Ernest Burgess put it: "A sect is a religious organization that is at war with the existing mores."[20]

Of course, being "at war" with others presents risks for sect members. Extreme deviance can result in social ostracism or worse. Even minor divergence prompts those in sects to prefer each other's company because of their difficulty fitting in to the general cultural milieu. But if it is so uncomfortable, why do people join sects? Among the major reasons is because sects offer rewards that are not available to them in other ways. For those with nonstandard theological beliefs, sects confer acceptance and understanding. The religious life of the sect might also be rich and rewarding. People considered social outcasts find family in sects; others whose secular ambition has been thwarted may earn status and positions of power and influence in the smaller, more homogeneous sect. And for the poor, sects may be the only source of physical survival.

Sociologists Stark and Bainbridge proposed a theoretical basis for the rewards of sect affiliation. According to their view, human beings are motivated by highly abstract and psychic rewards as well as those which are tangible and material. Religions attract followers on the basis of a system of incentives consisting of intangible promises that substitute for desired objective rewards. They called these rewards "compensators," which have "the character of an IOU, the value of which must be taken on faith."[21] Examples of compensators might include (1) a sense of superiority and status based on assumptions of who is "really" in God's favor, (2) promises as explicit as physical healing of ailments that do not respond to conventional medical treatment, or (3) promises as vague and unprovable as a "hereafter" free of pain and suffering especially available to those who were denied pleasures and comforts in this life.[22] Although compensators are available through many social institutions (politics, business, science, education, and others), only religions base their compensators on supernatural assumptions. In other words, the source of the compensators (the grantor of the rewards) is currently beyond human knowledge or apprehension.

Building on their theory of compensators, Stark and Bainbridge proposed a model for sectarian schism.[23] They began by recognizing that there are natural cleavages, or social divisions, occurring in all organizations. These cleavages are usually based on, or result in, differentials in power, wealth, and privilege. Those in leadership will inevitably be in a position to influence the organization in ways that produce compensators or rewards they find particularly attractive. The rewards those who already have power and wealth desire are usually more worldly (e.g. secular status, prestige, and monetary affluence) than those desired by people not in power (e.g. promise of a better life to come, assurances that they are God's chosen people, and that their faith is "God's faith"). Worldly rewards may be gained in all organizations, even churches, but the high degree of tension with the surrounding society that some people find rewarding, and which is characteristic of sects, is inimical to the acquisition of the secularly recognized rewards the leaders desire. Therefore, those in power and those with the greatest secular resources (often the same people) will tend to influence the sect, consciously or unconsciously, toward a position of reduced tension with society. Stark and Bainbridge summarized their theory:

> ... over time, the privileged faction will tend to get its way. It will use its control of the religious organization to reduce tension with the surrounding society, for such tension will tend to hamper the privileged. That is, to the degree that the religious group is in tension with the external society, it will limit powerful members' ability to realize their full potential for success in secular life and it will reduce the supply and value of the direct rewards the religious group supplies to its members.[24]

The process Stark and Bainbridge described appears historically viable. The Roman Catholic church of the fifteenth and sixteenth centuries was no longer theologically or socially in tension with society. It had not been for centuries. Instead, it was virtually coopted by society. The sale of indulgences Martin Luther so objected to was merely one evidence of traditional theological doctrine being bent to support church leaders' secular needs.

In the Reorganized Church evidence of reduced tension and increased accommodation to society is not as dramatic, but it is present. The First Presidency's support of ecumenical efforts is only one of many theological indicators of social accommodation.[25] Though still officially proscribed, open Communion is tolerated, even defended in some Reorganized Church congregations.[26] While the Book of Mormon is still revered and quoted, the church permits open criticism of traditional accounts of its origin and its theology.[27] The involvement of the church's founding prophet, Joseph Smith, Jr., in polygamy is no longer vigorously denied by church leaders familiar with institutional history.[28] The church no longer encourages the historic gathering principle; instead, it urges its members to be "leaven" in their home areas and work toward community betterment where they live. The cherished concept of Zion itself has become increasingly vague and less compelling to leaders and members alike.[29] And in perhaps its most emotional change, the church now admits females to its once all-male priesthood. Although church leaders insist that these changes do not involve its "central beliefs," each represents significant departures from traditionally exclusivist Reorganized Church theology and practice and further reduces the sense of uniqueness of the church relative to other Christian denominations.

The upward social mobility of the church and its changing theological stance toward a position of reduced tension with society is not an unexpected phenomenon to sociologists. The transformation of lower-class sects into middle-class churches is a long-observed phenomenon. For example, theologian H. Richard Neibuhr, from whom Stark and Bainbridge derived much of their conceptual foundations, early in the twentieth century observed that sects tended to reduce their tension with society over a period of time, thus allowing them to begin attracting middle- and upper-class members. Unfortunately he proposed no mechanism by which this transformation took place.[30]

As Stark and Bainbridge examined possible explanations for such transformations, they considered a theory based on Max Weber's classic work, *The Protestant Ethic and the Spirit of Capitalism*, suggesting that the Puritan ethic of hard work, thrift, and industry might account for upward economic mobility. However, they felt this theory was too limited in its application (to sects deriving from Puritanism) to explain sect mobility in general.

They then examined the psychological theory of "moral regeneration," which argues that socially dysfunctional individuals who find sects attractive are influenced by their membership in the sectarian community to become useful, contributing citizens of society. In their summary of this argument:

> ...persons adrift in society, lacking ties to the moral order, are strongly reattached to society by virtue of their recruitment into an intensely integrated moral community—a sect. It even can be argued that the very deprivations that cause people to join sects are abated by sect membership, thus enabling people to improve their circumstances.[31]

While they believed this theory had considerable statistical and logical support, they felt it only applied to a few individuals who were enabled to "reenter society," while failing to account for how the majority of sects themselves become transformed into more conventional religious movements.

Finally, they proposed their own theory based on the concept of "statistical regression towards the mean." In brief, this mathematical concept as applied to religious organizations holds that sects starting out as extremist gradually lose their sense of "over-and-againstness" when the original devotees pass out of the picture and are replaced by a second generation of members less zealously committed to the organization's original ideals. People born into a sect are seldom as intensely devoted as those who join voluntarily as adults. Over a period of time, the second and later generation followers gradually ignore the most extreme values and practices of their ideological ancestors and adopt those of the prevailing society, thus pulling the organization more into the mainstream of life.[32]

In the process of accommodating to the demands and values of the larger society, some of the sect's members, usually those with less social power and influence, begin to feel deprived of those elements they found attractive when they joined the movement. For many sect members, accommodation and reduced tension with society have no value for them. Instead, they find themselves longing for the very rewards (compensators) that the majority of the movement have rejected as no longer desirable or needed, such as concepts of chosenness and God's special favor and protection, and of unique insights and doctrines that would lead the world "to come unto Zion to learn of her ways." Stark and Bainbridge identified the consequences of such abandonment of traditional beliefs:

> To the extent a religious group reduces its tension with society, there will be a growing demand among its less powerful members for more efficacious compensators for scarcity. These less privileged members' concerns will have clear focus, for they will recognize that their grievance was caused by change. They will believe that their religious group has deserted them, as it has deserted its historic theology. They will not need to cast about for a more suitable faith. Rather, they will demand restoration of the tried and therefore true solution to their needs. Put another way, as religious movements

reduce their tension and thus better serve the needs of their dominant members, support in favor of a [dissident] sect movement grows. All that is needed then is leaders, people capable of mobilizing the discontented and organizing them into a counterforce.[33]

They went on to predict that those who lead dissident movements away from the parent body will usually be "clergy or at least prominent lay leaders" who have had extensive contacts with those needing the strongest sectarian compensators. Though dissident leaders stand to lose status in the original church, they expect to gain far more prestige as leaders of small, break-away groups. They concluded, "Those leaders who already have the closest contact with a potential sect constituency will have the most to gain by defection from the parent organization. Thus are sects born."[34]

The Reorganization's Future

What can one conclude about the future of the church from this analysis? For one thing, Reorganized Church members cannot deny that substantial change in what some people regard as essential doctrine and practice has occurred and will continue to occur in the future. The lesson of the Stark and Bainbridge analysis is that sectarian change is not only a common phenomenon but inevitable and likely unavoidable. Whether the changes are considered fundamental or peripheral to the major purposes of the church is a matter of interpretation, and whether the changes are welcomed or abhorred depends largely on whose needs are being met and whose are being ignored.

Given this analysis, one may speculate about a few issues over which future dissents and possible schisms may occur. They do not represent responses to significant changes in social paradigms. Because paradigm shifts represent new ways of thinking, such fundamental changes are notoriously hard to predict with a high degree of accuracy. In the social sciences, a paradigm refers to a standard way of thinking, a set of ideas, norms, and behaviors characteristic of a particular society at a given time. The society infuses these ideas and norms into people from infancy on through adulthood. Concepts of "right and wrong," "good and evil," and other such values become so much a part of one's personality that it is difficult to think in ways foreign to one's culture. A statement illustrating this point has been attributed, perhaps apocryphally, to Albert Einstein: The universe is not only stranger than we imagine, it is stranger than we *can* imagine. For most of us, that is the way it is about changing social paradigms. The reason they are so hard to see coming is that we are in effect prisoners of our own ways of thinking, limited to familiar images and language.

Nevertheless, without trying to imagine changing paradigms, one may still identify a few problems already pregnant with possibilities for strain and tension in the future. Two trends of the late 1980s especially suggest serious potential for dissent and schism. The first of these has to do with a reversal of the trend toward centralization of authority that has characterized the church in the twentieth century. Nearly 150 years ago the Reorganized Church began as a loose association of widely separated branches, virtually independent because of limitations imposed by difficulties in travel and communications. In the ensuing generations, however, the church crossed over the boundary from being a de facto congregationally based church to a hierarchically structured one. There is little evidence that such centralization was a long-term objective of church leaders (with the exception of the Supreme Directional Control controversy, of course). Rather, the transition appears to have come incrementally, as a result of many seemingly unrelated decisions dealing with short-term problems. Though the church officially recognized the value of reversing, or at least arresting, this process in a statement of institutional objectives in 1966,[35] the goal has been difficult to realize by administrative initiative alone. However, lean budgets during the latter half of the 1980s has forced the church to lay off many appointees and Headquarters staff. Many functions performed by the World Church must now be done by local jurisdictions. To cope with this, some local stakes and regions are establishing endowment funds to support local programming and employing salaried ministers for a variety of pastoral and missionary tasks. Long experience confirms that power resides at the level where the money is. The more programming and funding develops at the local level, the less influence the World Church will have on local decisions. At some point, it is inevitable that disagreements will arise between local and hierarchical interests. Schism is much more likely when the local areas are already self-sufficient.

Another potential arena of dissent comes from the church's rapid growth in Africa and the Caribbean. Sociologists have long noted a "demonstration" effect that occurs when economically deprived cultures come into contact with more affluent societies. As a result of knowledge gained from films and television, or even personal visits, persons in the deprived cultures often become envious of the standards of living they see in more developed societies. Rather than considering the historical and situational roots of such differences in economic wealth, they regard their relative deprivation as intolerably unfair and demand immediate justice. The shape such demands for justice might take in the context of the church are not difficult to imagine. Greater investment of church resources in its Third World jurisdictions and increased policy input from such areas are only two strong possibilities. If high membership growth rates continue in such nations as Haiti, Nigeria, and Zaire over the next generation, such demands will be hard to ignore when larger and larger proportions of the World Conference represent these jurisdictions. Should these demands be denied, mass defections from the faith would not be unprecedented.

Another sure source of future dissent and schism can be attributed to the church's doctrine of revelation. The concept that anyone may receive communication from God and that the church is led by a living prophet whose pronouncements may be characterized by disjunctive changes in theology and tradition gives potential legitimacy to anyone who can convince others that his or her message is from Divinity. Charismatic nonconformists can gain adherents much easier in such an atmosphere than in one in which the scriptures are the sole source of authority and must be interpreted and applied by a cadre of trained officials and priests. Most of the schisms from various factions of Latter Day Saintism have had such charismatic leaders claiming to be prophetic.[36] It would be naïve to believe that such a common and traditional cause of schism will cease anytime soon.

If one accepts the Vernon typology (table 1 above), it is apparent that the Reorganized Church of Jesus Christ of Latter Day Saints is gradually metamorphosing from a sect into a denomination. The process has been neither smooth nor completely linear, but it has been inexorable. Social theory identifies the source of many of the problems involving dissent and schisms the church has suffered in the past generation. It also predicts that changes will continue to occur and that dissent and schism will be the inevitable result.

The practical implication of this theory is that by understanding what engenders dissent and schism, some of it may be avoided. In other cases, when dissent grows to the point of schism, knowledge of its causes can allow people to disengage from emotional commitments to defending the faith and rationally assess the nature of the situation. While "divorce" is rarely a pleasant prospect, over the long term, some separations and divorces may be regarded as inevitable. Perhaps the best strategy for everyone would be to wish the "other side" well and move out in faith that when we do our best according to the knowledge, insights, and skills with which God has endowed us, that is simply all God can expect of us.

Notes

1. Fritjof Capra, "Paradigms and Paradigm Shifts," *ReVision* 9 (Summer/Fall 1986): 11. Capra's definition and work was closely based on Thomas S. Kuhn, *The Structure of Scientific Revolutions* (Chicago: University of Chicago Press, 1970 ed.), see especially pages 175ff.

2. See for example Paul M. Edwards, "Theocratic-Democracy: Philosopher-King in the Reorganization," in F. Mark McKiernan, Alma R. Blair, and Paul M. Edwards, eds., *The Restoration Movement: Essays in Mormon History* (Lawrence, Kansas: Coronado Press, 1973), 341-357; Clare D. Vlahos, "The Challenge to Centralized Power: Zenus [sic] Gurley, Jr., and the Prophetic Office," *Courage: A Journal of History, Thought and Action* 1 (March 1971): 141-158. See also Roger D. Launius, "Guarding Prerogatives"; Ken R. Mulliken, "The Supreme Directional Con-

trol Controversy"; William D. Russell, "The Fundamentalist Schism, 1958-Present"; and Steven L. Shields, "An Overview of Dissent in the Reorganization" in this volume.

3. Richard Price, *Action Time* (Independence, Missouri: Price Publishing, 1985), 2.

4. Rodney Stark and William Sims Bainbridge, *The Future of Religion: Secularization, Revival and Cult Formation* (Berkeley: University of California Press, 1985), 99. Copyright © 1985 The Regents of the University of California. Used with permission.

5. Roger Yarrington, "Changes in the Church," *Saints Herald* 137 (September 1990): 356, 362.

6. Richard Price, "RLDS Hierarchy Expels Minister for Warning Membership," paid advertisement in *The Independence Examiner* (15 August 1987): 12.

7. Vlahos, "The Challenge to Centralized Power," 141-158.

8. Edwards, "Theocratic-Democracy," 355.

9. Larry E. Hunt, *F. M. Smith: Saint as Reformer* (Independence, Missouri: Herald Publishing House, 1982), 387-463.

10. *Report of the Commission on Education*, Reorganized Church of Jesus Christ of Latter Day Saints (April 1970), 116. See also William J. Knapp, "Professionalizing Religious Education in the Church: The 'New Curriculum' Controversy," *The John Whitmer Historical Association Journal* 2 (1982): 47-59.

11. Charles D. Neff, "The Church and Culture," *Saints Herald* 119 (December 1972): 13-14, 51-52. See also Clifford A. Cole, "The World Church: Our Mission in the 1980s," *Commission* (September 1979): 42.

12. Donald D. Landon, *A History of Donald D. Landon While Under General Conference Appointment, 1951-1970: An Oral History Memoir* (Independence, Missouri: Department of History, Reorganized Church of Jesus Christ of Latter Day Saints, 1970), 94. See also Russell, "The Fundamentalist Schism, 1958-Present," in this volume.

13. First Presidency, "The Identity of the Church," First Presidency Meetings (9 January 1979), 12-13.

14. Milton V. Backman, Jr., *The Heavens Resound: A History of the Latter-day Saints in Ohio 1830-1838* (Salt Lake City, Utah: Deseret Book, 1983), 63-81.

15. *The History of the Reorganized Church of Jesus Christ of Latter Day Saints* (Independence, Missouri: Herald Publishing House, 1973) 6:614.

16. Roger D. Launius, *The Kirtland Temple: A Historical Narrative* (Independence, Missouri: Herald Publishing House, 1986), 106-107.

17. Reorganized Church of Jesus Christ of Latter Day Saints, *Report of the Commission on Education* (April 1970), 64.

18. *Information Please Almanac* (New York City: Simon and Schuster, 1980), 42.

19. Stewardship Commission, Reorganized Church of Jesus Christ of Latter Day Saints, *Membership and Financial Manual* (1989), Section D. "Contributor Statistics," p. D-2, Table: "Contributors to World Church Funds."

20. Robert E. Park and Ernest W. Burgess, *Introduction to the Science of Sociology* (Chicago: University of Chicago Press, 1921), 872.

21. Stark and Bainbridge, *Future of Religion*, 120.

22. Ibid.

23. Ibid., 101-109.

24. Ibid., 104.

25. See Howard J. Booth, "Recent Shifts in Restoration Thought," in Maurice L. Draper and Clare D. Vlahos, eds., *Restoration Studies I* (Independence, Missouri: Herald Publishing House, 1980), 162-175.

26. Howard J. Booth, "For We Being Many, Are One Bread, And One Body ... " in Marjorie B. Troeh and Eileen M. Terril, eds., *Restoration Studies IV* (Independence, Missouri: Herald Publishing House, 1988), 249-252.

27. See for example William D. Russell, "The Historicity of the Book of Mormon and the Use of the Sermon on the Mount in III Nephi," in Maurice L. Draper and A. Bruce Lindgren, eds., *Restoration Studies II* (Independence, Missouri: Herald Publishing House, 1983), 193-200.

28. Richard P. Howard, "The Changing RLDS Response to Mormon Polygamy: A Preliminary Analysis," *The John Whitmer Historical Association Journal* 3 (1983), 14-28.

29. A. Bruce Lindgren, ed., *Leaders Handbook, 1991* (Independence, Missouri: Herald Publishing House, 1990), 1.6.

30. Stark and Bainbridge, *Future of Religions*, 150.

31. Ibid., 151.

32. Ibid., 150-152.

33. Ibid.

34. Ibid, 105. Stark and Bainbridge's analysis of psychological factors affecting dissent concentrates primarily on factors relating to one's conception of doctrine. Another interesting approach has been suggested by Stan L. Albrecht, et al., in "Religious Leave-Taking: Disengagement and Disaffiliation Among Mormons," in David G. Bromley, ed., *Falling From The Faith: Causes and Consequences of Religious Apostasy* (Beverly Hills, California: Sage Publications, 1988), 62-80. In their essay, Albrecht and his

coauthors take the position that "falling away" from a faith takes place along three dimensions. In the behavioral component people "disengage," i.e. "cease or discontinue their active participation in a religious group." In the affective component, persons "disaffiliate" by either joining another religious group or not affiliating with any group. "Apostasy" is the cognitive component that reflects changes in belief about doctrine and is the area in which the Stark and Bainbridge analysis concentrates. According to Albrecht et al., the primary factors affecting disengagement and disaffiliation have to do with such influences as (1) lack of family commitment or other similar problems such as religiously divided households, and (2) life-style changes in which persons decide that the church is no longer "relevant" in their lives. Albrecht et al. suggest that doctrine plays little part in individual decisions to disengage or disaffiliate from a faith.

35. First Presidency, *Statement on Objectives for the Church*, approved by the Joint Council of the First Presidency and Council of Twelve on 14 April 1966, and read to the World Conference on 17 April 1966, *World Conference Bulletin* (18 April 1966): 240. See also the "Report of the First Presidency," *World Conference Bulletin* (Monday, 10 April 1972): 199.

36. See Steven L. Shields, *Divergent Paths of the Restoration: A History of the Latter Day Saint Movement* (Los Angeles, California: Restoration Research, 1990 ed.).

Suggestions for Further Reading

The subject of dissent in American religion has not been studied with much depth or concentration in the recent past. The most readable and comprehensive overview is presented in Edwin Scott Gaustead, *Dissent in American Religion* (Chicago: University of Illinois Press, 1973), one of the "Chicago History of American Religion" series. The only overview of the issue in Mormonism is a single article. Clearly there is considerable need for additional work. The problem of apostasy is discussed in Leonard J. Arrington, "Centrifugal Tendencies in Mormon History," in Truman G. Madsen, ed., *To The Glory of God: Mormon Essays on Great Issues* (Salt Lake City, Utah: Deseret Book, 1972), 165-77. General discussions of the subject for the Utah and Reorganized churches are in Thomas F. O'Dea, "Sources of Strain in Mormonism Reconsidered," in Marvin S. Hill and James B. Allen, eds., *Mormonism and American Culture* (New York: Harper and Row, 1972), 149-155, and Wayne Ham, "Let Contention Cease: An Overview of Past and Present Dissent Among the RLDS," unpublished address presented at the annual meeting of the Mormon History Association (5 May 1986), Salt Lake City, Utah.

Although not specifically oriented toward dissent, a good general history of Mormonism is James B. Allen and Glen M. Leonard, *The Story of the Latter-day Saints* (Salt Lake City, Utah: Deseret Book, 1976). More than thirty years old now, a still significant sociological study of the religion is Thomas F. O'Dea, *The Mormons* (Chicago: University of Chicago Press, 1957). A recent work with a provocative thesis is Jan Shipps, *Mormonism:*

The Story of a New Religious Tradition (Urbana: University of Illinois Press, 1985). Another lively work, offering a thesis which places Mormonism within the context of American religious history, is Klaus J. Hansen, *Mormonism and American Culture* (Chicago: University of Chicago Press, 1981).

Although outdated, Inez Smith Davis's book, *The Story of the Church* (Independence, Missouri: Herald Publishing House, 1986 ed.), originally published in 1934, does have considerable information on various dissenting factions of Mormonism that arose following the death of Joseph Smith, Jr., in 1844. More scholarly and recent, though less voluminous, is the one-volume narrative history of the church by Paul M. Edwards, *Our Legacy of Faith: A Brief History of the Reorganized Church of Jesus Christ of Latter Day Saints* (Independence, Missouri: Herald Publishing House, 1991). Although it does not go into great detail on the dissent issues, it deals with the major historic periods of dissent in an objective manner. An outstanding shorter study of the development of the Reorganization has been presented in Alma R. Blair, "The Reorganized Church of Jesus Christ of Latter Day Saints: Moderate Mormons," in F. Mark McKiernan, Alma R. Blair, and Paul M. Edwards, eds., *The Restoration Movement: Essays in Mormon History* (Lawrence, Kansas: Coronado Press, 1973), 207-230. A compendium of various dissenting groups in the Restoration is Steven L. Shields, *Divergent Paths of the Restoration: A History of the Latter Day Saint Movement* (Los Angeles, California: Restoration Research, 1990 ed.). Shields's *The Latter Day Saint Churches: An Annotated Bibliography* (New York: Garland, 1987) presents a useful set of bibliographical citations on the many Mormon factions that have evolved during the 160 years since the church's origin.

The specific incidents of significant dissent in Mormonism have been analyzed in various publications by scholars. The first serious instance of dissent in Mormonism took place in Kirtland, Ohio. This episode has been analyzed in Marvin S. Hill, *Quest for Refuge: The Mormon Flight from American Pluralism* (Salt Lake City, Utah: Signature Books, 1989) and especially in the brilliant article by Hill, "Cultural Crisis in the Mormon Kingdom: A Reconsideration of the Causes of Kirtland Dissent," *Church History* 49 (September 1980): 286-297. The aftermath of Zion's Camp has been shown to be the beginnings of the Kirtland dissent. This episode has been discussed in Roger D. Launius, *Zion's Camp: Expedition to Missouri, 1834* (Independence, Missouri: Herald Publishing House, 1984). For the general history of the church in the area, see Milton V. Backman, Jr., *The Heavens Resound: A History of the Latter-day Saints in Ohio, 1830-1838* (Salt Lake City, Utah: Deseret Book, 1983). The life of the church in Kirtland as reflected in its principal physical structure is described in Roger D. Launius, *The Kirtland Temple: A Historical Narrative* (Independence, Missouri: Herald Publishing House, 1986).

The problems that cropped up in Kirtland were continued in Missouri in the latter 1830s. During that era all three witnesses to the Book of Mormon were lost to the church, as were more than half of the Quorum of Twelve Apostles and the presiding bishop, Edward Partridge. An undocumented number of others also withdrew or were expelled from the church during this period. On this subject, see the outstanding book by Stephen C. LeSeuer, *The 1838 Mormon War of Missouri*

(Columbia: University of Missouri Press, 1987). A dated but still useful shorter study of this subject is F. Mark McKiernan, "Mormonism on the Defensive: Far West, 1838-1839," in McKiernan, Blair, and Edwards, eds., *The Restoration Movement*, 121-140. Phillip R. Legg, *Oliver Cowdery: The Elusive Second Elder of the Restoration* (Independence, Missouri: Herald Publishing House, 1989), emphasizes the dissent of the era.

In Nauvoo during the mid-1840s a major dissenting movement arose around the William and Wilson Law brothers. Intended at first as a reform movement, it eventually became a rival church organization in 1844. The standard work on Nauvoo remains Robert Bruce Flanders, *Nauvoo: Kingdom on the Mississippi* (Urbana: University of Illinois Press, 1965), which reviews the issue of dissention in the city. On William Law, see Lyndon W. Cook, "William Law, Nauvoo Dissenter," *Brigham Young University Studies* 22 (Winter 1982): 47-62; and John Fredrick Glaser, "The Disaffection of William Law," in Maurice L. Draper and Debra Combs, eds., *Restoration Studies III* (Independence, Missouri: Herald Publishing House, 1986), 163-175. Law began publication of a rival newspaper in 1844, *The Expositor*, and the destruction of the press after its first issue led directly to Smith's death. On this subject, see Dallin H. Oaks, "The Suppression of the *Nauvoo Expositor*," *Utah Law Review* 9 (Winter 1966): 862-903.

At Joseph Smith, Jr.'s death in 1844 at least fifteen groups emerged to claim a portion of the legacy of Mormonism. The two most successful of these were the Utah Latter-day Saints and the Reorganized Church. There have been and there remain significant differences between these groups over such issues as succession in the presidency. On the succession question, see Ronald K. Esplin, "Joseph, Brigham, and the Twelve: A Succession of Continuity," *Brigham Young University Studies* 21 (Summer 1981): 301-341, which makes a strong case for Brigham Young's leadership. Several works by D. Michael Quinn make a sustained investigation of leadership and its transference between quorums and individuals: "The Evolution of the Presiding of the LDS Church," *Journal of Mormon History* 1 (1974): 21-38; "The Mormon Succession Crisis of 1844," *Brigham Young University Studies* 16 (Winter 1976): 187-233; and "Joseph Smith III's Blessing and the Mormons of Utah," *The John Whitmer Historical Association Journal* 1 (1981): 12-27. The succession of Joseph Smith III and the leadership he offered has been described in Roger D. Launius's two award-winning books, *Joseph Smith III: Pragmatic Prophet* (Urbana: University of Illinois Press, 1988), and *Father Figure: Joseph Smith III and the Creation of the Reorganized Church* (Independence, Missouri: Herald Publishing House, 1990).

Another major difference between the two major Mormon churches has been the manner in which they interpret the issue of democracy and Zion, subjects which bear directly on dissent. The Reorganized Church has adopted a system that has been generally democratic, while in the Utah church authority tends to flow from the top down to the membership. A fascinating comparison of this and other developments in the two churches can be found in Douglas D. Alder and Paul M. Edwards, "Common Beginnings, Divergent Beliefs," *Dialogue: A Journal of Mormon Thought* 11 (Spring 1978): 18-28. This theme has also been traced in Edward A. Warner, "Mormon Theodemocracy: Theocratic and Democratic Elements in Early Latter-Day

Saint Ideology, 1827-1846" (Ph.D. Diss., University of Iowa, 1973). On the Reorganization's stance on this issue, see Maurice L. Draper, "Theocratic Democracy—Restoration Church Government," *Saints' Herald* 115 (1 December 1968): 800-801, 814; 115 (15 December 1968): 842-844. Joseph Smith III's role in fashioning the government of the Reorganization is analyzed in Clare D. Vlahos, "Moderation as a Theological Principle in the Thought of Joseph Smith III," *The John Whitmer Historical Association Journal* 1 (1981), 3-11; Roger D. Launius, "Joseph Smith III and the Quest for a Centralized Organization, 1860-1873," in Maurice L. Draper and A. Bruce Lindgren, eds., *Restoration Studies II* (Independence, Missouri: Herald Publishing House, 1983), 104-120; and some of the works already mentioned.

This environment has been a potent seedbed for disagreements in the church over its nature and direction. In the nineteenth century the most serious debate in this regard was the rebellion of Jason W. Briggs and Zenos H. Gurley, Jr., two apostles who eventually withdrew from the Reorganized Church. Various aspects of this subject are illuminated in Clare D. Vlahos, "The Challenge to Centralized Power: Zenus [sic] H. Gurley, Jr., and the Prophet Office," *Courage: A Journal of History, Thought and Action* 1 (March 1971): 141-158; William D. Russell, "The RLDS Church and Biblical Criticism: The Early Response," *The John Whitmer Historical Association Journal* 7 (1987): 62-68; Alma R. Blair, "The Tradition of Dissent—Jason W. Briggs," in Maurice L. Draper and Clare D. Vlahos, eds., *Restoration Studies I* (Independence, Missouri: Herald Publishing House, 1980), 146-161; and Clare D. Vlahos, "Images of Orthodoxy: Self-Identity in Early Reorganization

Apologetics," in Draper and Vlahos, eds., *Restoration Studies I*, pp. 176-186, as well as publications already mentioned.

A second major dissenting episode in the church took place during the Supreme Directional Control controversy of the 1920s. In this arena the personality of Frederick Madison Smith was at center stage. On Frederick M. Smith, see Paul M. Edwards, *The Chief: An Administrative Biography of Fred M. Smith* (Independence, Missouri: Herald Publishing House, 1988); Larry E. Hunt, *F. M. Smith: Saint as Reformer*, 2 vols. (Independence, Missouri: Herald Publishing House, 1982); Norman D. Ruoff, comp., *The Writings of President Frederick M. Smith: The Zionic Enterprise*, Volume III (Independence, Missouri: Herald Publishing House, 1981); Ruth Lyman Smith, *Concerning the Prophet: Fredrick [sic] Madison Smith* (Kansas City, Missouri: Burton Publishing Company, 1924); and Frederick M. Smith, *The Higher Powers of Man* (Independence, Missouri: Herald Publishing House, 1968 ed.). Although it did not seem so at the time, the controversies between Frederick Smith and R.C. Evans in the 1910s foreshadowed some of the difficulties arising in more serious form nearly a decade later. On Evans, see Roger D. Launius, "R. C. Evans: Boy Orator of the Reorganization," *The John Whitmer Historical Association Journal* 3 (1983): 40-50. Specifically on the Supreme Directional Control controversy, see Paul M. Edwards, "Theocratic-Democracy: Philosopher-King in the Reorganization," in McKiernan, Blair, and Edwards, eds., *The Restoration Movement*, 341-357.

Beginning after World War II the Reorganized Church began to move into mission fields for the first time beyond Western civilization, began to change as an entity with greater resources and standing, and set up the parameters for what became the fundamentalist dissent in the church. The first vestiges of this controversy arose in the educational curriculum of the church. This subject has been admirably treated in William J. Knapp, "Professionalizing Religious Education in the Church: The 'New Curriculum' Controversy," *The John Whitmer Historical Association* 2 (1982): 47-59. The nature of the changes has been discussed and critiqued in Larry W. Conrad and Paul Shupe, "An RLDS Reformation? Construing the Task of RLDS Theology," *Dialogue: A Journal of Mormon Thought* 18 (Summer 1985): 92-103; Howard J. Booth, "Shifts in Restoration Thought," *Dialogue: A Journal of Mormon Thought* 13 (Fall 1980): 79-92, reprinted as "Recent Shifts in Restoration Thought," in Maurice L. Draper and Clare D. Vlahos, eds., *Restoration Studies I* (Independence, Missouri: Herald Publishing House, 1980), 162-175; and Maurice L. Draper, "Sect-Denomination-Church Transition and Leadership in the Reorganized Church of Jesus Christ of Latter Day Saints (M.A. Thesis, Kansas University, 1964). A semiofficial position on this restructuring can be found in Clifford A. Cole, "The Cause of Zion: Today and Tomorrow," Part I, *Saints Herald* 121 (August 1974): 486-489, 508; Part II, 121 (September 1974): 558-561, 570, which suggests that the church's mission requires change. More recently Roger Yarrington, "Changes in the Church," *Saints Herald* 137 (September 1990): 356, 362, editorialized on this subject. Controversies in the church have been played out especially significantly in the church's World Conferences. On Conferences generally, see M. Richard Troeh and Marjorie Troeh, *The Conferring Church* (Independence, Missouri: Herald Publishing House, 1987). On one such difficult Conference, see William D. Russell, "Reorganized Mormons Beset by Controversy," *Christian Century* (17 June 1970): 770, dealing with the 1970 meeting.

Many problems of dissent in the recent church have related to the difficulties inherent in dealing with the issue of modernity and its effects on culture and society. On this topic in religion generally, see Martin E. Marty, *Modern American Religion, Volume 1: The Irony of It All, 1893-1919* (Chicago: University of Chicago Press, 1986); John MacQuarrie, *Twentieth Century Religious Thought* (New York: Harper & Row, 1963); James Barr, *The Scope and Authority of the Bible* (Philadelphia: Westminster Press, 1980); Rodney Stark and William Sims Bainbridge, *The Future of Religion: Secularization, Revival and Cult Formation* (Berkeley: University of California Press, 1985); and Ernest R. Sandeen, *The Roots of Fundamentalism: British and American Millenarianism, 1800-1930* (Chicago: University of Chicago Press, 1970). On the Restoration's difficulties with this aspect of society, illuminating insights are offered in Louis Midgley, "The Challenge of Historical Consciousness: Mormon History and the Encounter with Secular Modernity," in John M. Lundquist and Stephen D. Ricks, eds., *By Study and Also By Faith: Essays in Honor of Hugh Nibley on the Occasion of His Eightieth Birthday, March 27, 1990* (Salt Lake City, Utah: Deseret Book, 1990), 2:502-551. The church's confrontation with non-Western culture in the mission field and its significant effect on the church has been discussed in Maurice L. Draper, *Isles & Continents* (Independence, Missouri: Herald Publishing House, 1982); Clifford A. Cole, "The World Church: Our Mission in the 1980s," *Commission* (September 1979): 41-46; and Charles D.

Neff, "The Church and Culture," *Saints Herald* 119 (December 1972): 13-14, 51-52.

The social explanations of dissent have been profitably analyzed in Meyer N. Zeld and Roberta Ash, "Social Movement Organizations: Growth, Decay, and Change," *Social Forces* 44 (March 1966): 327-341; William R. Dill, "The Impact of Environment on Organizational Development," in Sidney Mailik and Edward Van Ness, eds., *Concepts and Issues in Administrative Behavior* (Englewood Cliffs, New Jersey: Prentice-Hall, 1962), 94-109; Richard T. LaPiere, *Social Change* (New York: McGraw-Hill, 1965); W. Loyd Warner, *The Corporation in the Emergent American Society* (New York: Harper and Brothers, 1962); Warren G. Bennis, *Changing Organizations* (New York: McGraw-Hill, 1966); Peter Blau, *Bureaucracy in Modern Society* (New York: Random House, 1956); Max Weber, *The Theory of Social and Economic Organizations*, A. M. Henderson and Talcott Parsons, trans. (New York: The Free Press, 1964); and Fritjof Capra, "Paradigms and Paradigm Shifts," *Re-Vision* 9 (Summer/Fall 1986): 11.

Central to recent dissent in the Reorganized Church has been the reevaluation of the church's history and theology. On the theology issue, see such works as *Exploring the Faith* (Independence, Missouri: Herald Publishing House, 1970 and 1987); Wayne Ham, "Problems in Interpreting the Book of Mormon as History," *Courage: A Journal of History, Thought and Action* 1 (March 1971): 15-22; Peter A. Judd and Clifford A. Cole, *Distinctives: Yesterday and Today* (Independence, Missouri: Herald Publishing House, 1983); Peter A. Judd and A. Bruce Lindgren, *An Introduction to the Saints Church* (Independence, Missouri: Herald Publishing House, 1976); C. Robert Mesle, *The Bible as Story and*

Struggle (Independence, Missouri: Herald Publishing House, 1989); Lloyd R. Young, "Concerning the Virgin Birth: Comments on the Doctrine," *Saints' Herald* 111 (1 February 1964): 77-78, 94, as only a few examples of the reconsideration of many of the traditional conceptions of the church. Likewise, the church's history has been completely revised in the last generation, under the auspices of what has been called the "New Mormon History." On this subject, see Martin E. Marty, "Two Integrities: An Address to the Crisis in Mormon Historiography," *Journal of Mormon History* 10 (1983): 3-19; Paul M. Edwards, "The New Mormon History," *Saints Herald* 133 (November 1986): 472; Thomas G. Alexander, "Toward the New Mormon History: An Examination of the Literature on the Latter-day Saints in the Far West," in Michael P. Malone, ed., *Historians and the American West* (Lincoln: University of Nebraska Press, 1983), 344-368; Thomas G. Alexander, "Historiography and the New Mormon History: A Historian's Perspective," *Dialogue: A Journal of Mormon Thought* 19 (Fall 1986): 25-50; and Richard P. Howard, "New Currents in Mormon History," *Saints Herald* 135 (November 1988): 483. Only two subjects of this reconsideration are the methods of the translation of the Book of Mormon and Joseph Smith's involvement in plural marriage. On these, see James E. Lancaster, "By the Gift and Power of God," *Saint's Herald* 109 (15 November 1962): 798-802, 806, 817; reprinted as "The Method of Translation of the Book of Mormon," with minor revisions in *The John Whitmer Historical Association Journal* 3 (1983): 51-61; and Richard P. Howard, "The Changing RLDS Response to Mormon Polygamy: A Preliminary Analysis," *The John Whitmer Historical Association Journal* 3 (1983): 14-29.

Traditionalist response has been significant. Such dissenters as Richard Price have prepared detailed critiques of the church's "errors." Among other materials, see Richard Price, *Saints at the Crossroads* (Independence, Missouri: Cumorah Books, 1974); Richard Price, *Decision Time* (Independence, Missouri: Cumorah Books, 1975); Richard Price, *Action Time* (Independence, Missouri: Price Publishing Co., 1985); Richard Price and Larry Harlacher, *Restoration Branches Movement* (Independence, Missouri: Price Publishing Co., 1986); and Merva Bird, *Women's Ordination—NO!* (Independence, Missouri: School of the Saints, 1990). The institutional church has not been silent on the dissent. See Standing High Council, "The Ethics of Dissent," *Saints Herald* 135 (April 1988): 141-146, as an official statement on what is allowable in opposing the church's administrative leadership.

Roger D. Launius